CRIMES AND PUNISHMENT

VOLUME
20

Crimes and Punishment takes a hard and objective look at crime and criminals—their ways and methods and the means by which they are caught and punished. This authoritative edition combines material from *Murder Casebook, Science Against Crime,* and *Crimes and Punishment* which were originally published in the United Kingdom. This new compilation casts a penetrating eye upon the violence around us with which we must live.

CRIMES AND PUNISHMENT

The *Illustrated* CRIME ENCYCLOPEDIA

VOLUME 20

H. S. STUTTMAN, INC. *publishers* Westport, CT 06889

CONTENTS

PIRATES	The Swashbucklers	2361
POISONERS	The Macabre Minds of the Poisoners	2367
POOK AFFAIR	The Girl-Chaser and the Housemaid	2373
PRESIDENT GARFIELD ASSASSINATION	"God Killed the President"	2377
PRICE, Harry	The Most Haunted House in England	2385
PROTECTION RACKETS	Pay Up or Else . . .	2393
RANDOM KILLERS	Slaughter at Random	2399
RAPE	Psychology of the Sex Killer	2409
RAPE EVIDENCE	What is Rape?	2415
RED BARN MURDER	The Mystery of Maria Marten	2452
RED LIGHT BANDIT	Caryl Chessman	2461
REINSCH TEST	A Trace of Arsenic	2469
RICE, William Marsh	An Old Man's Money	2473
RICHARDSONS, The	The Fraternity of Torture	2479
CRIME FILE	Peter Hurkos	2392
MURDER CASEBOOK	Bodies in the Undergrowth	2419

Arthur Shawcross: he liked to go fishing and seemed a homey, harmless sort of man. In truth he was seeking watery graves for his victims, using his friendly manner as a bait to hook his human catch.

Published by H. S. STUTTMAN INC.
Westport, Connecticut 06880
© H. S. STUTTMAN INC. 1994

Murder Casebook material
© Marshall Cavendish Limited 1989, 1990, 1991, 1994

Science Against Crime material
© Marshall Cavendish Limited 1982, 1994

Crimes and Punishment material
© Little Brown & Company 1973, 1974, 1975, 1976, 1994

No part of this book may be reproduced in any form or by any electronic or mechanical means, including information storage and retrieval devices or systems, without prior written permission from the publisher, but brief passages may be quoted for reviews.

PRINTED IN THE UNITED STATES OF AMERICA

PIRATES
THE SWASHBUCKLERS

To the age of cinema, fed on romantic tales of "gentleman" buccaneers of the Douglas Fairbanks mould (right), who sweep young ladies off their feet, the pirate is a hero. But, as history tells us, real pirates, like the notorious Francisco Lolonais (left), were more interested in murder, pillage . . . and rape.

IT WAS the great Hollywood dream factory that turned the pirate into a figure of romance. When Douglas Fairbanks Senior leapt aboard a Spanish galleon with a cutlass between his teeth, or Errol Flynn bowed with elaborate courtesy to a captive lady in crinolines, who could believe that the original buccaneers were mostly criminal degenerates? But that is the unromantic truth. Throughout the history of civilization, pirates, like brigands and highway robbers, have been a kind of vermin, as useless to the human race as the cholera germ.

As soon as men decided to live in cities for their mutual protection, the bandits began to infest the roads between the cities. And as soon as enterprising merchants started to link the cities of the Mediterranean and North Africa, the bandits of the sea began to waylay their ships. There was one basic difference between the pirate and the brigand. If a brigand committed wholesale murder, he was likely to enrage the authorities into hunting him down at all costs. If a pirate killed everybody on board a merchant ship then burned the ship down to the waterline, he was lessening his chances of being detected. So piracy made for a kind of sadistic criminality seldom met with among brigands.

The earliest and most notorious of the pirates were Greeks—the people we now think of as the founders of European civilization. The trade of piracy was still flourishing when the Romans came to power, and Rome finally decided it had to be got rid of at any price. The Rome of Julius Caesar depended on Egyptian wheat, and there were so many pirates plundering the supply ships that the country was starving. The pirates were literally terrorists. They would often besiege a fortified city, then burn everybody in it; other cities would take warning, and everybody would flee before the pirates arrived, leaving them to pillage at leisure.

Then the day came when the Romans decided it was time to forget internal squabbles and destroy the pirates. They selected their greatest general, Pompey, whose huge forces descended on them, and gave them a taste of their own tactics.

There was mass slaughter; the strongholds were turned into smoking ruins, full of corpses. The sea wolves were no match for Roman legions. In 40 days, all the major pirate villages had been destroyed. Then, having shown that he could be cruel and merciless, Pompey announced that Rome was prepared to pardon all pirates who surrendered voluntarily. Most of them had no alternative; forced off the major sea routes, they would have starved to death. They surrendered by the thousand. Pompey had cleared the Mediterranean for many years to come.

Vengeful mood

Pirates were like lice, who need to batten onto a host. When the Roman Empire collapsed, there was no one for them to rob. So, during the Dark Ages, the seas were fairly safe. The Arabs controlled North Africa and Spain; life was stable and free from pillage. Then, in 1492, the year Columbus discovered the Bahamas, the Spanish finally hurled the Arabs back into their own country. But North Africa was poor; it could hardly support its own people. In a vengeful mood, the Arabs decided to wreck the commerce of the Christian world.

Overnight, the Mediterranean was full of fast, light vessels that could overtake most merchant ships. Equally suddenly, the Christians realized that their rejoicing about the conquest of the Infidels had been premature.

In 1504, for example, Pope Julius II sent two great warships loaded with treasure from Genoa to Rome. They lost sight of one another. All at once, a tiny, fast craft appeared; within minutes the unprepared Roman ship was overrun. The Arabs then made the prisoners strip, and dressed in their clothes. Next they caught up with the other treasure ship, and signalled it to wait.

Suspecting nothing, the crew allowed their companions to draw alongside—and only realized there was something wrong when a storm of arrows killed most of the men on the decks. The slaves who rowed the Roman treasure ships were Arabs; they were released, and Christians put in their place. Then the three ships sailed for Tunis with a fortune in Vatican treasures.

The exploit reverberated from end to end of Europe. So did the nickname of the captain of the pirate ship, Red Beard—Barbarossa. His career was bloody and fairly short. He persuaded the Emir of Tunis to give him protection, in exchange for a share of the booty. The Emir was delighted; Barbarossa was a national hero among the Arabs. Barbarossa repaid him by strangling him one day (with only one hand—he had lost the other in battle) then proclaiming himself Emir.

Charles I of Spain sent an army of 10,000 against him, and Redbeard was literally hacked to pieces. But his younger brother remained, and he went on to make the name of Barbarossa as feared as that of Attila or Genghis Khan. He decided it was too dangerous to be a king or sultan; so he approached the Turkish Sultan of Constantinople, and offered to retake Tunisia and present it to him. The Sultan provided a huge army, with which Barbarossa II reconquered all the land his brother had lost. Then he went on to become the most successful pirate in world history.

His ships raided from Spain to the Black Sea. Majorca and Minorca were overrun so often that the coastal inhabitants moved their villages inland and fortified them. The seaside towns of Italy were next subjected to a reign of terror like the one they had known 1600 years earlier. Because Barbarossa regarded this as a Holy War, he would have whole towns destroyed; everyone who was too old—or too young—to be carried off

DARING DEEDS were the hallmark of famous pirates. Pierre Legrand (left) was the first openly to take on a war ship. Others (above) followed his lead.

as slaves was murdered. On one occasion, he heard about the charms of a famous beauty, the Duchess of Trajetto, in Italy. He decided that he would like to present her to his master, the Sultan of Constantinople; so his ships swooped on Calabria—a fleet of 60 galleys. The Duchess was warned just in time, and fled in her nightdress, riding until her horse dropped from exhaustion at Fordi. When she returned a few weeks later, the town was just a few smoking ruins, full of horribly mutilated and crucified corpses of women and children. Barbarossa was a man of violent temper, who did not like to be thwarted.

Married bliss

When he was finally tamed, it was not by the armies and fleets which the Europeans threw against him, but by a beautiful Christian girl. His ships were sailing past Reggio, in Calabria, when someone in the shore battery was reckless enough to fire a defiant shot. Barbarossa had not intended to land, but this insult so enraged him that he took 12,000 men and besieged the town.

The daughter of the governor was taken prisoner; she was 18, and very beautiful. Barbarossa was an elderly man—in his sixties—and he fell violently in love. He could have had the girl sent to his harem and then raped her. Instead, he begged her to marry him, offering to show mercy to the townspeople. She had no choice. Barbarossa found married bliss so satisfying that he retired to Constantinople, built himself a magnificent mausoleum, and died happily in his bed—of sexual over-indulgence.

By this time the whole of Europe was nauseated by the corsairs.

The Pope summoned all the knights of Europe to a major crusade—even the Protestant Queen Elizabeth of England sent one of her best seamen, Sir Richard Grenville. Spain supplied a large fleet—and on one of its galleys sailed Miguel Cervantes, the future author of *Don Quixote*. On October 7, 1571, two enormous fleets—of about 300 vessels each—faced one another in one of the most significant sea battles of the world, Lepanto.

Moslem sea power in the Mediterranean was broken as decisively as Pompey had earlier broken the pirates. The world's second great age of piracy was over. Ominously enough, however, the third age was just beginning—the age of the "Spanish Main".

The defeat of the Turks meant that Spain was now one of the leading nations of Europe. It might have gone on to become the master of Europe if it had not been for the defeat of the Armada in 1588. But Spain was still a meaningful power in the New World across the Atlantic. It held Cuba, Puerto Rico, Santo Domingo, and parts of the mainland known as the Spanish Main. The Spaniards were determined to retain their new empire at all costs. A French settlement in Florida was wiped out in 1562; in 1604, two British ships were captured in the West Indies, and the Spaniards cut off the hands, feet, noses and ears of the men, smeared their bodies with honey, then left them tied to trees to be bitten by flies and ants as they bled to death.

The same kind of ruthlessness had destroyed most of the native population of the West Indian islands. Various Europeans began to drift in, mostly French and English, escaping from religious persecution at home and hoping to make new lives. There was plenty of meat on Santo Domingo, Haiti, in the form of wild hogs; French settlers—many of them criminals fleeing from justice—made some kind of a living by killing and skinning the hogs. They dried their skins in smoking-huts called *boucans*; so they became known as "boucaneers" or buccaneers.

Playing cards

When the Spanish tired of these seventeenth-century "hippies" living on their island, they drove them off, and the buccaneers retreated to a small island called La Tortuga. They now had no pigs to skin, and took to piracy for a living. Again, the Spaniards had made a rod for their own backs.

One of the first buccaneers on record

Pirates

KNIGHTED for his work on behalf of the British Crown, Henry Morgan (right) was a national hero and personal friend of the King of England. Victor of many battles and daring raids (above and opposite) he was, nevertheless, a notorious pirate who plundered and murdered as much for personal gain as for service to his country. He died a wealthy man.

was Pierre Legrand, who is unusual because he stayed in his profession for such a short period. He managed to assemble a boat and a small crew in Tortuga, then set out to find ships to rob. For weeks they had no luck, until they were running short of food. One day, they saw a heavily armed convoy of treasure ships sailing past—and Legrand decided to try and equal Barbarossa's feat with the Pope's galleys.

Under cover of darkness, they sailed up to the last ship. The watch was asleep—no one expected a warship to be attacked. Legrand found the captain and three Spanish grandees playing cards; they were shot down when they resisted. Twenty of the crew were killed before the rest surrendered. Then the pirates turned the ship in the darkness and sailed off. The treasure on board was enough to make most of them rich, and Legrand retired to Normandy, where he lived in comfort until his death.

One of the most brutal and vicious of the pirates of Tortuga was Jean-David Nau, known as Lolonais, an ex-slave, who appears to have been motivated by a desire for revenge on the Spaniards. One chronicler describes how he became so enraged with one of his Spanish captives that he slashed open his chest with a cutlass, tore out his heart, and began to gnaw it with his teeth. It is certainly in character. Lolonais raided towns in Spanish possession—Maracaibo and Gibraltar—and inflicted horrible tortures on their inhabitants to make them reveal where they had hidden their money. Then the captives were executed.

Cabin boy

The fortunes of the Spanish went from bad to worse. Charles I of England was a Catholic and friendly to Spain, but when he was executed, Oliver Cromwell sent an expedition to the West Indies, and captured Jamaica. The British were glad to help anybody who made the lives of the Spaniards a misery, so they encouraged the buccaneers. They encouraged a man whose name has become almost synonymous with the history of piracy—Henry Morgan. Morgan was a Welshman, who went to sea as a cabin boy and landed in Jamaica. It was with the aid and the blessings of the governor of Jamaica, Sir Thomas Modyford, that Morgan began his career as a pirate.

Living shields

There was actually a treaty of non-aggression with Spain in 1667, but Modyford heard that the Spaniards were preparing a huge expedition to conquer Jamaica. So he sent out Henry Morgan in charge of 12 ships to get in the first blow. Morgan marched 50 miles inland to the town of Puerto del Principe, took it by storm, and tortured the inhabitants until he extracted a confession that 70 men *had* been forced to join the army for an expedition against Jamaica.

His men then made the citizens reveal the whereabouts of their treasures. Delighted by success and eager for more riches, they attacked the strongly-fortified towns of Puerto Bello and La Gloria; they captured the latter by driving monks and nuns in front of them as living shields as they advanced on the walls.

Morgan's most daring raid was on

Panama, which involved a nine-day march through jungles and up rivers. This caused trouble with the British government, and Sir Thomas Modyford was ordered to arrest Morgan and send him to London. Morgan went – voluntarily – and arrived in the capital to find himself a national hero, like Drake. He spent three comfortable years in London, became a friend of the king, and was finally sent back to Jamaica with a commission to wipe out the buccaneers. Morgan's conscience was not disturbed. He persecuted his former shipmates with the same ruthless ferocity he had shown towards the Spaniards. He was knighted, and died a rich man. So the passing of the greatest of the buccaneers brought the era of buccaneers to a close.

Not, however, the end of piracy. Now that it had ceased to be profitable on the Spanish Main, the pirates moved across the Atlantic to the Indian Ocean. The East India Company had opened up the trade routes to India, and the seas around Africa were as full of vulnerable shipping as the Mediterranean had been a few centuries earlier. The most famous of the Indian Ocean pirates was again an Englishman, Henry Every (sometimes spelt Avery). His most famous feat was the seizure of two ships of the "Mocha fleet" in 1695.

Turkish harem

Mocha used to be one of the greatest ports of southwestern Arabia, and the ships that sailed from Mocha to India were usually laden with treasure. According to a legend that made Every's name famous in England, one of these two ships contained the daughter of the Grand Mogul of India – who was so beautiful that Every married her.

The truth was less romantic and more brutal. The ships *were* full of treasure, and beautiful Turkish girls who were being taken to a harem. Most of the women, young and old, were raped – some of them so sadistically that they died. One old lady who was raped *was* a relative of an Indian king, which may have given rise to the story of the beautiful princess.

The pirates obtained some £1000 each from the exploit. Every then took refuge in the Bahamas, and applied for a Royal Pardon. Unfortunately, his action had caused so much trouble in India that the British government offered a reward of £500 a head for Every's crew. As soon as they heard this the men split up and fled. Twenty-four of them were caught, and six of these hanged – but Every vanished completely, to become another of the great legends of piracy.

The pirate who gained the most evil reputation of all, "Blackbeard", was, in fact, one of the least vicious of all the corsairs. He started his career round about 1700, serving on "privateers" against Spain. A privateer was a privately owned warship, permitted by its own government to prey on the ships of an enemy government. Blackbeard's real name was Edward Teach, and when the war with Spain ended in 1713, he continued as a pirate in a captured French ship.

He plied his trade up and down the east coast of America, with the active support of the Governor of North Carolina. The reason for this support was simple; England tried to force her colonies to trade only with her own vessels, so the resentful Americans didn't mind English ships being attacked.

For some time, Blackbeard enjoyed a profitable career as he also treated his captives with reasonable humanity. Finally, however, the Governor of Virginia – a richer state with no liking for pirates – despatched Lieutenant Robert Maynard with two sloops to search out Blackbeard. Maynard finally cornered him in an inlet, drove his ship aground, and captured it after fierce fighting. Blackbeard's head was cut off, and left to dry on the mainmast.

Chinese hatred

After the death of this last of the "pirate princes" there was another brief outburst of piracy after the Napoleonic wars. Eventually, most of the civilized nations banded together to put an end to it when they signed the Declaration of Paris in 1856 – making privateering internationally illegal. Piracy still continued in the China seas – rooted in the Chinese hatred of foreigners – until the coming of steamships put an end to it.

In all, it had taken mankind just over 3000 years to get rid of one of its most vicious habits, and some of its most vicious practitioners.

PIRACY SOON found its way from the high seas to the stage, and audiences responded with enthusiasm. Above, an early dramatic portrayal of "Red Rover".

POISONERS

THE MACABRE MINDS OF THE POISONERS

1 Marie Lafarge

2 Dr. Pritchard

3 Madeleine Smith

4 Adelaide Bartlett

5 Marquise de Brinvilliers

6 Schoolboy Graham Young

7 Cesare Borgia

8 Mrs. Nannie Doss

DOCTORS, noblemen, "innocent" young women, religious fanatics, old grandmothers and adolescent schoolboys: they plotted and killed with poison . . .

Poisoners

ONE OF the more enduring myths of criminology is that poison is the favourite weapon of the female criminal. All you have to do to disprove that is to glance at a representative list of female killers: Charlotte Corday, Catherine Hayes, Kate Webster, Lizzie Borden, Ruth Snyder, Maria Manning, Ruth Ellis, Aileen Wuornos – most of whom used axes, knives or guns. It is true that a similar list could be drawn up to include Lucrezia Borgia, Marie Lafarge, Madeleine Smith, Adelaide Bartlett, but this proves no more than that women have used poison as often as men.

Poison is not the prerogative of either sex. But the very fact that there *is* such a myth provides a key to the mentality of the poisoner.

A surprisingly high proportion of poisoners are daydreamers, fantasists — capable of telling splendid, elaborate lies to other people and to themselves. They would shrink from using anything as crude as a knife or a revolver. In short, poisoners usually have a touch of the artistic temperament; and the artistic temperament has more than a touch of the feminine — as Oscar Wilde showed in his essay on the nineteenth-century poisoner Thomas Wainewright, *Pen, Pencil and Poison*.

Weak-willed

Examine the above list of female murderers, and another interesting aspect becomes apparent. The last four names on it were acquitted, although most students of crime would agree they were probably guilty. Marie Lafarge — a fantasist if ever there was one — was very nearly acquitted. There is something oddly practical about these daydreamers: they get away with it.

And what of the other name on the list — the most notorious poisoner of them all, the woman whose name has become synonymous with evil and murder? Oddly enough, this is another example of myth-making. Poor Lucrezia Borgia almost certainly never killed anybody, and she was anything but a murderess by nature. A gentle, rather weak-willed girl with the temperament of a good housewife, her chief claim to fame is that she was the sister — and mistress — of one of the deadliest men in history, Cesare Borgia. It was Cesare who was the master-poisoner, and who is one of the most interesting examples of the criminal temperament since the Emperor Caligula (A.D. 37-41).

Lucrezia and Cesare Borgia were the bastards of a cardinal and a courtesan. The cardinal, who later became Pope Alexander VI, was Roderigo Borgia. He was rich, powerful, easygoing, and he kept his mistress, Vannozza Cattanei, in style in a *palazzo*. Vannozza bore him five children. Of these Lucrezia, the youngest, was born in 1480. Of the sons, Juan inherited his father's carefree temperament; but from the beginning, Cesare was violent and headstrong. Handsome, charming, vital, and energetic, he had the spoilt child's compulsion to have his own way in everything. He was very definitely a High Dominance Male. And Lucrezia, with her pretty oval face and slightly receding chin, was very much a medium-dominance female.

This is, of course, the classic combination for producing crime—Snyder and Gray, Fernandez and Beck, Brady and Hindley, are all examples of this explosive mixture of the Dominator and the Dominated. Lucrezia seemed made to be dominated, and she adored both her brothers—particularly Cesare. She probably lost her virginity to him before she reached her teens. Cesare was the sort of person who needed frequent sexual conquests—not

POISONER'S PALACE (left) . . . where Cesare and Lucrezia Borgia were born. Cesare (below) was the mastermind behind the poisonings which made his sister (inset) a legendary criminal.

so much out of sensuality, as a desire to prove his power and potency.

There are plenty of such despots in the history of crime: men who have an insane compulsion to have their way in absolutely everything, and who cannot bear to be crossed in the slightest thing. Most of them, however, have to compromise with reality to some extent. They behave perfectly normally with the world at large, and take out their delusions of grandeur on their wives and families. Cesare Borgia is interesting because he was in a position where he could put his fantasies of godlike power into action.

He set out to sleep with every woman who attracted him—whether it was his own sister, or the wife of his younger brother. When he captured a town, he had 40 of its prettiest virgins sent for him to deflower. When invading Swiss soldiers looted his mother's house, he captured them, and had them tortured to death.

Later he spent some time at the French court where he suffered slights and humiliations. When he returned to Italy, he had most of the servants who had witnessed his humiliations murdered, so they couldn't mention what they had seen. The slightest frustration drove him to murder. His father seemed to prefer his brother Juan to himself. Accordingly Cesare had Juan murdered, and his body thrown into the Tiber. When Lucrezia married Alfonso of Aragon—on her father's orders—Cesare was so frantic with jealousy that he had Alfonso killed. When Cesare called on her at her castle a few months later, Lucrezia, in spite of her grief, welcomed him, and probably slept with him. (Her first child was almost certainly Cesare's.)

Stripped and left

Cesare was an adept in the use of poisons. Some of them could make the victim die a lingering death, making his hair and teeth fall out; others could kill immediately, with all the symptoms of a stroke or heart attack. It is satisfactory to record that his downfall came through poison. Cesare and his father—the Pope—were invited to dine with a cardinal, Adriano de Corneto. They fell violently ill after the banquet. (So did the cardinal — but that was probably political wisdom.) The Pope died. And Cesare, who believed himself invincible and invulnerable, suddenly saw his castle of fantasy collapse.

His troops deserted him. He was made prisoner by a new Pope. He fled to Spain, and was imprisoned for his brother's murder. He escaped and joined a small army belonging to his brother-in-law; in a minor skirmish, he was seriously wounded, stripped and left to die. He was 32 years old, and had been responsible for dozens of murders. His sister Lucrezia married again, became famous for her kindness and piety, and lived happily ever after—

or at least for 11 years, until she was 39.

It is ironic that this gentle, affectionate girl should have become known as one of the great poisoners of history, when there is no evidence that she ever harmed anyone except, possibly, herself.

Cesare Borgia dispensed death by many other means beside poison; he also had his enemies strangled, stabbed, and hacked to pieces. Yet in a sense, he remains the archetypal poisoner. His portraits do not show an obviously evil ruffian; they depict a dreamer with an intelligent face. (He loved art, and was a patron of Leonardo and Raphael.) He believed—as did his sister and mother—that he could become the master of Italy, perhaps of the world. It was fantasy; he didn't have the realism of his namesake, Julius Caesar. His military successes were due to the backing of his father as much as to his own good generalship.

Childish act

Everybody, at one stage of their development, would like to impose their will upon the world. Everybody would like to see their enemies humiliated, their loyal friends rewarded. But most of us have to come to terms with a world in which this is not possible. If we learn to adjust well, we become decent, complex, mature human beings. Children don't *want* to adjust. As Freud points out, a child with infinite power would quickly destroy the world in a rage. Criminals are basically people who have failed to come to terms with this reality. Although they know they can't make the world obey their will, they still try to cheat it in minor ways—to steal what it refuses to give.

A man like Cesare Borgia never makes the slightest attempt to come to terms with reality from the beginning. He had two people who adored him—his mother and sister—and one who loved him self-indulgently—his father. So, like a spoilt child, he was allowed to indulge his tantrums all his life. This was a tragedy, for he had the intelligence and vitality to be a great man. But by the time he was 20, tantrums and violence had become such a habit that nothing could cure him. It was also a tragedy for the world that it had to put up with his monomania.

Here, then, is the basic picture of the criminal—but especially of the poisoner. For to kill by poison is perhaps the most *childish* of all criminal acts. It is an attempt to stay on good terms with the world while breaking its laws. At the same time, it is one of the cruellest forms of murder. Anybody who has ever had mild food poisoning knows how bad it can be—vomiting until you are exhausted, and then vomiting again, unable to think because even thinking makes you feel sick.

The poisoner can inflict this because he—or she—has decided to ignore the

2370 | Poisoners

victim, to pretend he is a mere object with no feelings. Nearly all the famous poisoners have been rather childish personalities — often delightful and charming, but fundamentally children determined to get their own way by stealth.

Lucrezia Borgia was innocent; the woman who *deserves* Lucrezia Borgia's reputation was another pampered aristocrat, Marie, the Marquise de Brinvilliers, executed in 1676. The eldest of five children, she was the daughter of a Councillor of State and Treasurer of France. Like Cesare Borgia, she was eye-catching and charming; and, like Cesare — and like many highly dominant women — she was a sexual experimenter. She later admitted to having had sexual intercourse with her brother while still a child.

At 21, in 1651, she married Antoine de Brinvilliers, Baron de Nourar, who turned out to be a gambler and a libertine. Eight years later, the Baron met a gambler and charming confidence man named Ste Croix, who soon became Marie's lover. The Baron didn't object to this liaison, but Marie's father did. He had Ste Croix arrested and thrown into the Bastille. There Ste Croix met an expert in poisons named Exili, and became his pupil and disciple. Released from prison after six months, he and Marie decided that the quickest way to lay hands on a fortune was to poison Marie's father.

It was here that Marie revealed the typical "dissociation" of the poisoner. She visited hospitals, giving poisoned fruit to the invalids, to see whether the poison could be detected at an autopsy. It couldn't — almost no poison *could* be at that date. Then Marie went to stay with her father, and he fell ill. She nursed him with apparent devotion for eight months, until he died. When she had inherited his fortune, she took a series of lovers. She resembled Cesare Borgia in another way: she couldn't bear to be crossed; when a creditor had one of her houses sold to pay a debt, she set it on fire.

Blackmail

The following year, 1667, she devoted to poisoning her two brothers. But her success made her careless. She revealed her plans to her lovers, who were more squeamish than she was. Ste Croix, for example, blackmailed her. Another lover, the tutor of her children, tried to dissuade her from further murders, and so became a prime target himself; he survived several attempts on his life. She now decided to poison her husband, so she could marry Ste Croix. But Ste Croix (wisely) didn't want her. Whenever her husband fell ill, he rapidly administered antidotes.

PIOUS but deadly, Marie de Brinvilliers escaped to a Dutch convent when her incriminating letters were discovered. She was finally arrested and executed.

Finally, Marie met her downfall. Ste Croix died — presumably of natural causes — and Marie's first thought was for the box containing her letters to him — with which he had been blackmailing her. Her concern was not misplaced. When the box was opened, orders for her arrest went out immediately, and one confederate was broken alive on the wheel. She then fled to the Netherlands, entered a convent, and managed to avoid arrest for three years. At last the law caught up with her. Her confessions were so frank and sensational that they had to be printed in Latin. After a trial lasting nearly three months, she went to the block. Her body was burned, and the ashes scattered.

The pattern should by now be clear. Not all poisoners have dominant personalities; but the element of fantasy and daydreaming seems common to most. Perhaps the most celebrated single case in the history of poisoning is that of Marie Lafarge. Marie poisoned her husband with arsenic in 1840, and the case is of interest to criminologists chiefly because it was one of the earliest cases in which forensic toxicology played a major part.

Fake affection

An English chemist, Marsh, had discovered that if arsenic — or anything containing it — is put into sulphuric acid and zinc added, a gas called arsine is formed. Then, if a narrow jet of this gas is burned and a cold porcelain dish placed in the flame, the arsenic is deposited on the dish. It was this that caused Marie's undoing, and led to her sentence for life imprisonment. But the real fascination of the case is the personality of Marie Lafarge — a spoilt, rather pretty young girl, brought up at an expensive private school with the daughters of aristocrats, but without any large fortune of her own.

She was pleased, therefore, when a coarse farmer and ironmaster, Charles Lafarge, approached her through a matrimonial agency. Although she disliked her suitor, she accepted him because she thought he was a rich landowner, and that she would be able to invite her friends to stay at their château. When she discovered that the château was a decaying house, and the estate was a muddy village, she was at first heartbroken. Then she apparently made up her mind, quite coolly, to escape from the situation by poisoning her husband.

In the months following the marriage — during which she faked affection for Lafarge — she carried out the poisoning with the callousness and deceit of a delinquent child. But several relatives of the doomed man saw her adding a white powder to his food. Even before his death, a medical expert called in to attend to Lafarge said he was dying of poison. Marie was duly arrested; experts on poison clashed at her trial; the case became a *cause célèbre*, splitting France into two factions: her accusers and her sympathizers. For a time, it looked as if she would be acquitted; but the evidence of the great poison-expert Orfila convicted her. She spent ten years in prison – during which she corresponded with her most influential supporter, the novelist Alexandre Dumas – and eventually died of tuberculosis at the age of 36.

This same streak of immaturity and fantasy can be seen in most of the major English poisoning cases, from Dr. Pritchard and Madeleine Smith to Londoner Graham Young, the "motiveless poisoner" who, in 1972, confessed to administering poison to his father, stepmother, and school friend. One of the most celebrated of English poison mysteries is that of the death of Charles Bravo, who died of antimony poisoning at his house, the Priory, in Balham, South London in 1876. His pretty wife Florence was tried for his murder, but finally acquitted. Yet in all the essentials described above, she had the temperament of a poisoner: the immaturity, the childish desire for her own way, the dreamy, romantic disposition. This does not prove her guilt; but, added to the other evidence, it makes it very likely.

Possibly the oddest thing about poisoners is that there is something in them that keeps them permanently immature, so they never grow up. This can be seen in America's classic poison case, that of Nannie Doss (sometimes known as "Arsenic Annie") who continued her literally poisonous career over nearly 30 years – and would probably have continued into old age if a doctor's suspicions had not mercifully been aroused.

Coy murderess

This fortunate event took place on October 6, 1954, when a 58-year-old man died in Tulsa, Oklahoma. He had been in hospital shortly before his death, suffering from stomach pains. He recovered and returned home with his wife, 49-year-old Nannie Doss. Nannie made him a large dish of stewed prunes, and he died the next day. His doctor, N. Z. Schwelbein, said he couldn't imagine what had killed Samuel Doss, and that there ought to be an autopsy. Nannie agreed enthusiastically. "Of *course* there should be. It might kill somebody else . . ."

When the police approached her some time later, and said that her husband's stomach had contained enough arsenic to eliminate ten men, she looked amazed and distressed. "How could such a thing

COY KILLER . . . smiling and happy, Mrs. Nannie Doss poses for camera in hallway of Tulsa Court with daughter and granddaughters. She was on trial for the murder of fifth husband – and ten others.

happen?" she gasped.

Nannie was a plump, bespectacled woman, who had obviously once been pretty; this was clear from the rather coy, soft manner, which seemed to suggest that she was younger and more desirable than she actually was. When asked if she had poisoned her husband, she stared at the police with wide open, innocent eyes, and said in a shocked voice: "My conscience is clear."

She talked openly and readily – so much so that the police had difficulty interrupting her. They began to wonder whether it was all a mistake – and then changed their minds when they asked her what she knew about a certain Richard Morton. With her customary wide-eyed frankness, she declared that she had never heard the name. They then showed her four insurance policies, which indicated that Richard Morton had been her previous husband, and that she had benefited by about $1500 from his death.

She giggled coyly. "Well, I guess I wasn't telling the truth. I *was* married to him." It took days of patient questioning, of gently bringing her back to the point, to get her to admit that she had poisoned Samuel Doss and Richard Morton.

When news of the case appeared in newspapers across the country, the Tulsa police were suddenly flooded with calls that made them realize they had apprehended a mass murderess. Samuel Doss was apparently husband number five, and

LADY KILLER with the motherly air. Mrs. Doss sits back after making the confession that she had poisoned four husbands. Left, a husband who survived.

four of the five had suffered mysterious deaths. Before Richard Morton, who died early in 1953, there had been Arlie Lanning, who was married to her from 1947 until 1952 – when he passed on of stomach pains – and Frank Harrelson, who died in 1945, the year he married Nannie.

Harrelson's two-year-old grandson had died a few months earlier in the same house; as Harrelson left the funeral he had prophetically remarked: "I'll be the next." A young nephew of Arlie Lanning's had also expired in the same house – of "food poisoning" – just before Lanning's death.

Further investigation revealed that Nannie's mother and two sisters had died with stomach pains when Nannie had been staying with them. Finally, detectives traced Nannie's first husband, George Frazer, whom she had married when she was 15. The union had been unhappy because Nannie had been wildly flirtatious, and had periodically run off with other men. She explained to the officers that she had been searching for her "dream man" all her life, and that her favourite reading was *True Romances*.

One day, it was revealed, George Frazer had come home to find two of his children dying on the floor. There was no inquest, and shortly afterwards, Nannie went off with another lover – whereupon Frazer divorced her.

Naughty girl

Under questioning, Nannie's manner never changed; she remained smiling and candid, admitting to poisoning four husbands with an apologetic giggle – as if confessing to being a naughty little girl. She indignantly denied murdering anyone except the four husbands, but gave way on this point when her mother's body was exhumed and found to be full of arsenic.

Sentenced to life imprisonment, she died of leukemia in 1965. Even as a convicted murderess, her manner never changed. Apparently nothing could make her admit that being responsible for the deaths of eleven people – four of them children – was at all wicked. Why had she committed murder? Because she was a romantic with a high level of sexual drive; she felt she deserved more of life than boring, ordinary husbands.

Most poisoners – unlike other types of murderers, whose methods are more direct and violent – kill in order to gain emotionally or materially. The wife slowly but lethally disposes of the husband she has grown tired of; the husband, in turn, gets rid of a faded and no longer loved wife, and replaces her with the latest model.

Poison is used by those who have carefully calculated the odds, and who believe they can get away with their crime. When they are caught no one is more surprised and nonplussed than the poisoners themselves – weak, cowardly, and avaricious people, who slay by stealth and are caught by the skill of detectives and doctors.

POOK AFFAIR

THE GIRL-CHASER AND THE HOUSEMAID

He was the prodigal son in the genteel household — a spoiled, foppish young womanizer despite his mild tendency to fits. She was the housemaid, naive and pretty. Their affair would end in tragedy, rocking Victorian England.

THE remarkable Pook affair — involving sex, murder, and police bungling — shook late Victorian England to its core. But it began with nothing more sensational than the hiring of 15-year-old Jane Maria Clouson as housemaid to Mr. and Mrs. Ebenezer Pook.

In 1869 the Pooks lived in a double-fronted house on London Street, Greenwich, a short walk from the south shore of the Thames and close to Blackheath in south-east London. Pook had been a compositor on the London *Times* before leaving with his modest savings to set up as a stationer and jobbing printer close to Greenwich Town Hall. His business was soon prosperous, providing employment for his two sons — Thomas James, a serious, competent man who had married, according to the father, beneath him —

and Edmund Walter, then 20 years of age, a good-looking youngster, an elegant dresser and an inveterate girl chaser.

The Pooks were social climbers, Mrs. Pook in particular. She maintained a style suitable to both the wife of a leading businessman and — in those days a great social asset — an ex-member of the staff of the *Times* newspaper. The position of Jane Clouson in the household was humble, if useful. She shared duties with an indifferent cook and a "boy", a child who lived out and whose tasks were menial. Jane was very pretty, and a good example of a lower-class Victorian girl of impeccable morality, respectability and obedience; her parents, who had put her out to the favoured work of the times, lived in the socially inferior Isle of Dogs where her father was a night-watchman.

This was Jane's first situation, and the Pooks employed her at a lower wage than usual while training her to cope with the long daily round as housemaid. Her eventual mastery of her job would mean that later she could move up a rank to the position of parlour-maid in a larger household.

Only a few details of her personality have survived. She was a gentle, romantic child, ingenuous as were young girls of her age; she behaved well and is said to have worked satisfactorily for the exacting, masterful Mrs. Pook, who also tried to soften her harsh Cockney accent.

Edmund was the centre of everything in the Pook household, a spoiled, indulged young man, adored by his mother. He was an epileptic, a sufferer from the *petit mal*, which is a less fearsome thing than the *grand mal*, manifesting itself in attacks comprising an alternation of consciousness at unexpected times, spasmodic muscular disturbances and a tendency to pass out suddenly, followed by a return to mental normality. Despite this, Edmund was a flirtatious and hopeful womanizer, courting several local girls simultaneously. He even kept a whistle with which to summon his lovers to their bedroom windows at night while he stood beneath in vigil.

It was not long before Edmund's eye turned to Jane Clouson. It was apparently a slow siege which required secrecy and subtlety, for the girl was highly cautious, and fearful for her position; but Edmund's bold and roving eye contributed to an association which grew with time. Jane, the unworldly innocent, must in the end have received Edmund in her bedroom—there were three attic rooms at the top of the house, Jane's being the smallest but closest to the head of the narrow upper stairs.

About Christmas, 1870, she confided to a friend that she feared she was pregnant; she did not name the putative father, but evidence pointed to Edmund Pook. Her behaviour proclaimed that she was in love with him. Up to then her fears were unfounded; she had either had a false pregnancy, or was biologically innocent; she was certainly in her normal health shortly afterwards.

The affair must have continued, but somewhere there was carelessness; for on Thursday, April 6, 1871, the day before Good Friday, an irate Mrs. Pook cross-examined Jane, and the maid told her that she was "certainly" pregnant.

Sex with a servant

Jane was instantly dismissed, told to pack her things and leave. Whether she accused Edmund or not is unknown; if she did, Mrs. Pook would never have considered a son of hers to be sexually associating with a servant. Through the friend to whom Jane had voiced the belief in her pregnancy at Christmas, a room was found for her in the house of a Mrs. Hamilton in Ashburnham Place, very close to the Pook printing and stationery premises in the parallel Greenwich High Road.

There Jane spent Easter with a landlady who took a great liking to her. Easter Monday she passed at the home of her mother's sister, a Mrs. Elizabeth Trott, who lived with her husband and daughter, Charlotte, in nearby Deptford; Charlotte was a close friend to Jane and knew all about the romance with Edmund Pook.

The proximity of Edmund at work meant that the pair would be able to indulge in secret meetings, but whether Edmund desired to see the girl or not was of no importance. Jane, now 17, was convinced that she was pregnant, as her women friends authoritatively advised her, and Edmund knew that she could not

"LET ME GO!" cried a girl at Kidbrooke Lane, a favourite trysting spot. Was it pregnant Jane Clouson struggling with her lover Edmund?

be shrugged off. On Sunday, April 23, Jane Clouson visited her cousin and, according to Charlotte Trott's later words, said: "... Edmund says I must meet him either tomorrow night or Tuesday to arrange with him to go into the country ... You must not be surprised if you miss me for some weeks, but you shall have the first letter I shall write to anyone. Edmund says ... I shall be happy." The rest of her talk with Charlotte revealed that Edmund was carefully anticipating future enquiries.

Judging by the hearsay of the time, Edmund Pook was unwillingly associating with the girl, covering his tracks and making sure his parents knew nothing. Whether he had murder in mind is not clear. He certainly bought a packing-case opener. This was a flat metal object about a foot long with, at one side of the head, a rounded axe for cutting through wood and, on the other side, a small hammer. At the top was a pronged "jemmy" for forcing out nails. This was a commonplace article of commercial and household use in those days.

Excitement and joy

On Tuesday, April 25, Jane Clouson had told most of the people in her small circle that she was meeting Edmund at seven o'clock that night at the foot of Crooms Hill, when her future was to be decided, a prophecy which she anticipated with excitement and joy. What happened after seven o'clock is not known in detail. In view of later events there is no doubt that Jane and Edmund must have walked across Blackheath Common on their way to the lonely fields favoured by courting couples.

Their final destination was Kidbrooke Lane, a quiet spot where the little Kid Brook crossed the road. It was here, on the same night, that a man claimed he heard a girl's voice crying: "Let me go! Let me go!"—not an unusual thing in that neighbourhood—and that he saw a man and a woman struggling, the woman wearing a dark dress and jacket, a dark hat, with a pink rose ornamenting the jacket. The evidence was dubious, for it was dusk and the sun had set around eight o'clock, but later the man was to identify Edmund Pook as the one who had struggled with the woman. Another man named Lazell claimed that he saw Pook in a cornfield that night with a female companion; other courting couples heard cries for help at about eight o'clock.

The certain fact is that P.C. Gunn, whose beat included Kidbrooke Lane, went along it twice at long intervals, seeing nothing. On his final journey, at 4.15 a.m., he came across a woman on the ground; in the light of his oil lantern he saw that her head was gashed and bloodied. Gunn did what he could, though the girl was beyond coherent speech; he covered her with his cape, and went some distance towards Eltham before he was able to contact a sergeant of police.

The pair commandeered a cab, and the willing cabman helped get the woman on board. At the house of Dr. John King, of Eltham, she was given attention and detained there while the doctor did what he could. The next day her condition had deteriorated and she was rushed to Guy's Hospital, where she died.

Wild and ferocious

The post mortem revealed the extent of her injuries. There were 11 incised wounds on the face, with two deep gashes on the left side, one of which had driven bone into the brain. One eye was almost torn from its socket. The overall effect suggested a wild and ferocious attack, either by someone anxious to hide the victim's identity or by a maniac. The corpse was that of a young woman, of the working class, quite definitely two months pregnant.

Somewhat casual police investigations were already on the move. At the scene of the crime footprints were found, which nobody attempted to preserve. There were blood marks near the brook, indicating that the killer had cleansed himself. Other minor objects were found, and, nearby, a packing-case axe-hammer, bearing blood and hairs.

Jane Clouson had not taken any baggage from Mrs. Hamilton's house, and a few days later the landlady talked to the Trotts and decided that something

Pook Affair

In memory of
JANE MARIA CLOUSON,
A MOTHERLESS GIRL
WHO WAS MURDERED IN
KIDBROOKE LANE, ELTHAM,
ON THE NIGHT OF TUESDAY
THE 25TH OF APRIL, 1871.
SHE WAS TAKEN TO GUY'S HOSPITAL
WHERE SHE DIED ON SUNDAY
APRIL 30TH 1871
AGED 17 YEARS
SHE WAS AGREEABLE IN MANNER,
AMIABLE AND AFFECTIONATE IN
DISPOSITION.
HER LAST WORDS WERE "OH LET ME DIE"
MAY GOD'S GREAT MERCY ...
MY MURDERER TO CONFESS HIS DREADFUL DEED,
THAT WHEN THE SECRETS OF ALL HEARTS ARE MADE
GUILT AND REPENTANCE MAY ...

THIS MONUMENT WAS ERECTED
BY PUBLIC SUBSCRIPTION

was wrong, in spite of Jane's warnings of her intended secret departure. Everyone in the area knew of the dead woman found in Kidbrooke Lane. The Trotts went to see the local police and, shown Jane's clothes, identified them, but her injuries were so appalling that the uncle and aunt were uncertain until a birthmark on the girl's body was found.

Diligent probing

All the hearsay facts came out now, and, immediately, the police went to see Edmund Pook, who behaved badly during the interview. No doubt his attitude nettled the police, placated at first by his family background. Their probings suddenly became far more diligent than their examination of the murder site. One suspicious fact after another joined together, and Edmund was arrested in May.

There was a lot of evidence against him—eye-witness facts, identification parade claims, bloodstains on his clothes, and an accumulation of important circumstantial detail. All that Jane had innocently and excitedly told her friends was

JANE'S MURDERER was not Edmund — according to the court. But public opinion thought otherwise, and the Pook family was ruined. . . .

carefully noted. The whole district turned against the Pooks; they were reviled in the streets, and Edmund's guilt was widely believed to such an extent that overexcited witnesses were to do the prosecution's case infinite harm in court.

The trial opened in the Central Criminal Court on July 12, 1871, before Lord Chief Justice Boville. Sir John Coleridge, Q.C., the Solicitor General, prosecuted, the defence being presented by the formidable James Huddlestone, Q.C. The judge was a strict interpreter of the law as it stood; he followed it rigidly, yet he showed partiality towards Edmund Pook. Certain witnesses and evidence were discounted, and hearsay, despite its cohesion and obvious importance, was not accepted by the court.

The Pook family were supporting their son to the limit. The history of his *petit mal* showed how he suffered from nosebleeds, and evidence was given to suggest that at the salient time he had been with another girl. Mr. and Mrs. Pook were formidable, a pair of unshakable if disliked witnesses. Contempt and scorn was poured on the idea of Edmund in any way associating with a "skivvy"; every fact offered by the prosecution was challenged by the Pooks.

It was never mentioned, as it could have been, that Edmund's epilepsy might well have played a part in the murder which, despite the cut and parry of evidence, was certainly committed by him. It is not unknown in medico-legal circles now —and then—that an "altered state of consciousness", known as an "epileptic equivalent" or "automatism", could well take the place of a fit; outside factors can even trigger this, during which an epileptic is capable of carrying out a murderous attack without knowing what he is doing.

Aura of public hatred

There was, of course, Edmund's prior possession of the packing-case instrument. Having it with him may have been irrational, melodramatic, or even intended as a weapon of "blackmail". However, so confused was the case and the evidence that the judge summed up distinctly in Edmund's favour. Apart from everything else, he may even have been unconsciously influenced by the tremendous aura of public hatred which had shown itself. The jury accepted his guidance and returned within 20 minutes to give Edmund Pook his freedom.

Greenwich exploded in an ecstasy of hate. Hundreds demonstrated outside the Pook home; there were street processions of protest, and violent manifestations of anger. The police did little to interfere with all this. It was said that they fiercely resented the court's remarks about their efficiency and its sharp criticisms of Inspector Mulvaney and Superintendent Griffin who had charge of the case, and certainly did not do all they could for its successful conclusion.

A rich Londoner, Newton Crossland, was so outraged at the verdict that he published a savage libel on the Pooks, bait for an action which he anticipated. When it came, and Ebenezer Pook brought suit, Edmund had to go in the box—which he could not do at his trial. Serjeant Parry, a celebrated counsel, tore Edmund to pieces and openly made it clear that here was the guilty man. A civil court could not interfere with a murder verdict; libel had been committed, so the Pooks were awarded £50 damages. There were other actions, but Edmund was never rehabilitated in the public eye. His family was ruined, and eventually dropped from sight. Local opinion never for one moment doubted the identity of Jane Clouson's murderer.

PRESIDENT GARFIELD ASSASSINATION

'GOD KILLED THE PRESIDENT'

A religious fanatic pumped two bullets into James Garfield. But when the President died nine weeks later, the gunman blamed his death on the inefficiency of the doctors . . . and the will of God.

President Garfield Assassination

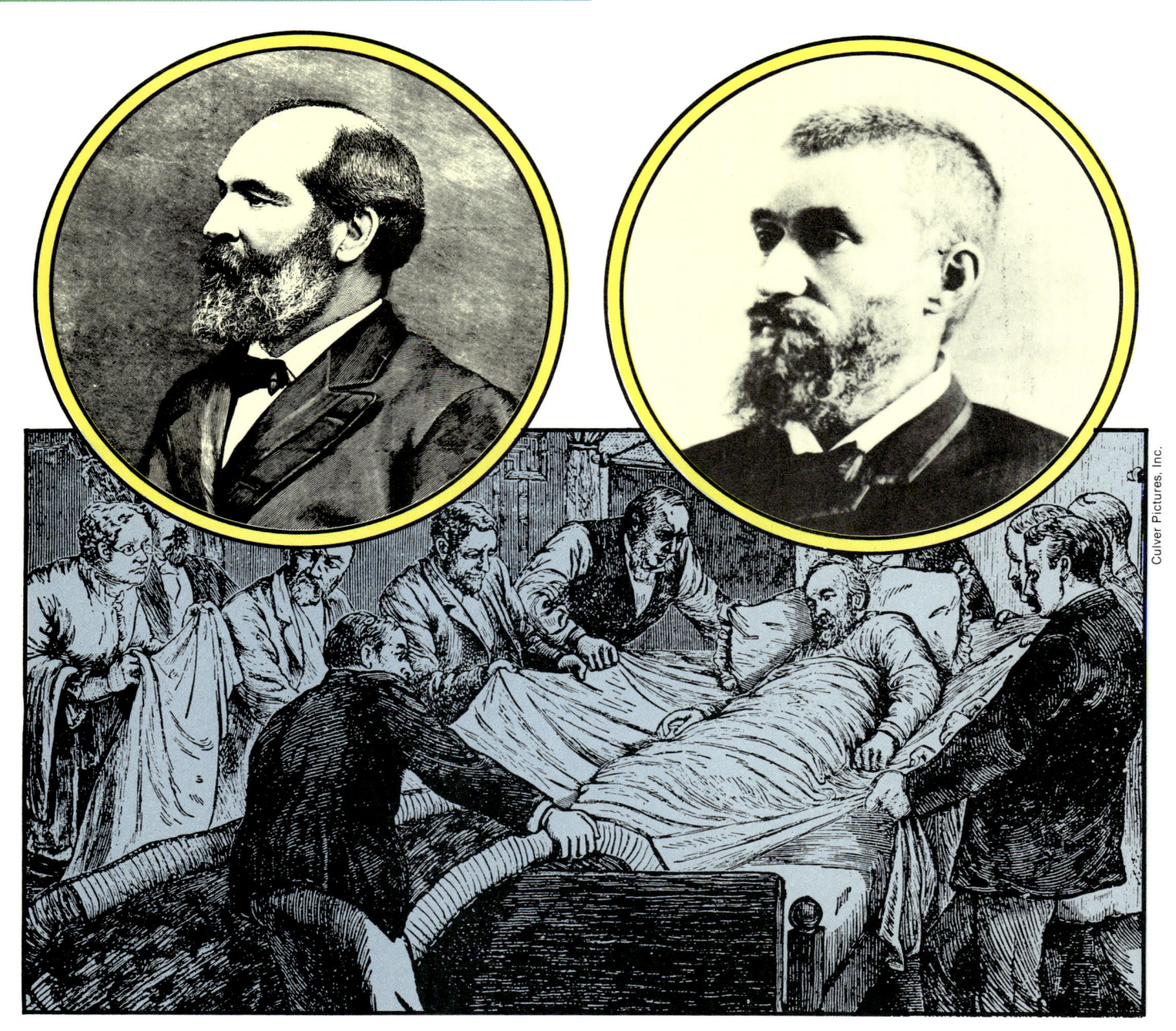

THE tragic episode which led to the trial of the crazy killer of James Abram Garfield, 20th President of the United States, took place in the ladies' waiting room of the Baltimore and Potomac Railroad station in Washington, D.C., on July 2, 1881.

Suddenly a shot rang out followed by another, and 49-year-old Garfield fell to the ground. The man who fired the shots from the crowd of spectators — which had gathered to see the President depart for New York — was promptly seized.

The President eventually died on September 19. He had been in office for less than seven months and was automatically succeeded by the Vice-President Chester A. Arthur.

The trial of Charles Guiteau for the murder of President Garfield began before

GUITEAU, THE MAN with the "bad face" (inset right) and his victim, the 20th U.S. President. Hit twice, Garfield is lowered into bed after the shooting. He died two months later from the wounds.

Judge Walter S. Cox, Associate Justice of the Supreme Court, in Washington, on November 14, 1881. Owing to frequent adjournments — caused by the prisoner's outrageous behaviour — the trial lasted intermittently for more than two months.

To begin with, the only lawyer whom Guiteau could find to undertake his defence was his former brother-in-law George Scoville. At the outset of the trial, however, the services of a more senior counsel, Mr. Leigh Robinson, were obtained. But on the opening day, after he had formally pleaded not guilty, Guiteau declared that Mr. Robinson had been briefed without his knowledge and demanded his retirement.

This the judge refused. The prisoner then produced a roll of manuscript and attempted to deliver a speech until stopped by the judge — who observed that "this was not the proper time" for such a recitation.

The jury was then impanelled, a long drawn out process, since many of those on the panel admitted that they had already formed the opinion that Guiteau should be hanged.

The prisoner continued to object to having Mr. Robinson as his leading counsel, and wrote to the newspapers amplifying his objections — an action strongly disapproved of by Scoville. Finally, on the third day of the trial, Dis-

U.S. MARSHALS rescue Guiteau from an angry crowd. America's morbid interest in the killer brought reporters from all over the country to see him in jail.

trict Attorney Corkhill opened the case for the prosecution and proceeded to call two witnesses who had been present at the time of the shooting.

These were James Blaine, who had become Secretary of State in the Garfield administration, and Señor Camacho, the Venezuelan Chargé d'Affaires; each gave his version of what had happened at the railroad station on July 2.

Guiteau's counsel clashed with another prosecution witness who had seen the shooting, when the latter was cross-examined about Guiteau's appearance at the time. "He had a bad face, according to my opinion," said this witness.

"I do not want an opinion from you," snapped Scoville.

Another angry scene occurred when Scoville asked the judge to take measures to prevent his client from giving out un-authorized communications to the press. Guiteau reacted furiously—abusing the judge, counsel, and the court officials. The judge then told him that if he did not keep quiet he would have him removed from court.

Shouting match

"I do not care if you do," answered the prisoner brazenly. "The Court of Appeal will reverse your decision and I will get a new trial. You have no right to remove me."

The shouting match terminated with an assurance from the judge that he had indeed authority to remove him and he would certainly do so if Guiteau persisted with his disturbances. Eventually the prisoner quietened down.

On the fifth day, Mr. Scoville announced that he wished to change the prisoner's plea to one of insanity, and this was accepted. In the course of his remarks to the bench, the defence counsel stated that his client acknowledged the killing.

Immediately Guiteau was on his feet. "No, your Honour," he protested. "We acknowledge the shooting but not the killing!" He went on to say that on July 25 the President's physicians had announced that their patient had not been fatally shot.

"My bullet was not fatal," Guiteau went on. "Garfield's death was caused by malpractice. I was only inspired to *shoot* the President. The doctors finished the work . . . It is the Deity's act, not mine, and I expect that He can take care of it. He has taken care of it very well so far."

When the court adjourned at the end of that day, Guiteau was placed in a prison van and taken back to the jail where he was being held in the malarial swamps on the banks of the Potomac River. On the

Members of the Press interviewing Guiteau AT POLICE HEADQUARTERS

way a man on horseback rode alongside the van and quickly discharged two shots directly into it, taking good aim at the prisoner.

A few days later another crackpot patriot named Sergeant Mason took aim at Guiteau through the window of his cell—but the bullet missed its target and flattened itself against the wall.

When the court reconvened next morning, Guiteau attributed his escape to "the intervention of Providence".

At this stage in the proceedings, Mr. Robinson intimated that he had had enough of his eccentric client and asked leave to retire from the case. "I want Robinson to stay now," exclaimed Guiteau. But the counsel insisted on withdrawing and the judge allowed him to do so.

Mental condition

When his leader had departed, Mr. Scoville rose to open the defence. He said that the plain question for the jury to decide was whether the prisoner had killed President Garfield, and if so whether his mental condition at the time was such as to render him responsible for his action.

In developing the argument in favour of his client's insanity, Scoville claimed that the burden of proof that he was sane at the time rested with the prosecution. "I never feign," the prisoner shouted at this point. "I act myself, sane or insane!"

His counsel went on to refer to Guiteau's career as a lawyer in Chicago, how he had given it up to join a socialist community, how he had helped the evangelists Dwight L. Moody and Ira Sankey, how he had been an unsuccessful lecturer and writer, and how he had depended on the Lord to pay his debts.

Again Guiteau interrupted his counsel, shouting: "I left a $5,000 a year law business to serve the Lord. I was happier than ever when I was selling my lectures on the street, for I was working for the Lord."

The prisoner's brother John Guiteau and a string of other witnesses, lay and medical, then took the stand and stated that in their view the prisoner manifested varying degrees of insanity.

Senator Logan of Illinois, the prisoner's home state, described how he had been "besieged" by the prisoner in Washington to get him a job. He thought, hardly surprisingly, that there was "something wrong in the prisoner's mental arrangement".

Guiteau's landlady then testified that he was nervous and abrupt in his actions and, moreover, that he had failed to pay his bill.

When it became known that Guiteau would next take the witness stand, the court was more crowded than ever—particularly with fashionably dressed women carrying opera glasses.

Guiteau began by reading from the written statement which he had brandished at the outset of the trial. "I propose that all the facts shall go to the jury and the court," he declared. "Any facts in my career showing whether I or the Deity fired that shot are of vital importance.

"I only did what the papers said ought to be done. Since the shooting they have deified the President. I want them and the doctors who killed him to share the odium with me. I never would have shot him of my own volition, notwithstanding the newspapers, had not the Deity commissioned me to do the deed . . .

"I am not a murderer. The Lord inspired my act, as in the case of Abraham and others in the Bible."

He went on to deliver a long, rambling speech, bringing in his allegedly lucrative practice as a lawyer; his work as a lecturer; and his unsuccessful attempt to establish a paper in New York called *The Theocrat*—which eventually got him "run down" and demoralized.

"When you are down," he said, "everyone gives you a kick!" Then, comparing his case to that of the Apostle Paul, he exclaimed, striking his fist on the table in front of him:

"I strove to frighten the world, just as Paul did. I had no money and no friends. I had just as rough a time as Paul did."

A WREATH from Queen Victoria rests on Garfield's coffin at his lying in state. "Since the shooting they have deified the President," said his killer.

Asked by his counsel about his unsuccessful application for public office, he said that he wanted to be appointed an American consul in France, either in Paris or Marseilles, on account of his French antecedents.

He had written on the subject to President Garfield and had gone to the White House to see him—when he handed the President a copy of a speech he had made in the recent Presidential election campaign.

"I wish it to be stated here," Guiteau declared, "that my getting or not getting office had nothing whatever to do with my removing the President. That was an act of inspiration, done as a political necessity. I was urged on by the Divine Presence, since the President's removal was necessary to save the nation from ruin."

Under cross-examination by the District Attorney, he admitted that he was "physically a coward, always keeping away from personal danger". But morally, he said, he was "as brave as a lion", particularly when he thought that "the Deity was backing him".

Ten Commandments

Asked whether he believed in the Ten Commandments, he said that he did.

"How about 'Thou shalt not kill'?"

At this question Guiteau bridled and pounded the table again. "I decline to discuss that with you," he shouted, adding that the jury's simple duty was to determine whether or not the Deity had inspired him to do what he did. He had no doubts himself. "The President's removal was an act of the Deity," he repeated.

"Are you insane at all?" the District Attorney asked bluntly.

"I am not an expert," the prisoner replied with some cunning. "Let the experts and the jury decide that."

"Do you feel any remorse?"

"Why of course I feel remorse—human remorse," Guiteau answered after a moment or two. "I feel sorrow."

On the nineteenth day of the trial, it was announced that President Arthur, who had been served with a subpoena by the defence, declined to appear in court as a witness. However, Garfield's successor agreed to testify by affidavit, and to answer any questions that might be put to him in writing.

The new President did so a few days later in a statement in which he said: Guiteau has rendered no services to the Republican Party that I know of, and there is no ground for supposing that he would receive political preferment."

When the prisoner's Congressman, Charles Farwell of Chicago, took the stand, he stated that Guiteau had proposed to him that if he would let him have $200,000 to purchase a Chicago news-

TROOPS AND SAILORS form a guard of honour for the President whose death was "inspired by the Deity . . . to save the nation from ruin".

paper called the *Inter-Ocean*, Guiteau "would make him President".

"That is false," the prisoner interrupted with another characteristic shout from the dock. "I never made such a proposition. I asked him to invest money in it."

Another witness called by the defence was the editor of the *Washington Gazette*, who swore that Guiteau had "made a perfect nuisance of himself about the Republican Headquarters". This produced another outburst from Guiteau.

"You were a nuisance yourself. I would rather be hanged as a man than acquitted as a fool. I will not have any more of this kind of evidence!" Then, turning towards his counsel, Guiteau added:

"If you put any more of these cranky fellows on the stand, I will score you again. I am no fool and will not allow you to make me out one."

A clergyman from New York, the Rev. Dr. McArthur, whom the prosecution called in rebuttal, gave what the newspapers covering the trial described as a shocking story of the prisoner's immorality—adding that he was divorced from his wife. "We present this testimony," the District Attorney informed the court, "to show that what the defence calls insanity is nothing more than devilish depravity."

This remark was greeted with loud applause in court. Guiteau responded by shaking his fist at the D.A. and shouting: "It is the unanimous opinion of the American people that you are a consummate jackass, Corkhill!" This was followed a little later by a further explosion when one of the medical witnesses advanced the theory that the prisoner's depravity was responsible for his having killed President Garfield.

From then on the court proceedings became more and more farcical. The prisoner suddenly showed unwanted solicitation for the jury's health. "It would be a great misfortune if anything happens to the jury," he said, and suggested that they should go for a four or five hour walk each day before breakfast.

He also frequently interrupted his counsel crying: "You talk and talk and you don't amount to a snap!" Then turning to the spectators in the gallery he exclaimed, "Scoville is making an ass of himself."

"It's an outrage"

On being told to keep quiet by a court official, he roared at him, "Mind your own business! I know my rights!" Once he called the judge an out-and-out liar, shouting and pointing his finger at him. "It's an outrage! God will curse you if you hurt a hair of my head."

On another occasion he brought the trial to a halt by screaming: "I have seven or eight hundred letters from sympathizers, many from ladies expressing their sympathies and prayers for my acquittal."

This was probably true, since women did mob him with morbid sympathy, and he was pestered by female autograph hunters in court to sign photographs of himself which they had thoughtfully provided for the purpose.

On New Year's Day, 1882, over two hundred persons, mostly women, responded to his public invitation to call on him in prison. One of his admirers sent him a poem, which he solemnly declaimed in court:

We hope that your hour of freedom is near,
For your stainless acquittal we heartily pray.
God has confirmed the act ...
Beware, ye Americans!

As the trial drew to a close, the prospects of an acquittal rapidly faded and a plaster cast was taken of his head. This necessitated shaving off his beard and moustache – which gave him an even madder and more haggard appearance.

The closing speech for the prosecution was made by a counsel from the District Attorney's office named Porter. This prompted Guiteau to intone every now and again, "A saint from Heaven could not stand Porter's abuse."

On January 25 Judge Cox summed up the evidence quite fairly, taking only an hour and a half to do so – a considerable feat of compression in view of the unusual length of time the trial had taken.

The jury were out for just under an hour, and when they filed back into the crowded courtroom it was clear from their faces that their verdict was one of "Guilty".

Asked by the judge if he had anything to say why sentence should not be passed upon him, Guiteau replied: "It was God's act, not mine. God will take care of it and won't let the American people forget it."

Judge Cox then sentenced the prisoner to death by hanging, the sentence to be carried out in Washington Jail on June 30 1882, between 12 noon and 2.00 p.m.

"May the Lord have mercy on your soul," yelled the prisoner when he heard the sentence. "I'm not afraid to die. ... I shall have a glorious flight to glory, but that miserable scoundrel Corkhill will have a permanent job down below where the Devil is preparing for him."

Guiteau was taken back to prison in a snowstorm. But when the day of the execution arrived the weather had changed to sweltering heat, and the hooting, jeering crowd which surrounded the prison refreshed themselves with lemonade and ice cream sold by itinerant vendors.

ABUSE and rambling speeches failed to help Guiteau at his trial, above. Even as the gallows trapdoor opened, right, he shouted "Glory! Glory!" through the hood.

Meanwhile the condemned man ate a good breakfast, had a bath, and read aloud to his spiritual adviser, the Rev. William Hicks, a poem he had composed entitled "Simplicity and Religious Baby Talk".

On the scaffold itself Guiteau recited another poem he had written with the refrain:

I'm going to the Lord,
I am so glad,
Glory Hallelujah!

As the executioner placed the black cap over his head and fixed the rope round his neck, the muffled words "Glory! Glory!" continued to be heard until the lever was pulled and the trap door fell open.

President Garfield Assassination | 2383

2384 | President Garfield Assassination

REJECTED for political office, Guiteau killed "to save the Republican Party".

PRICE, HARRY

THE MOST HAUNTED HOUSE IN ENGLAND

Things that went boomp in the night were no laughing matter for the terrified occupants of the sinister old rectory. The stones and bottles whizzing past their heads could be lethal. Locals told tales of the lascivious nun who had died horribly 700 years earlier. Did her ghost still thirst for revenge . . . ?

Harry Price Library

ON the night of February 27, 1939, the sky over the village of Borley in south-east England glowed red. The country lanes echoed to the sound of fire-bells as engines raced to the scene where angry flames were engulfing one of the most famous houses in Britain.

Borley Rectory, the haunted house that had baffled psychic investigators for 20 years, was burning—exactly 11 months after a "spiritual being" had threatened to destroy the building with fire.

Borley lies between Sudbury and Long Melford in Essex, and the Rectory was built in 1863. It was an ugly, red-bricked building, with dark, narrow windows that frowned over unkempt lawns. Tradition has it that the site was once occupied by a monastery, and there is a suitably grim tale told by the locals to explain some of the strange and terrifying happenings.

They say that in the thirteenth century a nun from a nearby convent fell in love with one of the monks.

The lovers tried to elope in a coach drawn by two bay horses, but were caught and punished. The monk was hanged, and the nun was walled up within the convent.

Certainly one of the most frequent apparitions seen at Borley was a nun. Sad and pale-looking, she appeared walking along a pathway that became known as "The Nun's Walk". A phantom coach had also been seen careering through the Rectory gardens.

Borley Rectory first made headlines in 1929, when the editor of the *Daily Mirror* contacted the famous ghost-hunter, Harry Price. The occupant of the house at that time was the Reverend G. E. Smith, and he had reported to the newspaper that strange things were occurring there.

Dragging footsteps

Ghostly lights appeared in locked rooms, dragging footsteps had been heard, and a maid said that she had seen the coach rushing across the lawn, before vanishing into thin air.

Price set off for Borley, where he was met by a reporter from the *Daily Mirror*, and upon his arrival he was told of other mysterious occurrences. Whispering voices . . . the sound of a woman crying. And the nun had been seen several times.

Price was told the story of the nun, which he quickly dismissed for a number of reasons. For one thing, he was unable to find any real evidence that a monastery had once occupied the site, or that a convent had existed nearby.

Even more conclusive was the fact that horse-drawn coaches were not invented until the fifteenth century, and although erring nuns were severely punished, it was not the practice to bury them alive.

Nevertheless, the nun persisted in being the most commonly seen apparition at Borley. She appeared on the lawn, in the gardens, and on her favourite pathway, and she often walked in full daylight.

Price did not have to wait long before he experienced for himself some of the frightening events. Indeed, his arrival was greeted with a feverish outburst of supernatural activity.

On the first evening a glass candlestick left an upstairs room, floated down into the hall and smashed itself at his feet. Pebbles, pieces of slate and mothballs followed, service-bells rang of their own accord, and keys jumped from locks.

While Price carried out his investigations, the *Daily Mirror* published a series of reports, and the Rectory became front-page news. Hordes of sightseers descended upon the house, trampling down the hedges and gardens in their attempts to see the "ghosts". At night cars jammed the lanes and a bus company ran trips to see "The Borley Ghost".

Within a month of writing to the newspaper, Mr. Smith moved out of the Rectory with his family to Long Melford. He had been driven out more by the behaviour of the sightseers than by any ghostly activities. The house then remained empty for 18 months, until October 1931, when the Rev. Lionel Foyster moved in.

Presented with new victims to plague, the Borley poltergeists went to town. In addition to their old pebble-throwing and bell-ringing tricks, they found new ways of scaring the wits out of the Foysters.

The violence became more physical, and on one occasion Mrs. Foyster received a ghostly black eye, delivered by a phantom fist as she walked along a darkened corridor.

Harry Price had not visited the Rectory since the Smiths had left, but Lionel Foyster lost no time in sending for him.

Once again the bells rang, pebbles flew and windows were smashed as the "spirits" greeted their old friend—or perhaps enemy.

Mrs. Foyster was in bed when suddenly she was heard calling for help. When Price and Foyster rushed to her room they found that the door was locked.

This, apparently, was not unusual, and did not seem to worry the clergyman, who "unlocked" the door in a manner that staggered and amazed even the hardened ghost-hunter. Placing a religious relic against the door, Foyster quietly recited the Lord's Prayer—and the bolt was heard to shoot back in the lock.

Unlike their predecessors, the Foysters stayed on, and Mr. Foyster carefully recorded every supernatural event. During the first 15 months there were more than 2000 of them, but not all were of a terrifying nature. Some of the "jokes" became a little tiresome, especially when household items began to disappear, and Mrs. Foyster's teapot was a favourite object of puckish attention.

A pile of hymn books

Sometimes the ghosts were quite helpful, like the time when a pile of hymn books was found in the kitchen. Nobody knew where they came from, but the church was short of hymn books, so the gift came in useful.

Appreciation of this little act of kindness was tempered when Mrs. Foyster's teapot disappeared again.

During a period of several weeks all was quiet: no bells, no pebbles, no footsteps, and the Foysters began to think that the haunting had ended. But it was only a lull, and when the activities started again they did so with renewed ferocity.

The Rector was awakened one night by a blow on the head from his own hair brush. The next day his wife was hit by a flying door-knob.

An attempt to exorcise the place was

BROODING Borley Rectory . . . and the famous ghost-hunter Harry Price. His arrival was greeted with a feverish outburst of supernatural activity. Herds of sightseers then descended upon the house, trampling down hedges and gardens. . . .

made by Lady Whitehouse, a friend of the family who lived in Sudbury. Mr. Foyster had already tried this, by burning creosote, but Her Ladyship chose a more fragrant method and used burning lavender.

The perfume was apparently not appreciated by the ghosts, and led to a fresh spasm of bell-ringing and stone-throwing.

In despair, the Rector sought the aid of a clergyman friend in a neighbouring parish, from whom he obtained some holy water for the purpose of trying another exorcism. The poltergeists objected to this even more strongly than they had done to the creosote and lavender.

As the Foysters moved from room to room, sprinkling and praying as they went, a large stone hit Mr. Foyster on the shoulder, and pictures fell from the walls.

During the next few days all hell was let loose. Mrs. Foyster was constantly under attack from stones, lumps of wood, and pieces of iron, and although she escaped physical injury she was reduced to a nervous wreck.

Wine on the floor

Between June and December 1931 the activities reached a peak, and on November 13 Mrs. Foyster, in the company of her maid and the nephew of Lady Whitehouse, witnessed a series of hair-raising spectacles.

The three people were having supper in the kitchen, while awaiting the return of Mr. Foyster, who was in London. Suddenly a wine bottle appeared, apparently from nowhere, and smashed into fragments under a chair.

Hardly had the maid finished sweeping away the pieces before it happened again, and a few seconds later a bottle "materialized" from thin air, hovered for a moment and then fell to the floor.

Petrified with fear, the trio stood motionless as the sound of someone—or something—was heard approaching the half-open door. As they watched, another bottle rolled into the room, circled the floor and came to rest without breaking. This episode was also played out against a background chorus of bells.

It seems incredible that the Foysters could have endured this unnerving situation for so long, yet they stayed at Borley for four years. When they moved out, in October 1935, it was decided that the Rectory should no longer be used by the church, and this gave Harry Price the chance to rent the house, so that he could carry out a thorough investigation.

APPEALS FOR HELP to tenant Marianne Foyster were perhaps the most convincing demonstration that there really was a ghost at large in Borley Rectory. But the B.B.C. crews found plenty of other kinds of frightening evidence....

He needed a team of unbiased, logically minded people, even sceptics and disbelievers—people who had never heard of Borley Rectory and would not be influenced by its past history.

His advertisement in *The Times* brought replies from scientists, university graduates, doctors of medicine, engineers—in fact people from all walks of life. The B.B.C. sent sound engineers to Borley with recording equipment.

The team's findings were published in a book by Harry Price entitled *The Most Haunted House in England,* and they make incredible reading. Price's men were hand-picked for their integrity, and for their scientific approach to the investigation.

They were not easily convinced that supernatural forces existed, either at Borley or anywhere else, yet many of the things reported in Price's book defy logical explanation. The nun was seen frequently, footsteps and knockings were heard, and various objects were mysteriously moved from one place to another.

One member of the team had a particularly nasty experience. He was alone in the Base Room when he heard the key turn in the door, locking him in. But the key was on the inside. Whatever had turned it was in the room with him.

Perhaps the most convincing demonstrations were the appearances of writing on the walls. Two men, one a B.B.C. engineer, actually saw marks appear on a wall as they stood and watched.

The philosopher and broadcaster Dr. C. E. M. Joad found pencilled scribblings on a wall that had been clean a few moments before. During the time of the Foysters, messages had been found, sometimes on scraps of paper, addressed to Marianne, Mrs. Foyster's christian name. They always appealed for help: "Marianne-help-get", and "Marianne-light-Mass-prayers", but the writings seen by the investigators were always unintelligible scrawls.

Some messages had been received by using a planchette, a device used for automatic writing, and through this it was established that the nun's name was "Marie", that she was French and had been murdered.

Threatening doom

On the night of March 27, 1938, Miss Helen Grenville, sister of one of Price's observers, picked up a message on her planchette that brought the story of Borley Rectory to its climax. She was holding a seance at her home in Streatham, south London, when the planchette began to move. Slowly the words were spelt out that threatened doom for the Rectory.

The house would be burned by the spirits that night, and under the ruins would be found the bones of a murdered person.

The fire did not occur exactly as was predicted, and two months later Price moved out of the Rectory. The next tenant was a Captain Gregson.

Marianne
light Mass
prayers

marianne

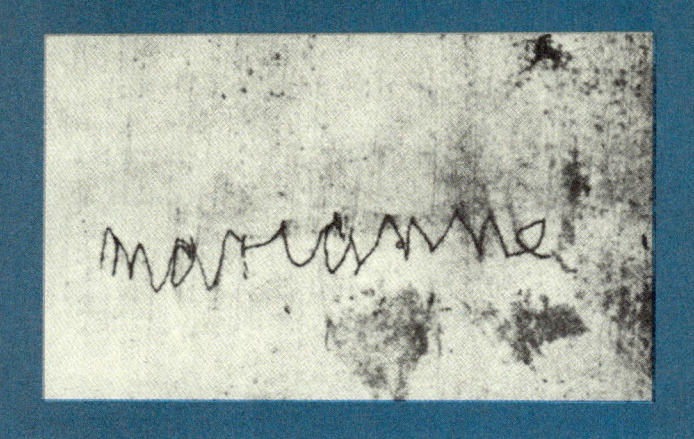

Marianne
Please help
get

Marianne

I CANNOT UNDERSTAND
TELL ME MORE

Marianne

I STILL CANNOT UNDERSTAND
PLEASE TELL ME MORE.

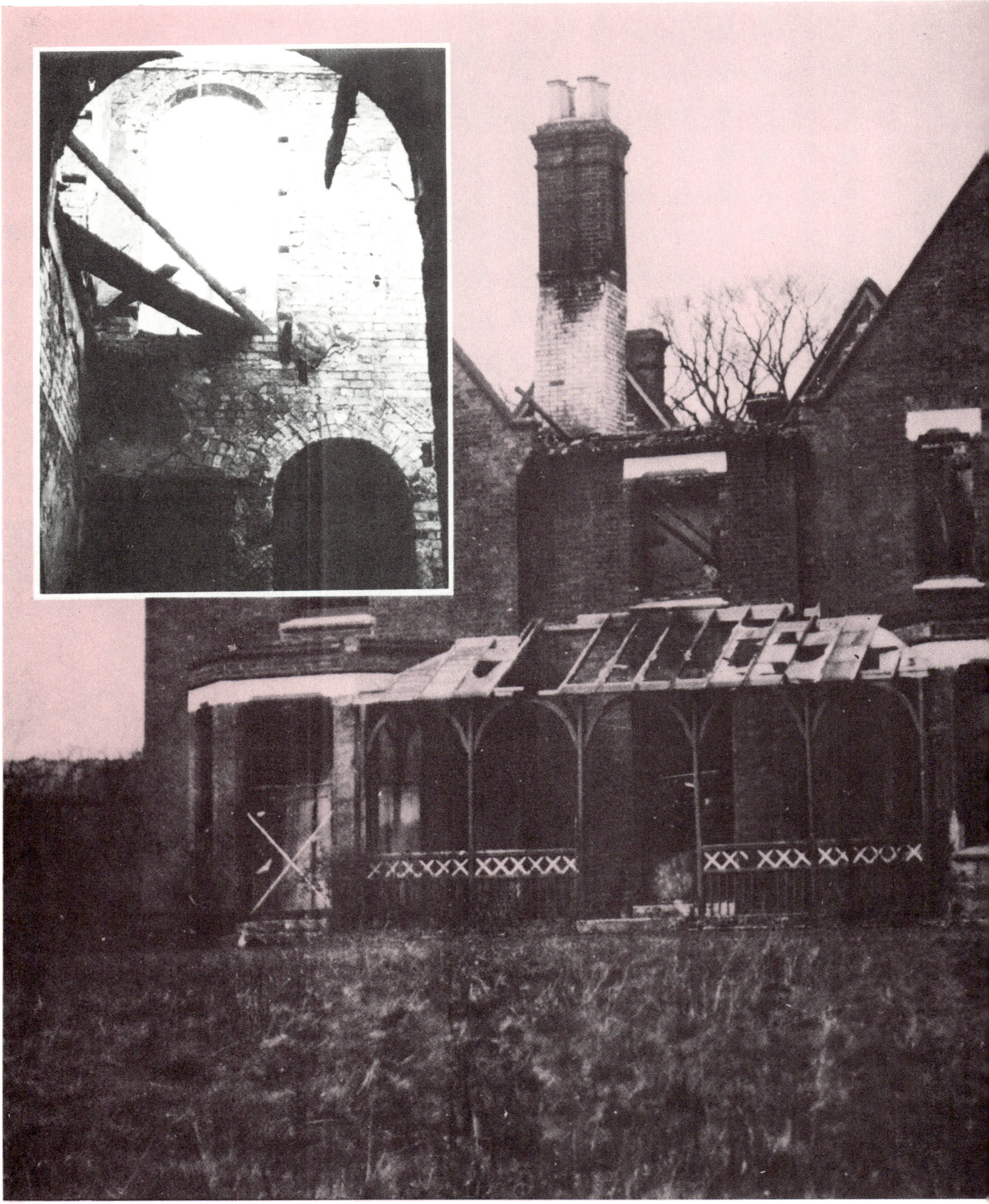

BONES found under the ruins were assumed to be all that remained of the nun. The fire that destroyed the house did not destroy its legend. Where there's smoke...

Gregson lived at Borley for 11 months, until the night of February 27, 1939. He was sorting some books in the hall when a pile of them fell from the bookcase onto a paraffin lamp. The lamp burst into flames, and within minutes the room above the hall was ablaze.

As the flames lit up the night sky the news spread through the district that Borley Rectory was on fire. The house that had struck terror into the hearts of the locals, and had made the tiny village famous throughout the world, was coming to a fitting end.

But was it the end of the ghosts? Did they ever really exist? If they did, then the flames did not destroy them. Some people claimed that they had seen weird, mis-shapen figures moving about in the burning building, and later psychical research in the gutted remains provided enough material for Price to write a second book, *The End of Borley Rectory*.

Harry Price died in 1948. Shortly after his death he was attacked by a journalist on the *Daily Mail,* who claimed that Price had organized a series of fake phenomena when he visited the place in 1929.

A fitting end

This was followed by a letter to the *Daily Mail* from Mrs. Eric Smith, whose husband had started the 20-year saga of Borley when he wrote to the *Daily Mirror*. She claimed that the poltergeist activities had only occurred when Price was at the Rectory, and said that, in her view, the house was not haunted.

In 1956 the Society for Psychical Research issued a report on the haunting of Borley Rectory, which also criticized Price. The report also suggested that Mrs. Foyster was responsible for many of the things that happened there.

But to dismiss the whole thing as a gigantic hoax is to ignore the testimonies of hundreds of people. That ghostly prediction was 11 months out – but does time mean anything to a ghost?

The fire started in the hall, whereas the message had said that it would start in the room above. Bones were found under the ruins. They were assumed to be all that remained of the nun and were reburied in Liston churchyard.

Was Price a hoaxer? Did Mrs. Foyster really "invent" all the strange happenings at Borley? There is no smoke without fire, and the fire that destroyed the house did not destroy its legend. Many people still believe that no satisfactory answer has ever been found for the mystery of Borley Rectory.

Crime File

PETER HURKOS

PSYCHIATRIC detection may seem a long way from modern police methods more accustomed to the use of science, but Peter Hurkos was taken seriously, even though he later turned to show business.

THE detectives investigating the case of the Boston Strangler—the maniac who killed and sexually assaulted thirteen women, the youngest 19 and the oldest 85, between June 1962 and January 1964—had gathered in a hotel suite in the city to go over their list of suspects. Some 300 police photographs of the Strangler's victims had been placed face downwards on the bed—the women in grotesque and shocking poses—and stockings, scarves, brassieres and blouses belonging to the murderees were in a box on the floor.

They had been brought there for the attention of the most unusual detective in the room—a tall, thickset, dark-haired Dutchman named Peter Hurkos. As a psychometrist—someone who can divine facts about people simply by touching some possession or item of their clothing—Hurkos had been called in to help identify the killer.

By passing his right hand to and fro above the photographs he could tell what position the woman was in. "Legs apart," he uttered after moving his hand over one particular stack. "I see the dead woman legs apart—one hand up, one hand down, in a funny way." His guttural accent made it difficult for the investigators to understand his every word, and to demonstrate his "vision" Hurkos lay on the floor. He spread his legs, crooked a knee, rolled his head sideways. "That woman," he exclaimed, "like this!"

Time and again he passed the photographic "test". Later, after running his hands over the nylon stockings and underwear—and after feeling a letter written by one of the suspected men—he stated definitely who the murderer was, how he looked and how he acted. He saw a small, effeminate, middle-aged man with a sharp nose—a man somehow connected with women's shoes. In fact the authorities had already placed such a person—whom they gave the alias of Thomas P. O'Brien—in psychiatric detention. Hurkos interviewed the suspect—a door-to-door salesman of nurses' shoes—and was convinced that the Strangler had been caught.

Six days later—after losing 15 lbs through his exertions—Hurkos left Boston. "My work here is finished," he stated. "The Strangler will not strike again." However, despite the profound impression he had made, the police were still not sure that O'Brien was their man. Later, Albert DeSalvo, 29, married, a small-time burglar, was arrested and then confessed to the crimes. Many people—led by Hurkos—believed him to be guilty of a number of things, but *not* the Boston stranglings. For although the psychometrist could "see" nothing about himself, he was rarely wrong when it came to revealing the truth about others.

Peter Hurkos was not born with his strange powers—they came to him literally by accident later—but he *was* born with a caul, or membrane, covering his head. He came into the world blind, in the seaport of Dordrecht, Holland, on May 21, 1911. Within minutes he almost died, and he didn't gain his sight until he was six months old. After a brief career as a sailor, he became a house painter like his father. And it was then—on July 10, 1941—that he fell from a ladder while painting a four-storey building in The Hague. He was taken to hospital with brain concussion, and was unconscious for four days. When he came to he found that his brain acted like radar, that he would never be "normal" again.

During the Second World War he worked for the Dutch resistance movement against the Nazis, and with the declaration of peace began to give psychic "readings" to women in The Hague. His sixth sense so astonished them that his fame surged throughout Holland, and early in 1951 he travelled to England to help Scotland Yard unofficially on a case. On Christmas Day 1950 a group of Scottish Nationalists had taken the Stone of Scone—used in the coronations of the early Scottish kings—from its place in London's Westminster Abbey. The Stone had been brought south from its home in Perthshire by Edward I in 1296, and its presence in the English capital was a torment to every true Scot.

After visiting the Abbey—and the Coronation Chair under which the Stone had rested—Hurkos "felt" where the missing relic was. "I see it in the remains of an old church," he said. "It has gone north of the border to Scotland. It was taken by students. It will be found within a month." Sure enough, four weeks later the Stone was recovered from the ruins of Arbroath Abbey, where the young Scotsmen had taken it. But, as was to happen later in America, the law did not altogether appreciate Hurkos's psychic deductions. He was harried and persecuted by customs men, and Scotland Yard issued a statement denying that they had asked him for help. He had done no more, they said, than "offer us information".

But if the English didn't want Hurkos, then the French did. He spent most of the next five years working with the Sûreté in Paris. In 1957 he paid his first visit to the United States, and in October of the following year became involved in a double murder in Florida. He was asked by the Miami police to give his impressions on the shooting of a local cab driver. Not only did Hurkos "see" the murderer—"A man called Smitty, tall and thin, who walks like a sailor"—but added that the killer had shot another man, a navy commander, in his apartment in Key Largo. Within a month Charles Smith, a merchant seaman with a criminal record, had been charged with the cabby's murder and jailed for life.

It was not until his much publicized work on the DeSalvo case that Hurkos became an internationally known figure. After a clash with the F.B.I. (who accused him of impersonating an agent) he moved away from crime and into the world of Hollywood and show-business. He appeared on television, got together a night club act, became the psychic adviser to such stars as Marlon Brando and singer Tony Bennett, and spent a brief period as special consultant on the film, "The Boston Strangler", with Tony Curtis as DeSalvo.

Before his death in Los Angeles in 1988 Hurkos was associated with two more macabre murder probes: the Ypsilanti-Ann Arbor slayings of six co-eds and two other young girls; and the brutal hacking to death of Sharon Tate in 1969.

PROTECTION RACKETS

To the festering slums of the New World they came — first the immigrants, then the violent parasites fattening on the hard work of their industrious brothers . . .

PAY UP OR ELSE . . .

Protection Rackets

IN the year 1880, an English clergyman named Rose was travelling with two Italian companions through Sicily. They were about a mile from the railway station of Lecrera when, quite suddenly, they found themselves surrounded by bearded, rough-looking men who carried knives and carbines. This was the gang of a notorious brigand, Leoni, whose name was feared all over Sicily.

The gang released Rose's companions, who were told to go to the Italian authorities in Palermo and report that the Rev. Rose was being held for a ransom of £5000. The authorities were concerned, but penurious; they reported the incident to the British Consul, and forgot it. A few weeks later they received a parcel containing one of Mr. Rose's ears.

The British government, stirred by the clamour in the newspapers, decided to pay the ransom; but before they had completed the endless formalities the brigands had grown impatient, and sent another ear, together with a note saying that if the ransom still wasn't paid Mr. Rose would be chopped up piecemeal.

The British were now enraged; they paid the £5000 and recovered the earless Mr. Rose; and they also made such threatening noises that the Italian government sent an army into the mountains. There was a bloody battle, Leoni himself was killed, and most of his men captured. The British newspapers congratulated themselves for forcing the inefficient Italians to do something they should have done years ago, and the affair was almost forgotten.

Small and evil-looking

But not entirely. For the most dangerous of the gang had escaped, together with six companions. His name was Giuseppe Esposito, and he was a small, evil-looking man with a cruel mouth and a low forehead. Friends in Palermo smuggled Esposito on to a ship bound for the United States, and he landed in New York and made his way to New Orleans with a few selected followers. There, under the name of Radzo, he rented a house in Chartres Street, bought himself a boat—probably with his share of the clergyman's ransom—and dredged for oysters. He was so confident that he was a free man in America that he called the boat *Leoni* and flew the bandit's flag from the mast.

But respectability bored Esposito; he had been a bandit for too long to enjoy making money legitimately. There were no mountains here to hide in, but there were plenty of wealthy Italians in New Orleans. Giuseppe Esposito called on some of them, and explained that he needed money to finance a fleet of boats; when they asked what guarantee he could offer in return for a loan, Esposito would casually take out a revolver and cock it, peering down the sights. Then, with slow deliberation, he would pull the trigger. The hammer clicked on an empty chamber. Pretending not to notice the trembling of his startled host, he would say deliberately: "Protezione"—protection.

It is possible that Giuseppe Esposito was not the originator of this popular euphemism, but he was certainly one of the first of the American "gangsters" to employ the method. In fact, he got his "loan" from Italian grocers and restaurateurs who understood the value of Esposito's good will, and he proceeded to organize his local "Black Hand gang" along the same lines as the great Leoni.

He began by deposing the leader of the local Mafia, Tony Labruzzo, who lacked Esposito's casual ferocity. Then he bought a fleet of boats and ships, and conducted elaborate piracy operations on the Mississippi and in the Gulf of Mexico. With his brigand's instinct for a hide-out, he had huts constructed in the depths of the swamps. He intended to conduct his protection racket along Italian lines: that is, to kidnap anyone who refused to pay, and hold him for ransom—the Italians with their regard for property, would only use vandalism as a last resort.

However, Esposito was never to achieve his ambition to become the Leoni of Louisiana. His deposed rival, Tony Labruzzo, told the Italian Consul that Leoni's chief lieutenant was in New Orleans, and the Chief of Police, Thomas Boylan, kept Esposito under surveillance. He learned that two New York detectives, James Mooney and D. Boland, had been hired by the Italian government to find Esposito.

For weeks two of Boylan's best men, the brothers David and Mike Hennessy, shadowed Esposito, and one day, when they received the word to pick him up,

THE FIVE POINTS GANG (named after New York neighbourhood, above) was one of many in close alliance with the bosses at Tammany Hall (top), whose protection and vote-buying rackets flourished in the slums.

they quickly moved in on their quarry as he walked across Jackson Square, pushed guns into his ribs and rushed him to the police station. It had to be done quickly: the Mafia were capable of storming the jail. Early the next morning Esposito was taken down river, and put on board a ship for New York.

Deported to Italy, he was tried, and sentenced to life imprisonment—in irons. But before he went on trial, Tony Labruzzo, the man who had betrayed him, was already dead, shot down in the street by a Mafiosi. The Black Hand knew that if it was to maintain its stranglehold on the Italian community it had to gain a reputation for absolute ruthlessness and terrible efficiency. The two Hennessy brothers left New Orleans; but Mike was killed in 1886, and David in 1890, both by Mafia gunmen.

Of course, Esposito was not the inventor of "protection". It had been known on the border of England and Scotland as far back as the sixteenth century, when bands of wanted men, led by local chieftains, extorted a "second rent" — or "mail" — from local farmers by threatening to burn their farms and destroy their crops; this was the origin of the word "blackmail".

In Sicily and Corsica — both islands with a violent history — brigands maintained themselves by extorting food and other necessities from the population. But "protection" was rare for an obvious reason: the wealthy citizens lived in the towns, where they were fairly well protected by the police, and the brigands were in the mountains. In Naples, there was a flourishing secret society called the Camorra, which certainly included "protection" among its many activities, and in Sicily, the original Mafia was basically an alternative to the police, providing quite genuine protection and other favours for those who paid a certain sum. In its early stages, it was a "protection racket" only in the same sense as is Securicor.

Dead Rabbits, Plug Uglies

In America, gangs had always abounded; in the early nineteenth century, the New York slums were full of outfits with names like the Dead Rabbits, the Plug Uglies and the Five Points. These specialized in burglary, theft from docks and warehouses, receiving stolen property, intimidation of prostitutes and all the usual extra-legal activities of slum-dwellers with more than the customary share of dominance.

The same was true of San Francisco, Chicago and other fast-growing towns — Los Angeles was, at this time, a tiny and peaceful village with no law enforcement problem. Politicians discovered the use of gangs to bully voters, and by the 1850s, the New York gangs and the Tammany Hall bosses were in close alliance. A man about to enter a polling booth was likely to be stopped by a man with a cosh and asked how he intended to vote. If he mentioned the wrong name, he never got inside; the roughneck would do the voting instead.

In the 1860s, the Chinese in the goldfields near Marysville, California, organized themselves into secret societies called "tongs"; the first two were known as the Hop Sings and Suey Sings, and they came into violent conflict when the mistress of a Hop Sing member was

Protection Rackets

stolen by someone from the Suey Sings. The girl was only handed back after many men on both sides had died. The tongs moved to railroad construction camps, then to the larger towns — the chief of which was San Francisco, known for its brothels and gambling houses.

Traffic in girls

The average Chinese in America were a docile and well-behaved people — too docile in many ways, for the whites preyed on them unmercifully. Their two chief necessities were opium — which had been introduced into China by the British — and girls. There was a flourishing traffic in girls, who were glad to get away from the terrible poverty of their own land to the relative luxury of sharing a cellar with 20 other "slaves".

The tongs were probably the first large-scale protection racket in America, and this was largely because they organized the lives of their fellow citizens in this foreign country, and got them to pay a proportion of their wages. If a Chinese established himself enough to want to bring his wife to America, the tong demanded a certain payment.

The tongs had a simple way of enforcing their will: murder. Their assassins preferred hatchets — hence the term "hatchet man" — but also carried a silk rope around the body, like the Thugs of India. Their "protection" was genuine, like that of the Mafia in Sicily. In San Francisco in 1875, a hatchet man named Ming Long, of the Kwong Dock Tong, came upon Low Sing, a member of the Suey Sing Tong, holding the hand of a pretty "slave girl" named Kum Ho, and split his skull with a hatchet.

Before he died, Low Sing gasped out the name of his killer to the head of his tong. Formal challenges were sent, and the next day at midnight the deadliest hatchet men of both tongs met in a certain street in Chinatown, and fought earnestly and bloodily until the police — mostly Irish — arrived with their whistles and night-sticks. No one was killed — although some died later. The Suey Sings were held to have won, because they had injured a large number of the enemy.

Payment was made to Low Sing's relatives; Ming Long was formally ejected from the tong, which meant that he was fair game for any hatchet man, and fled to China, where the tongs did not exist. The historian of San Francisco, Herbert Asbury, points out that both the tongs and chop suey were invented by the Chinese in America.

The Italians were the next great wave of immigrants to arrive in New York, fleeing from political troubles at home. The first generation settled down to hard work, running shops, restaurants and small businesses, and eventually many became prosperous. It was then that new arrivals like Giuseppe Esposito began to prey on these more successful countrymen, and the "protection racket" as we know it today came into being. The rise of the gangs was very slow, and most non-Italian Americans knew very little about them until the year 1890.

A life in chains

After Esposito had been deported back to Italy — and a life in chains — two New Orleans brothers named Charles and Tony Matranga decided that there were better ways of making money than in the saloon business. Inspired by Esposito's efficient take-over of New Orleans crime, they settled down to the business of organizing the gangs, and extorting "protection" from their fellow Italians.

Many Italians in New Orleans worked in the docks at the fairly reasonable wage of 40 cents an hour. A rich and influential family named Provenzano had a monopoly of the unloading of fruit ships from South America. Charles Matranga approached them, and suggested that, in future, they might like to obtain their dock labour through him. Naturally, the labourers also paid the Matrangas a "kick back" for their good services.

The Matrangas had discovered what Esposito knew: that a few "dominant" human beings can always lead a large number of non-dominant ones by the nose. In those days, zoologists knew very little about animal dominance, and had certainly never heard that precisely 5% of any animal group is "dominant". Most human beings make the very natural assumption that most other human beings

THE TONGS had a simple way of enforcing their will: murder. Their gangs fought pitched battles in San Francisco's Chinatown, while in New York the Short Tail Gang (right) plotted more violence in the docklands. . . .

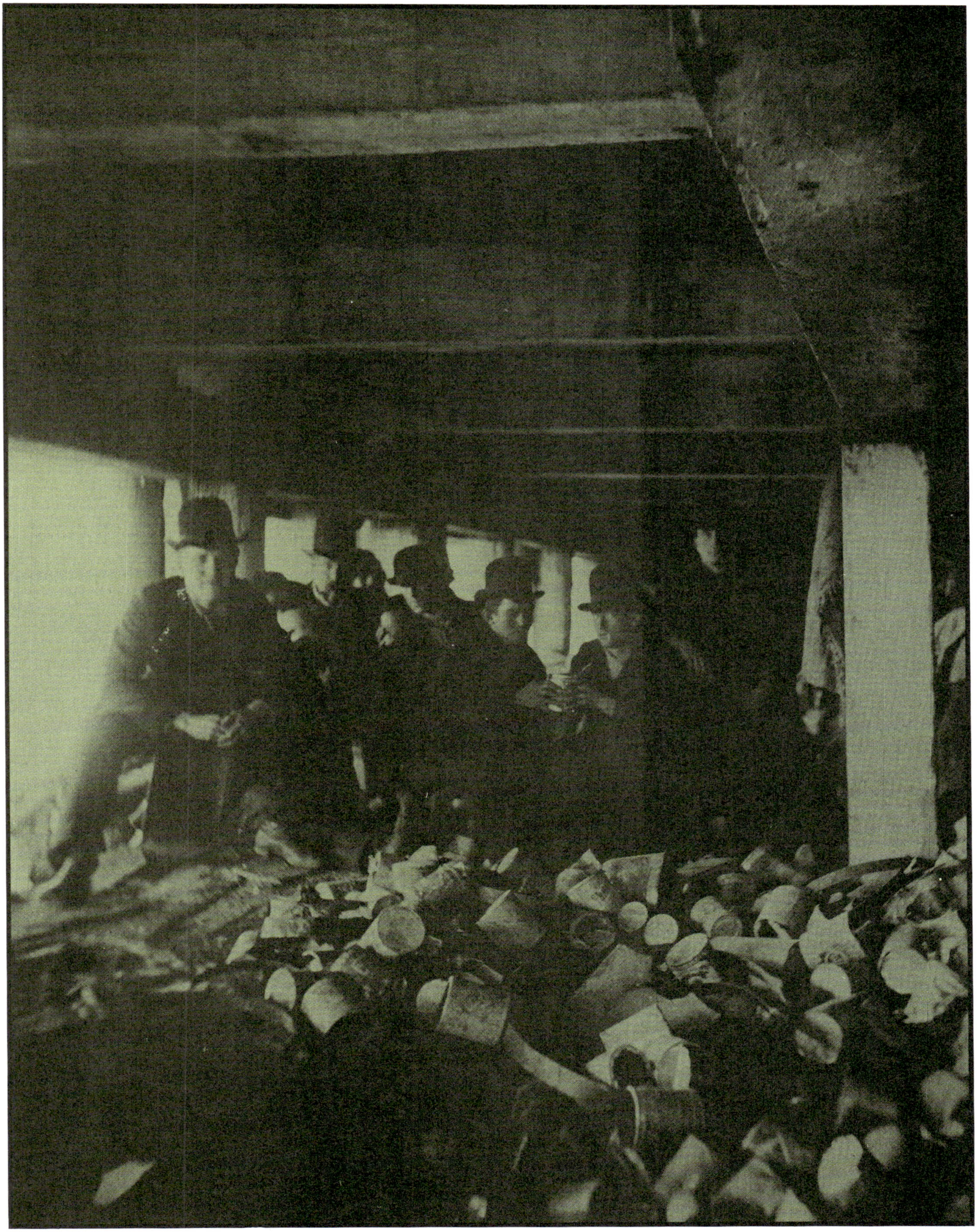

love their independence and will fight for it, and it is true that all animals, including humans, will fight grimly for their own "territory".

But it is also true that in any casually chosen group of 20 people, one is a leader and can impose his will on the other 19. Dictators like Stalin, Hitler and Mussolini owed their power to this biological peculiarity; and so did the Matrangas. If there had been any concerted resistance, no doubt they would have gone back to keeping a saloon and brothel. But their army of labourers handed over 10 per cent of their wages without protest; the Provenzanos paid the Matrangas for their services as a labour exchange, and suddenly the latter were on the road to being rich.

New Orleans masters

One day it struck them that the reason the Provenzanos didn't mind paying them "protection" was because they were making such an excellent income from the fruit ships they unloaded: after all, the labour force belonged to the Matrangas. So the Matrangas told the Provenzanos that from now on they would cease to act as middle men. Instead, the Matrangas would take over the loading and unloading of the ships. To underline the point, Provenzano managers and foremen were badly beaten up, the Provenzanos gave in to the blackmail, and the Matrangas, still slightly astonished at the ease with which it had all been accomplished, were masters of all the Italian casual labour in New Orleans.

But the Matrangas made the mistake of carrying on their war against the Provenzanos; they began to harass their grocery business. In desperation, the Provenzanos hired their own gunmen, and there were clashes in the streets. David Hennessy, one of the brothers who had captured Esposito, knew and liked the Provenzanos. He had an intense dislike of the Matrangas' organization of murder and extortion, which had killed his brother Mike in Houston, Texas, five years after Esposito's arrest.

When he was appointed chief of police, Hennessy decided he would stamp out the Mafia. One morning in 1890, a truckload of Provenzano men were on their way to work at a dock that had still not been taken over by the Matrangas. Suddenly, men with shotguns appeared out of the darkness and began firing indiscriminately. Since they were using buckshot, the darkness made no difference; two men were killed, and many others wounded.

Hennessy decided this was the last straw, and he began collecting evidence of Mafia activity in New Orleans. An anonymous letter warned him that he would be killed if he continued, but he ignored it. He corresponded with the Rome police, asking for names and photographs of some of Esposito's old gang. In April 1890, the Provenzanos retaliated by ambushing Tony Matranga and two of his henchmen. They succeeded in wounding them. Matranga identified two of his assailants as Joe and Pete Provenzano.

The police had no alternative but to arrest them, and their trial was set for October 17. David Hennessy declared publicly that he would appear in the witness stand for the Provenzanos, and make their trial the opportunity to divulge infortion about the Mafia in New Orleans.

He never reached the court room, for at midnight on October 15, 1890, Hennessy turned into Basin Street, and three men jumped out of a doorway, to riddle him with bullets. The dying man pulled out his own revolver and succeeded in firing four shots at the fleeing assassins; but he died as he reached the hospital.

This was too much—to shoot down a chief of police who was doing his best to stamp out organized crime. It was a direct confrontation between the criminals and the rest of society. Hennessy's investigations had disclosed that, in Sicily, the Mafia was stronger than the police, but it should never happen in America. Feeling against Italians became so intense that they began to be afraid of venturing outdoors during daylight; many were attacked in the street.

Eleven strong suspects

Hennessy's files quickly provided the police with 11 strong suspects. The 11 men were arrested the day after the police chief's murder. One of them was a man called Antone Scaffide. On the day after his arrest, a young man named Duffy walked into the jail and asked to see Scaffide. When the prisoner was brought out, Duffy suddenly produced a revolver and fired. The bullet only wounded Scaffide. Asked why he had done it, Duffy said that if there were more men like him in New Orleans, the Mafia would soon cease to exist. Naturally, his sentence was light.

Twenty-one Italians were eventually arrested, including Charles Matranga, and a 14-year-old boy who was accused of signalling Hennessy's approach to the killers. The law-abiding citizens of New Orleans sighed with relief—it looked as if justice would be done after all. The trial of nine of the Italians, including Matranga, was set for February 1891, but soon the citizens began to suspect that Justice was not going to have it all her own way. The Matrangas could afford expensive lawyers, and a great battery of legal talents was lined up for the defence.

The evidence at the trial was overwhelming. Many witnesses came forward to say they had seen some of the defendants running away from the scene of Hennessy's murder. One defendant broke down and confessed to being present at a meeting of the Mafia when Hennessy's death was decreed. It ought to have been an open and shut case. But halfway through the trial the judge ordered the acquittal of the 14-year-old boy, and also of Charles Matranga. The jury retired; when they returned, their verdict was that four of the accused were not guilty, and that they were unable to agree about three others, including Scaffide. It was obvious that the jurors had been either bribed or intimidated and that the same applied to many of the lawyers on the case.

The flag of Italy

The Italian colony added insult to injury by holding parties in the street to celebrate the acquittal of the nine—which everyone expected to be a prelude to the dismissal of the case against the others. A gang of Sicilians tore down an American flag, trampled it in the mud, and then hung it upside down below the flag of Italy.

For the citizens of New Orleans, that was the final indignity. In the morning newspapers of March 14, advertisements requested "all good citizens" to attend a mass meeting that evening, and to come "prepared for action". It was signed by 61 prominent citizens. That evening, a seething crowd filled Canal Street. The 61 citizens appeared, and some of them spoke briefly from the pedestal of a statue of Henry Clay, declaring that it was necessary for the people to take justice into their own hands. The men led the crowd to a gun store and handed out rifles. Then they marched to the prison.

The prison governor locked all prisoners in their cells except the Italians, who were told to find hiding places. The execution squad, led by William Parkerson, a well-known public figure, broke open a wooden door at the back of the prison, stationed armed guards there, then went deliberately through the jail, seeking out 11 Italians who were believed beyond doubt to be guilty of the murder. (Oddly enough, this list did not include Charles Matranga.)

These 11 men were dragged out and killed—nine shot, two hanged. Then, in good order, the "avengers" marched out. The mob dispersed quietly. It was the end of Mafia power in New Orleans. There was an attempted revival in 1900 when the "Black Hand" kidnapped the child Walter Lamana and killed him. But when the gang members were arrested and tried, this second "rebirth" also came to an end.

Sadly, this is only the beginning of the story of the Mafia and protection rackets. Today the Mafia's tentacles touch every facet of international crime, and it seems that organized crime — like the poor — will always be with us.

RANDOM KILLERS

SLAUGHTER AT RANDOM

These three men have a terrible factor in common... Robert Irwin (left), Salie Lineveldt (below left), and William Heirens (below) all butchered randomly selected women with a complete lack of compassion.

2400 | Random Killers

NO man or woman can ever be completely confident that they will not finish as victims of murder. That fact has been horrifyingly underlined through the years in every part of the world. A man may have nothing worth stealing. He may have made no enemies. There may be no possible motive for anyone to kill him. But there is always a chance, remote but still there, that he will stumble against the unlikely and the unknown—that he will meet Death from a Stranger.

Mrs. Dorothy Tarling was typical of the millions of respectable women who feel it would never happen to them, but hardened lawyers winced when a shattered skull was produced in court as a key exhibit at the trial of the man who had killed her. That man saw the skull only as an object of fun and giggled at the sight of it. Relatives of four women he had butchered in such a depraved and sadistic manner collapsed in tears as they gave their evidence, and their distress made him grin with delight. Detectives who had arrested him were not surprised, for this was the reaction they had grown to expect from 21-year-old Gamat Salie Lineveldt.

Lineveldt was the most perverted homicidal maniac they had ever encountered—a modern version of Jack the Ripper who for six nightmare months had brought a wave of terror to Cape Town. There was one significant difference between Lineveldt, a motherless Malay, and his hero the Ripper—all of the victims that he mutilated, and apparently violated, were immensely respectable women.

Bestial attacks

Women were not safe on the streets or in the parks—or even in their own homes. For Lineveldt—believed to be impotent with women who were not drenched in blood—took the most amazing chances when launching into his bestial axe attacks. Thousands of women, young and old, were terrified that they might be among his next victims.

Lineveldt's activities started in such a comparatively innocuous way that they did not rate even a line in the local newspapers. In September 1940 he walked into the backyard of a house in Wellington Road, Wynberg, and shouted to a woman in the kitchen that he wanted to use her lavatory. His manner, aggressive and impudent, frightened her, and she ordered him away. He opened the door and grabbed her by the throat, but her screams aroused neighbours, and, muttering obscenities, he ran away.

Exactly 19 days later, on October 3, Mrs. Ethel Marais—the young wife of a soldier—became his first murder victim. She had been to Cape Town railway station to see her husband off to join his unit at Johannesburg and had taken a trolley-bus home. After leaving the bus, she had a short walk to the house where she lived with her sister—but she never reached home.

The following morning she was found

SINK OF INIQUITY. 17-year-old Heirens faces the washtub in which he cut up six-year-old Suzanne Degnan. Her father wept at his daughter's abandoned bedside.

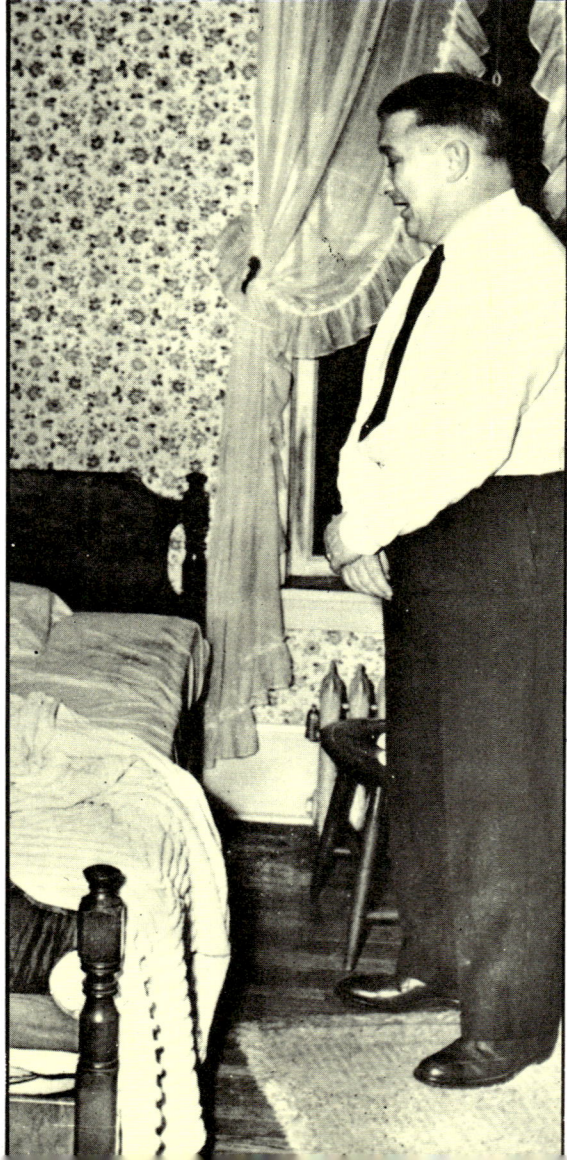

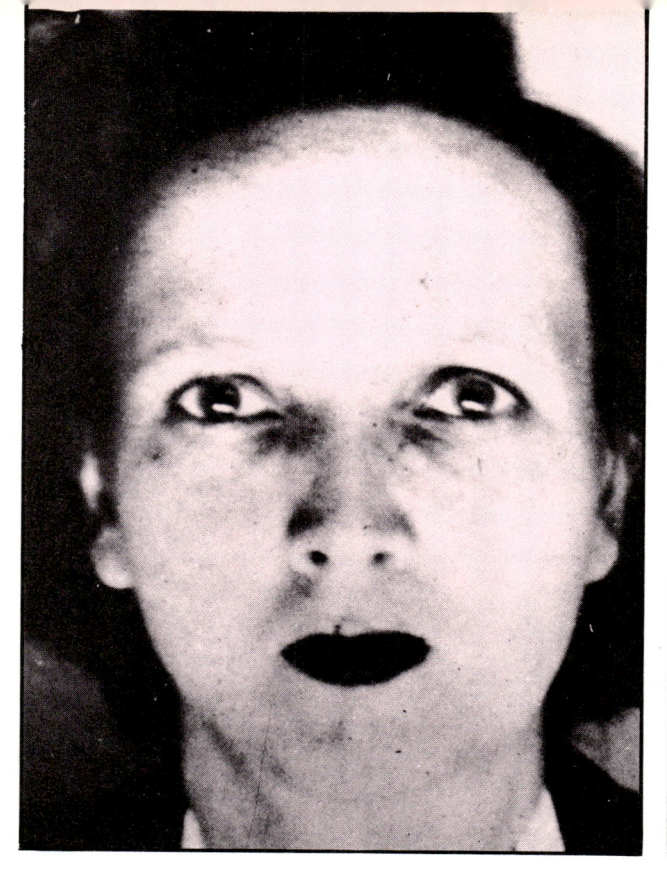

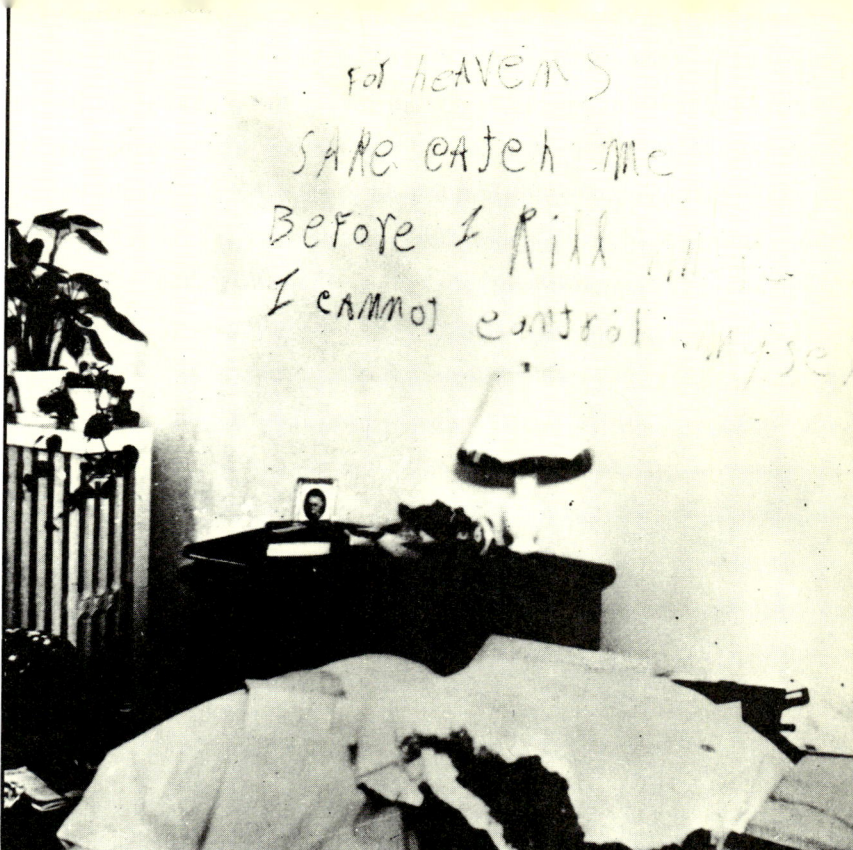

lying behind bushes, unconscious and close to death. Her face and head had been battered in, and her clothing from the waist down had been ripped away. One of her stockings had been used to bind her wrists, but the other stocking and her panties had been taken by Lineveldt for his own secret and perverted pleasures. A ring with a distinctive snake design was also missing, and there were indications that Mrs. Marais had been sexually violated as she lay unconscious.

Homicidal lunatic

Only 19 days later the mysterious Cape Town maniac struck again. This time his victim was Mrs. Dorothy Tarling, whose shattered body had been subjected to even more elaborate perversions. She was found in her own home by a servant girl — her brain lacerated by splinters of her skull. The lower part of her body had been bared and pillows had been pushed under her head and buttocks. Finger impressions were found in the blood on the inside of her right thigh, but they were too indistinct to be of any value.

However, in addition to stealing her underclothing Lineveldt had ransacked the house for valuables — and had left a perfect impression of his left thumb on a drawer. That print did not match any known to the police, and, in fact, they later discovered that, having read about it in the newspapers, Lineveldt had tried to protect himself by chopping off the top of his thumb.

Panic raged through the peninsula like a bush fire. The authorities were convinced that they were dealing with a

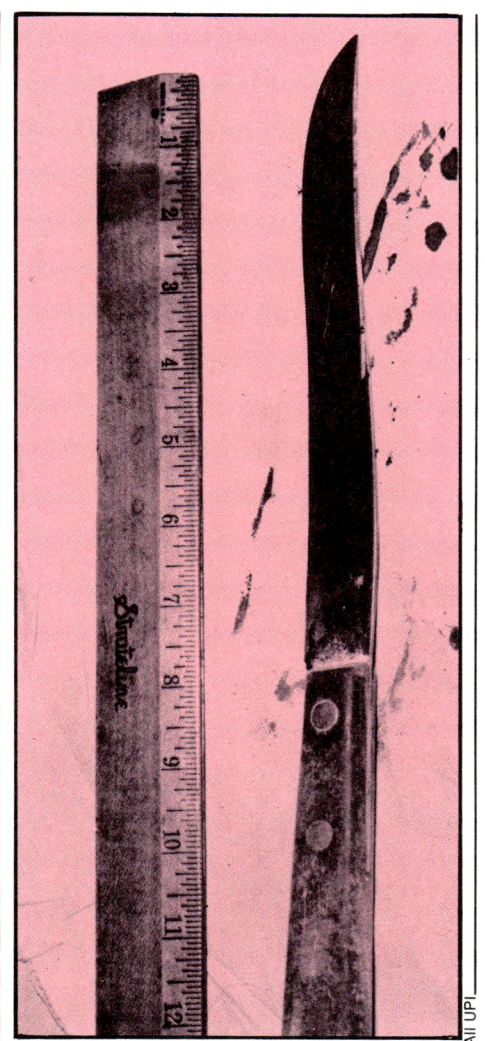

THE WRITING ON THE WALL. Heirens scribbled his plea in lipstick after stabbing ex-WAVE Frances Brown to death in her bedroom with an 8-inch bread knife.

homicidal lunatic and one who could apparently seem perfectly normal when not in his fits of savage madness. Many women were forced to live alone because — as in the case of Mrs. Marais — their husbands were in the Forces. Windows were locked and shuttered at nights, and there was a clamour for guns and ammunition. Groups of women arranged to sleep together in one of their houses for mutual protection, and there were pistols under many pillows.

Despite every precaution, however, Lineveldt claimed his third victim — just 20 days after the slaughter of Mrs. Tarling. The police saw great significance in the time-lapse. A pattern of horror was being clearly established.

Broad daylight

The third victim was 28-year-old Miss Evangelina Bird, who was living with Mr. and Mrs. Oswald Spolander in Wetton Road, Wynberg, and this time the outrage had an additional startling dimension, for it occurred in broad daylight at the Spolanders' home while potential witnesses were present. The blatant style of this killing — one that almost seemed to invite capture — later made criminologists wonder if the motivation was not curiously similar to that of the American psychopathic monster William Heirens.

Heirens was the Chicago man who, after murdering his second woman in

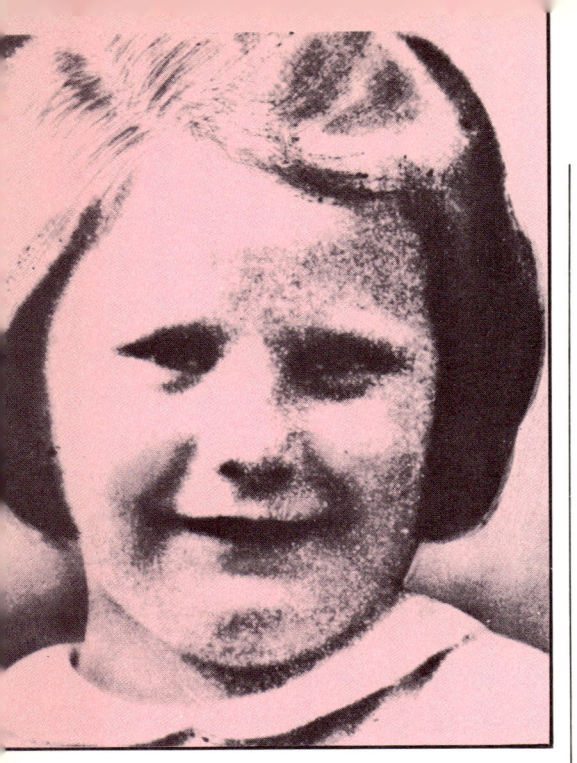

CHILD VICTIM. Little Suzanne Degnan was strangled in her bed before being cut to pieces with a hunting knife. Killer Heirens had never seen her before.

gruesome circumstances, scrawled a lipstick message on her bedroom wall: "For heaven's sake catch me before I kill more; I cannot control myself." Did the slaying of pretty Evangelina Bird contain, in its awful way, the same desperate appeal? Did Lineveldt, even as he was carrying out his killings, have a subconscious urge to be caught and stopped? Although his later attitude savoured chiefly of proud amusement over his "achievements", the circumstances of her death provide grounds for that thought.

Bloodstained hands

A grocer's delivery boy, Achmat Rawoot, called at the house at 10 a.m. and was given an order by Miss Bird. The boy left, and, barely five minutes later, Mrs. Spolander came down from her bedroom and saw blood on the front step. Nearby was a shoe. Miss Bird was soon found in a broken-down summerhouse behind a shrubbery, in almost exactly the same state as Lineveldt's other victims. The attack had been so frenzied that two of her teeth were completely knocked out; her dress had been tugged up to her breasts and her underclothing was down to her knees. But she had not been raped while unconscious — presumably because of a last-minute panic by Lineveldt.

Now, for the first time, the police had a description of the killer. He had been seen approaching the house by the delivery boy Achmat Rawoot, and had also been spotted by a woman called Johanna Pieterson as he had left, with bloodstained hands, on a bicycle with distinctive red tyres. None of this information was jigsawed fast enough to save a middle-aged woman called May Overton Hoets. On November 25 Mrs. Hoets was found in her home. Her body had been revoltingly mutilated, and a pillow with seminal stains had been put under her buttocks.

Jaunty pride

If Lineveldt had stopped at that fourth murder he would very likely never have been brought to justice, but the twisted urges which dominated him forced him on, and although there were no more murders, the police received a spate of complaints from women about the indecent behaviour of a black youth — and those complaints led them to Lineveldt. They found in his possession the distinctive snake ring stolen from his first murder victim, Mrs. Marais. At first he denied all knowledge of the murders, but eventually made a statement, saying: "I never saw any of the women I killed before the day I killed them.... I don't even know the names of the women I killed. I never saw any of them at any time before I killed them.... I never watched the houses before the assaults. I just walked in."

He refused to allow his attorney to enter a plea of insanity, and all through the three-day hearing he took a jaunty and grinning pride in being in the spotlight. He maintained that attitude right up until the moment they placed the noose around

TELL-TALE HANDWRITING. Spelling mistakes and eccentric handwriting on the ransom note (below left) tallied with samples of Heirens' penmanship.

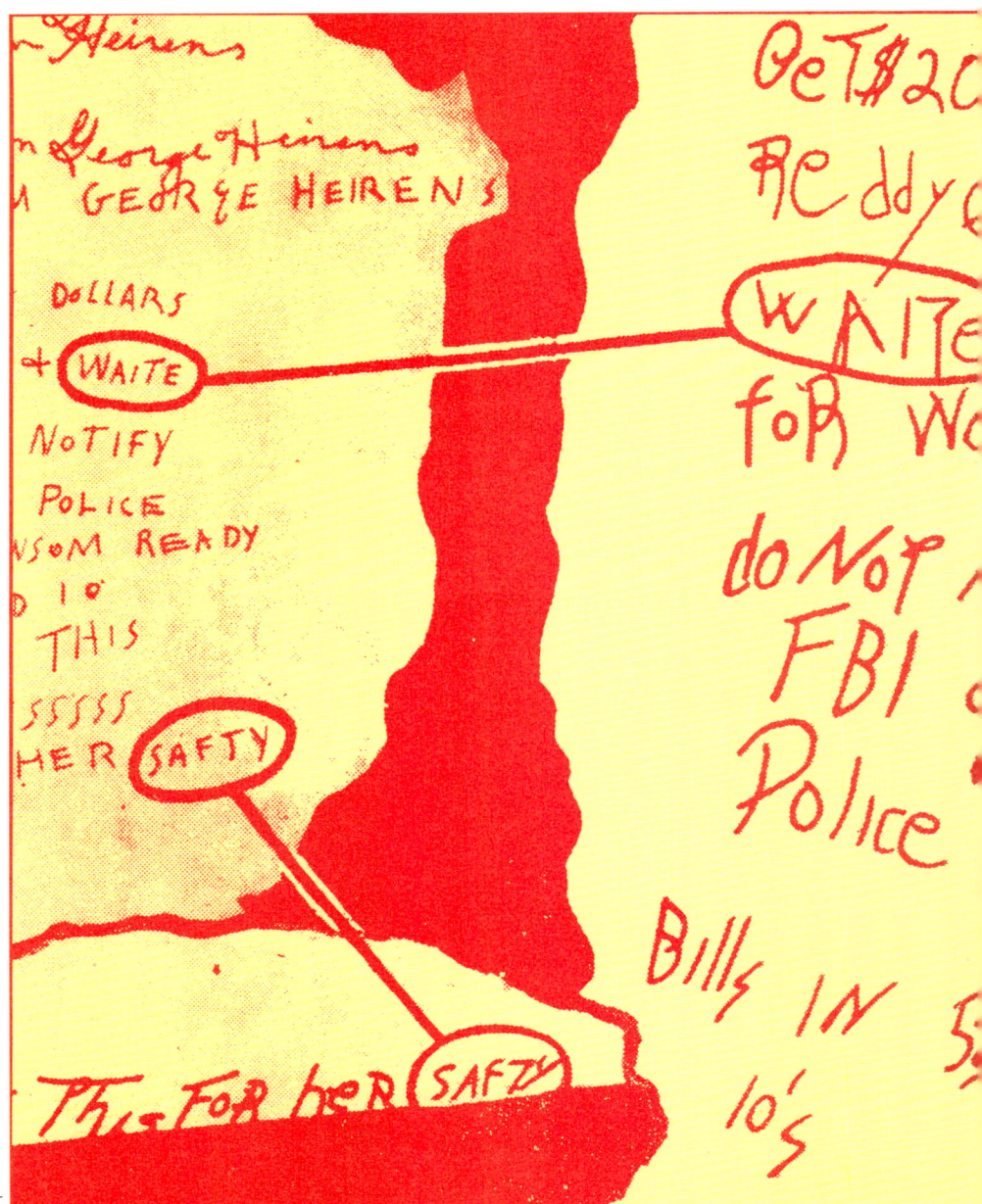

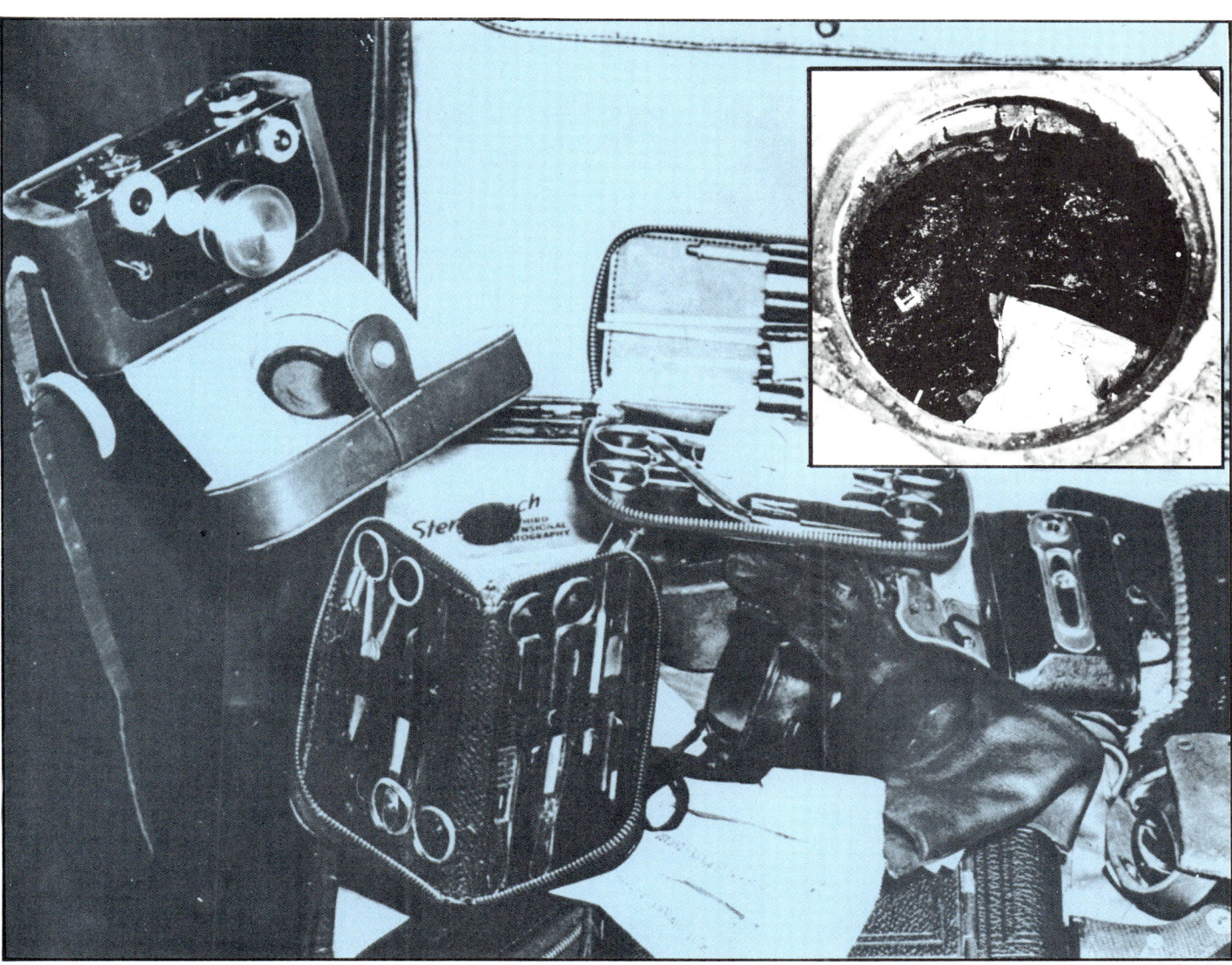

his neck; a prison officer who witnessed the execution said later that he had never before seen a man die so happily.

Apart from the victims he had taken with such vile and bestial force, Lineveldt had not experienced sexual intercourse previously, except on one occasion with a prostitute. He was "no good" with women. In that respect he was the same as 28-year-old Patrick Byrne—a church-going Irish labourer whose inadequacies goaded him to a crime which horrified Britain.

Nervous tension

Byrne, although he was a quick-tempered blusterer with men, was desperately shy with women. He blushed easily when they spoke to him and, according to a former girl-friend, was too bashful even to kiss her during the six months they went out together. Women made him feel uncomfortable—and for that he could never forgive them.

Just before Christmas 1959 the beheaded and savagely mutilated body of a shorthand-typist called Stephanie Baird was found in a cubicle in the Y.W.C.A. hostel at Edgbaston, Birmingham. Byrne, who was sentenced to life imprisonment for the atrocity, was said to have told the police: "I wanted to get my own back on women for causing my nervous tension through sex. I felt I only wanted to kill beautiful women."

A sacrifice

He had gone to her room after watching her as a peeping-Tom, and he said in his statement: "Before she could say 'no' I kissed her. She tried to shove me away, but couldn't, and for a second I got her round the waist. She only had her underskirt on. She screamed, and then I put my hands around her neck. . . . I heard a couple of small noises in her throat but kept on kissing her." After Stephanie was dead, Byrne stripped to his shoes and socks and attacked her body with a table knife. "I scored her back with the knife a few times, but it didn't go very deep. Her back seemed beautiful before, and I

REVOLVER, CAMERA and surgical knives were found in Heirens' room. Inset shows the open sewer with the paper bag in which Suzanne's torso was dumped.

felt I wanted to score it. It surprised me how easily the head came off. . . ."

There were thousands of girls in Birmingham that night. Any one of them would have served Byrne as a sacrifice to satisfy the sickness in his degenerate mind, but it just happened to be Stephanie, who had probably thought, like most men and women, that murders only happen to "other people", who chance to attract death from a stranger.

Bizarre appeal

Lineveldt and Byrne had a common bond in many of their mental quirks. This bond was also shared by William Heirens, a 17-year-old student in 1946 when he became known as the Jekyll and Hyde monster of Chicago. He, like Lineveldt, was abnormally obsessed with women's underclothing. This fetish began when he was

Random Killers

nine, and at first he merely stole the clothing from washing lines; then he started stealing them from strange houses and derived satisfaction from wearing them and hiding them with his treasures.

Alter ego

When he was about 12 he developed the habit of collecting them by climbing through windows, and found that this unlawful entrance through a forbidden opening—with all its symbolical undertones—gave him additional stimulation. Like Byrne, he also found it impossible to enjoy any normal healthy relationship with a girl-friend and complained to a psychiatrist: "They wanted to kiss; I didn't."

Heirens was lonely and introverted, and he tried to lay all the blame for his horrendous crimes on his alter-ego, "George". It was this George who, according to him, was in control on a night in January 1946 when he climbed up a ladder and into the bedroom of six-year-old Suzanne Degnan in one of Chicago's most elegant suburbs. He had never seen the child before, but he strangled her in her bed and carried her body down a ladder to dump it in a coal bin. Then, with a hunting knife, he hacked off her head—just as Byrne did with Stephanie Baird. He also cut off Suzanne's arms and legs and distributed the pieces of her in various sewers around the city.

Heirens, impotent with women because of his fear of normal sex, needed knives and guns to demonstrate his masculinity. He demonstrated it to Mrs. Josephine Ross when he killed her in her Chicago flat, and Miss Frances Brown, on whose wall he scrawled that bizarre lipstick appeal for his own capture, was yet another girl who received death from this particular stranger. In September 1946 he was sentenced to life imprisonment for each of these three murders, and he knew that under Illinois law he could not be released on parole until the year 2007 at the earliest.

Eight years before Heirens went on his final rampage of madness another triple murderer called Robert Irwin was given a sentence which, technically, could keep him behind bars until the year 2077. That was singularly ironic, because he had turned killer for one reason: he wanted to die but lacked the courage to commit suicide, and hoped the law would help him by arranging his execution.

Passport to eternity

Irwin, the son of a minister, was born in a marquee near Los Angeles during a summer religious convention. His childhood was singularly unhappy, and as a youth he became obsessed with religion. He repeatedly asked surgeons to castrate him so that his sexual energies could be "conserved for higher purposes", and in October 1932 he was severely injured trying to perform the operation himself.

At the age of 29 he started studying

IN LIFE AND DEATH. Veronica Gedeon was a model. Inset shows her body in death. Left, Stephanie Baird and her killer Patrick Joseph Byrne.

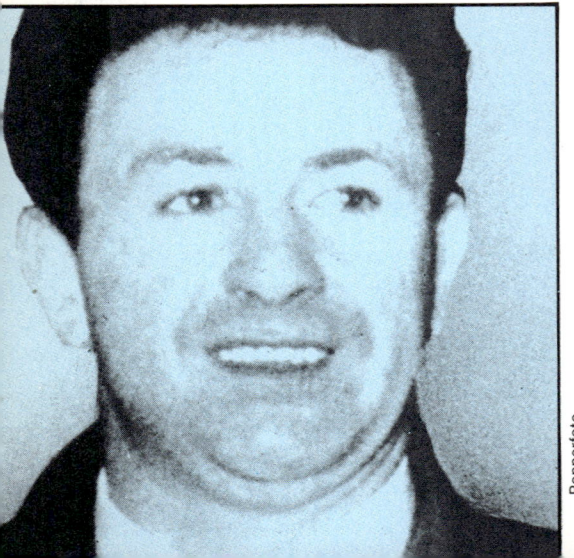

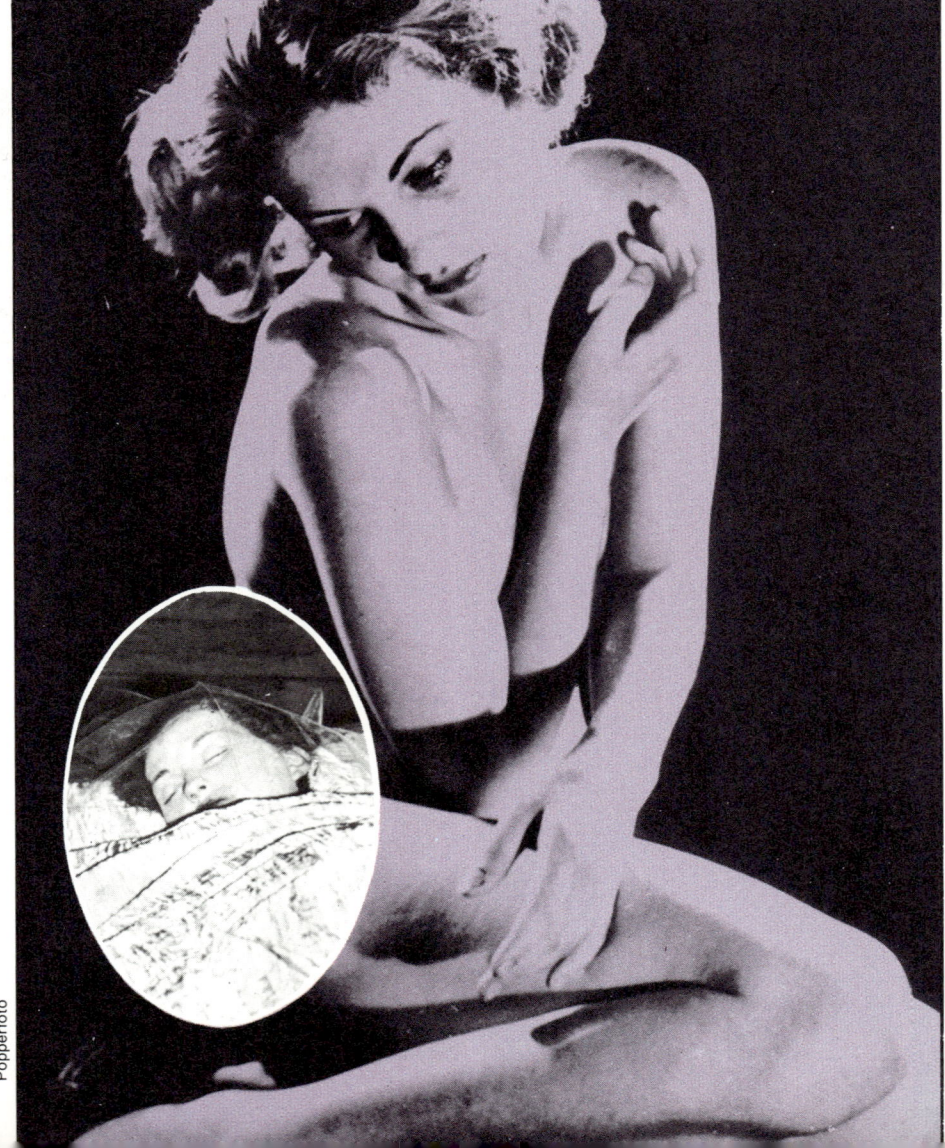

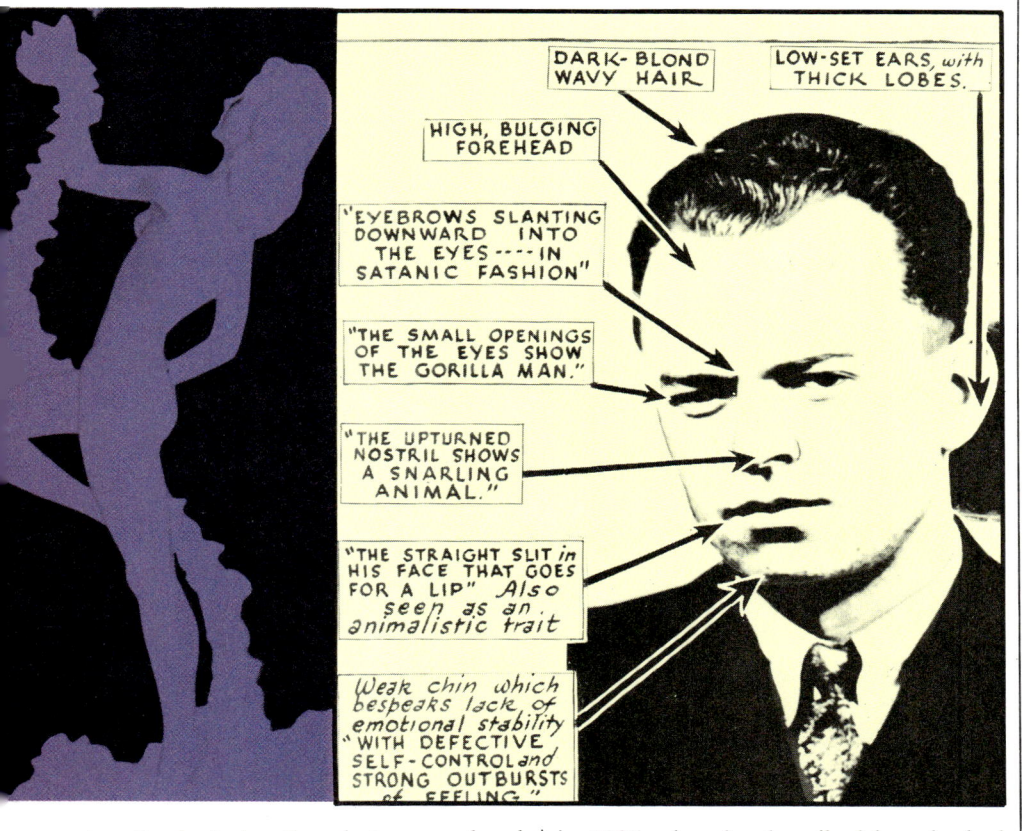

SMILING KILLER. Composite shots, left, of Robert Irwin in court. Below left is a sample of his sculpture, with a police picture detailing his facial character.

Field said he had strangled Beatrice Sutton, whom he had never seen before, because he was "fed up" with being short of money and wanted to end his own life. "But I hadn't the guts, so I thought I'd stick myself in a position where somebody else would have to do it," he said. "I went into her place, and she got ready to let me have intercourse with her, but I never meant to do that. I then done her in and, as you might say, put myself on the spot." Field, unlike Irwin, got what he wanted. A few weeks after his trial at the Old Bailey he was executed.

Fatal "accidents"

Other men of Field's type have found it comparatively easy to murder strangers — purely because they are strangers. They do not know their victims as *people*. They do not know their hopes and ambitions, their problems and their cares. There is a greater sense of detachment. It is more a question of destroying an object of little importance rather than of bringing death to a real human being.

Scruples of that sort never bothered Belle Gunness, the "lethal lady" of Indiana. Husbands, lovers, employees and strangers; to her they were all equal in the grave. She was 24 when, in 1883, she arrived in America from her native Norway and quickly married a man called Mads Sorenson. Mr. Sorenson did rather well and managed to survive nearly 17 years of marriage to her. He died rather suddenly in 1900 — officially of an "enlarged heart" — on a day which proved to be financially fortunate for Belle. For on that day it just so happened that two separate insurance policies on his life overlapped, and Belle was suddenly wealthy enough to buy a large farm at La Porte, Indiana.

BLOODY BED where Veronica Gedeon's naked corpse was found stabbed. Her mother was found under the same bed.

at a theological college but was ordered to leave after a fight with a fellow-student. That was when he decided to die — and so sealed the fate of an innocent man who did not even know he existed. Irwin had known a girl called Ethel Gedeon in New York, and he felt that she would prove his ideal passport to eternity. On March 27, 1937, he went to Ethel's home, but she was away on a visit so he had to amend his plans, and instead strangled her mother and her sister Veronica. While these killings were taking place a boarder called Byrnes was sleeping heavily upstairs. Byrnes never did wake. He was still snoring contentedly when the stranger called Irwin slammed an ice-pick into his head.

Irwin's motive was identical to that admitted in London by Frederick Field in 1936 when he described how he had killed a prostitute called Beatrice Vilna Sutton. She was found in her flat at Clapham 12 hours after she had been strangled. For 11 of those 12 hours Field had been in police custody, having been arrested as an absentee from the Royal Air Force, but no one suspected that he had been connected with the crime.

Unlucky coincidence

Field was taken under escort to his station at Hendon Aerodrome, and on the Monday evening a Metropolitan Police officer arrived there to charge him with the theft of four cheques. He was an unimportant small-time crook. At least, that was what they thought, until he surprised them with his detailed confession of the murder at Clapham.

Two years later she married a man called Peter Gunness, but he did not have the same luck as Mr. Sorenson. Within 12 months of the ceremony he suffered a fatal "accident" involving scalding brine and a blow from a meat grinder, and, thanks to another fortuitous insurance policy, Belle picked up a further 4000 dollars. That was when she launched into her real career as an expert in mayhem. Her main method for finding strangers worth murdering was the placing of lonely hearts advertisements, for, officially, she was trying to find a replacement for Mr. Gunness.

Laced with strychnine

Her letters to men in distant parts of the country were eloquent and persuasively worded. She kept up a skilful courtship-through-correspondence with several of them at the same time—promising each of them a life of unruffled domestic bliss. "You won't need your home any more, so sell it. We can live happily here on the farm." That was her stock line, and a surprising number of men accepted it without even meeting her. They would arrive at the farm, loaded with cash, and given a warm welcome, laced with strychnine.

Headless body

Neighbours who had seen the strangers arriving were regularly told that the "romance" had not worked out and that the latest man had gone home. Poor Mrs. Gunness—she seemed to be so unlucky in love. Some of her farm employees also left mysteriously—after she had become bored with them in bed. In fact they, like the men who had come a-courting, were axed into convenient sizes and buried around the farm.

In 1908 her headless body was found in her burned-out farmhouse. A coroner recorded a verdict of "death by felonious homicide—perpetrator unknown". One of her workers, Ray Lamphere, who admitted that he had been jealous over her succession of men, was found guilty of arson but not of murder. But later,

OPEN GRAVES are indicated by letter in the picture of Gunness Farm, Indiana. Mrs. Belle Gunness, inset above, was probably killed by accomplice Lamphere.

when he was in prison, he said he had been Belle's accomplice in murder and mentioned 42 victims. Some of them were dug up and identified, but some were never found.

No one was ever charged with Belle's murder. Lamphere was the principal suspect, but there was not enough evidence. It has been suggested that he found her dead, and, desperately conscious of all the bodies littered around, illogically thought he might avert any intensive homicide investigation if he could make it seem as if she had died in an accidental fire. It has also been suggested that Belle received what she had so often dealt out—death from a stranger—that one of her gentlemen callers beat her at her own game.

The urge to "get something for nothing"—as demonstrated so graphically by the case of Belle Gunness—is one of the standard motives of people who murder strangers. Harmless old men have had their skulls shattered for the sake of the loose change in their back pockets, and grandmotherly widows have been bludgeoned by thugs surprised whilst robbing from gas-meters. A particularly pathetic example of this motive was seen in March 1961 in London. The body of a saleswoman, Elsie May Batten, was found in an antique shop in Cecil Court, off the Charing Cross Road. She was on her back with an antique dagger, still bearing its price tag, stuck in her chest. Another, identical, dagger was in her neck.

"Fainted woman"

Mrs. Batten was a cheerful and friendly sort of woman, popular with her neighbours and with her colleagues. Murder, to her, was something remote, something she could read about in books or newspapers, but something which could never affect her. Yet, in broad daylight on that March morning, in a busy area of London, she had become the victim of a singularly brutal murder. No attempt had been made to sexually assault her. The fact that the murder weapons had obviously been snatched in a murderous impulse from their place on the shelves ruled out the likelihood of the killing being the work of a personal enemy. Robbery seemed to be the most likely motive, but her handbag and the box "till" appeared to be untouched.

When pathologist Dr. Keith Simpson examined the body he found there was another stab wound in the back, and a third dagger was, in fact, found underneath the woman. A 15-year-old boy told the police that he had seen Mrs. Batten on the floor when he had gone into the shop to buy a billiard cue at 11.30 a.m. At first he had thought she was a dummy, but when he realized it was a woman he felt she had probably just fainted—and left the shop. It apparently never occurred to him to get help for the "fainted woman". The only clue which the police could find was the impression of heel and sole marks on a piece of wood under the dead woman's legs.

Suspicious manner

Neighbouring shopkeepers were quizzed, but not one of them could recall seeing anyone going into the antique shop that morning. Opposite the shop, however, were the premises of a gunmaker whose 19-year-old son described how a young Indian had walked in and tried to sell him a dress sword. The man had said: "I paid 15 pounds for it, but I'll take 10." The gunmaker's son had suggested that the Indian should come back later to discuss business with his father. The Indian had said he would, and

SMALL-TIME CROOK Frederick Field (above) killed prostitute Beatrice Sutton (top right). Teenagers Fugate and Starkweather had "death orgy".

had gone away—leaving the sword with the boy—and had not returned.

The sword was identified as one missing from the antique shop, and the shop's owner, Mr. Louis Meier, remembered that a man who said he was half-Indian and half-English had been in the shop the day before the murder—asking about a £15 dress sword. He had left without buying one. Mr. Meier's description of the man tallied with that given by the gunmaker's son, and Identikit pictures were issued. Four days later a police constable in Soho saw a man who he felt matched the description and challenged him. The man was 21-year-old Edwin Bush—half-Indian and half-English—who reacted casually to the policeman: "Yes, I saw the photo in the papers. It did look a bit like me." There was something in his manner which heightened the policeman's suspicions, and when impressions of the soles and heels of his shoes were seen to match those found at the shop, he knew he had got his man.

Edwin Bush had murdered a woman he did not know for the sake of a £15 sword. Then, only a few minutes later, he had left that sword at the gunmaker's premises and had been too frightened to go back for it. His crime brought him nothing—except a rope around his neck.

Depraved killer

Nobody can ever be sure from where the next murderer or maniac will spring. Mrs. Batten had felt perfectly safe in that London shop. Salesman Merle Collison of Great Falls, Montana, probably felt he was perfectly safe on the morning of January 29, 1958, when—feeling tired after a long drive—he pulled his car to the roadside at Douglas, Wyoming. Soon he was fast asleep. And in his sleep he was murdered by one of the most depraved killers known in America—19-year-old Charles Starkweather.

Random Killers

Collison just happened to be in the wrong place at the wrong time, for he was seen sleeping by Starkweather and his 14-year-old accomplice Caril Fugate as they were reaching the climax of their orgy of death. The corpses of 10 people, including Caril's mother, step-father and her baby half-sister, were already littered across the trail of terror which they had blazed, and so Starkweather had no compunction about shooting Collison.

Suppressed hatreds
He shot him once in the nose and twice in the cheek; he shot him once in the neck and once in the left arm; he shot him in the wrist and in the left leg, and afterwards he said: "That salesman just happened to be in there... when soldiers have to take a place or do something they don't ask if there's any children and old people, women, or is anybody asleep... anyhow, whoever it was, he would have hated me if he had'a knowed me. How could he be different from everyone else?"

This, then, was Starkweather's justification for killing Collison. Collison did not know him, but if he had known him he would not have approved of him—and therefore he had to die. There was also another reason. Starkweather had difficulties in sustaining friendships with girls, and he was frightened that, once the high-peak excitement of the slayings was over, Caril would turn her back on him like so many others had done.

As a small boy Starkweather was always seething with suppressed hatreds. He hated school, home, people and life. His imagination was crowded with grotesque and cruel images; of people prostrate and helpless at his feet; of himself exercising the supreme heady power of life or death over everyone he met. A psychiatrist said of him: "Pumping bullets into a human is no different to Starkweather than pumping bullets into a rabbit." Other psychiatrists disagreed intensely. There was a world of difference. There was, for Starkweather, not the same erotic thrill in butchering a rabbit as in butchering an intelligent human being.

Gruesome rampage
Starkweather's reign of terror began and ended with the murder of a stranger. His first victim was a 19-year-old filling-station attendant on December 1, 1957. But his homicidal career did not start to gather momentum until January 21, 1958, when he shot Caril's mother and stepfather, Mr. and Mrs. Marion Bartlett, and clubbed their baby daughter to death. Caril told suspicious callers at the door that they could not come in as her parents had influenza. On January 27 he had three more victims—a 70-year-old man, a 17-year-old boy and a 16-year-old girl who, according to an autopsy report, had also been subjected to an "unnatural sexual attack".

The following day, January 28, brought yet another trio of victims—a Mr. and Mrs. Lauer Ward and their maid Lillian Fencl. Starkweather and Caril had forced their way into the Wards' house while the two women were there alone and murdered them, Starkweather also broke the neck of the Wards' pet dog and had waited with his gun for the husband to get home. The killer did get money from the Ward house—seven dollars from Mrs. Ward and ten dollars from her maid. While the life-blood was still pumping out of these bodies in Lincoln, Nebraska, the salesman Collison was innocently driving to Douglas, Wyoming. There, the following day, he met his death. The obscene and gruesome rampage of Charles Starkweather was over, and shortly after midnight on June 25, 1959, he was executed at the Nebraska State Penitentiary.

Perfect murder
Many killers have a powerful streak of arrogance in them, and while he was waiting for his execution, Starkweather boasted that his crimes would ensure that he would be remembered. He had done something which would never be forgotten, and, although his body would soon be rotting, the name Charles Starkweather would live on.

That type of arrogance also resulted in the death of a married, middle-aged woman called Mabel Tattershaw near Nottingham, England, in 1952. She was killed by a drab unknown called Herbert Leonard Mills—a "nobody" who nurtured secret dreams of becoming a "somebody" and who thought he could achieve them by committing the Perfect Murder. He had, as he admitted later, been brooding over his plan for a long time. The Perfect Murder, as he saw it, did not involve passion, hatred, greed, revenge or any other comparable urge. It was simply murder for the sake of murder. It was murder which proved that you were far more clever than all the famous killers—such as Heath or Haigh—who had been caught. It was murder which completely baffled all those brilliant detectives and left you with a secret self-hugging feeling of superiority.

But who could he murder? Mills had no idea—until one evening he chanced to sit next to Mabel Tattershaw in a Nottingham cinema. Her husband was in prison for shop-breaking, and she was lonely. She started a conversation with him, and, indeed, she made it all too easy for him by suggesting that they might meet again. She was old, and not attractive, but he began to realize that, as a complete stranger, she was perfect for his needs. She meant nothing to him, absolutely nothing, and no one need ever know he had ever spoken to her. He explained to her that he had to rush home, but that he would like to meet her the following night.

The following evening they went straight to a place known locally as The Jungle—a lovers' haunt in a wood. When they were far enough away for her screams not to be heard, he strangled her and left her dead in a ravine. Later he said: "I was satisfied I had found the perfect victim. No motive. No clues. I was proud of my achievement."

The initial surge of exultation, however, the euphoria of revelling in the triumph of it all, was soon to pass. Days went by and Mabel Tattershaw was reported missing but was not found. Mills had hidden her body too well. There seemed to be little glory in committing a murder—even the Perfect Murder—if no one was even aware that it had been committed. It was all such a terrible anti-climax.

Gallows
Finally, unable to stand the suspense of waiting any longer, he telephoned a newspaper and told a reporter that he had found the body of a murdered woman. What would the paper pay for an exclusive story? He was beginning to realize the possibilities of achieving double satisfaction—cash in addition to the wonderful secret fame. The reporter asked for his name, and Mills readily gave it. The police were quickly contacted, and, under their interrogation, Mills broke down and confessed the whole scheme. There were no histrionics when he walked to the gallows. He just went very quietly. Mabel Tattershaw was just another mound in the cemetery—like the other unlucky few who have met Death from a Stranger.

"PERFECT MURDERER" Herbert Mills killed to "become somebody". Then he went to the police and told of killing stranger Mabel Tattershaw.

RAPE

PSYCHOLOGY OF THE SEX KILLER

Dean Corll's house (below) in Pasadena was stocked with elaborate torture tools (inset). He was a vicious, homosexual rapist who slew his victims. . . .

2410 | Rape

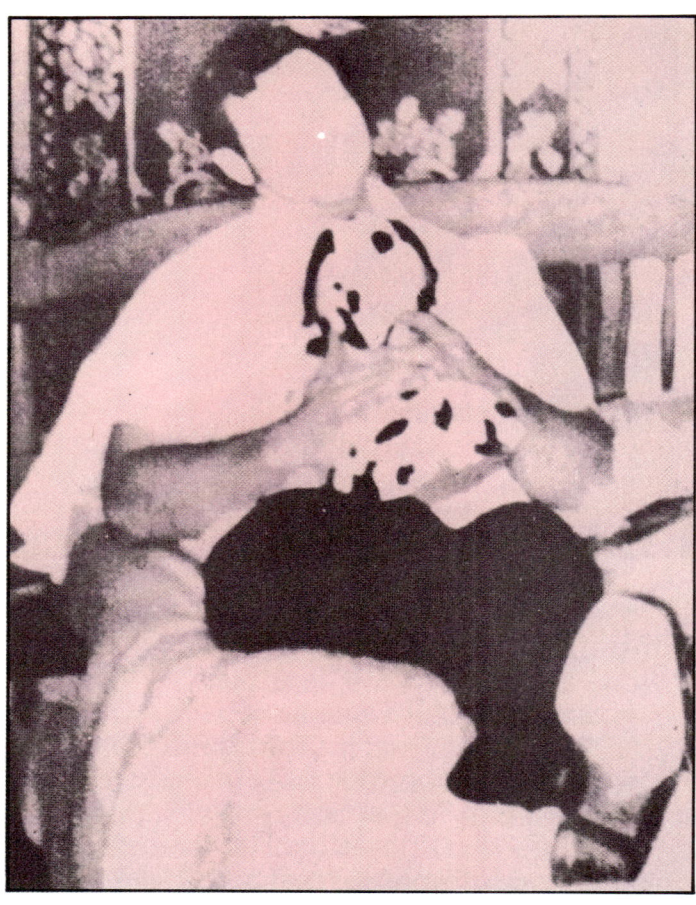

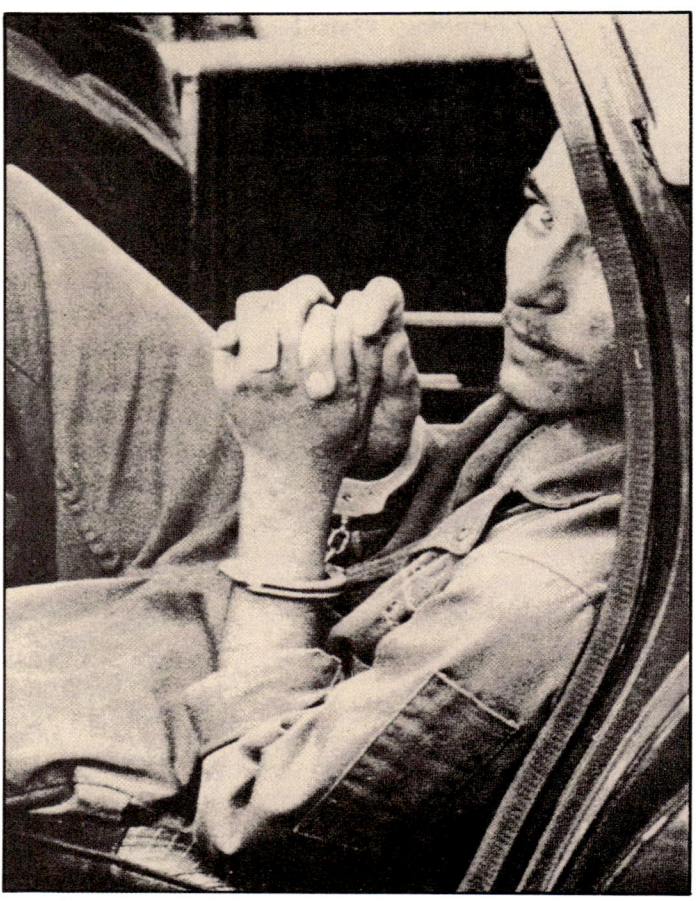

CLUTCHING a stuffed dog, Dean Corll (left), the homosexual mass killer, is all smiles. Seventeen-year-old Elmer Henley (right) finally shot him dead.

IF A list was made of the most notorious murderers in criminal history, there would be very few rapists among them. This statement may seem incredible: what about Christie, what about the Boston Strangler, what about Werner Boost, what about Joseph Vacher, the French Ripper? But having named these, even the memory of the criminologist begins to run short of examples. Of course there have been thousands of rapists; but most of them are commonplace criminals whose names are difficult to recall.

A large proportion of the sex killers whose names everyone can recall were not rapists: Jack the Ripper, Neville Heath, the American-born Peter Manuel. Even the man who probably ranks as the most notorious sex killer of all time, Peter Kürten, "the Monster of Düsseldorf", seldom performed the act of rape on his victims; he derived his sexual pleasure from the stabbing or throttling.

This underlines the basic point about sex murderers. When a man is prepared to kill for sex he can be considered sufficiently abnormal that ordinary sex may not interest him. Many men think that they understand the sex killer: but they are usually wrong. He is not just an over-sexed man carried away by desire, he is a man whose desires cannot be fulfilled by the normal sexual impulse.

The ordinary rapist is a different matter. In the United States, statistically, about one woman in every thousand can expect to be raped; and this excludes the vastly under-reported cases of "date rape". Despite these alarming figures, most rapists are not murderous, although the act of rape is considered to be an act of violence. Sociologist and writer Peter Parker cites an example in his book *The Twisting Lane* – that of Andrew Brown, a garbage collector in his mid-thirties.

Knock at the door

Brown had no record of previous sexual offences when, one summer in the late 1960's, he committed ten rapes or attempted rapes during a period of four weeks. They were all within 15 miles of his home. In one case – that may be taken as typical – he knocked on a front door and asked the woman who answered some question. She said she couldn't help him, and closed the door. He went round to the back door and into the house, looking for something to steal. The woman was in a bedroom. She told him he could take her jewellery, but he ordered her to lie on the bed.

"You're not going to rape me, are you?" she asked. "I said I didn't know, because I didn't," Brown reports. She tried to talk him out of it, but after ten minutes gave way. "I had an intercourse with her and then I went. She was crying a bit." In only one case did the girl resist violently, then Brown ran away. He was caught one day after his workmates had been discussing the case, and Brown told them the newspaper reports were exaggerated; one of the men went to the police. Brown was identified and sentenced to life imprisonment.

In *The Sexual Criminal* – a classic study by Paul de River – it is clear that the general pattern in the United States is similar. De River quotes a multiple rapist: "Well, I went by this girl's window, or not window, it was a walk, and her shade was up and I saw her and I just went into the building and went into her room. Then I showed her the knife and I told her to keep quiet and lay down. She laid down and I don't remember whether she took her lower underclothes off or not, or whether I helped her . . . Then I had intercourse with her. One thing, I told her to keep her mouth shut, then I left . . ."

What emerges clearly from these and other similar case reports is that the rapist is often in a somewhat confused, indefinite frame of mind. There is no need to disbelieve Andrew Brown when he says: "I said I didn't know (if I was going to rape her) because I didn't." De River describes another sexual offender who was apparently impotent and incapable of having an erection. He explained that he started to rob automobiles because he wanted money.

"The first people I held up I got an idea that it would be nice to undress them so there would be no chance they would follow me . . . When I undressed the first girl I got excited and I started to pet and love her. I tried to assault her but I couldn't get it in . . ."

He claims that this girl—like others—became so excited by his petting that she began to enjoy it. Whereupon the unsuccessful rapist ordered her male companion to have intercourse with her. "It exhilarates me to see that." Later the same evening, he held up another couple, and again petted the girl. He explained: "I wanted to do something for them, and she got hot and I tried to give her relief. I took no money from them."

Horrific case

So the original motive of robbery was forgotten. This kind of confusion seems typical of many rapists. So does the rather apologetic tone, and the slightly prudish wording: ". . . she took her lower underclothes off". In crime fiction, the rapist is usually a hard-eyed monster driven by inhuman lust; in reality, such men are exceptions. Most rapists, like Andrew Brown, are not sure whether they intend to go through with it or not; it often depends upon the attitude of the woman. She may talk him out of it, or frighten him away by resisting, or give in.

But in our present age of often violent sex, rape is frequently not restricted to savage attacks on young or even old women. A particularly horrific and notorious criminal case was that of Dean Corll, the 33-year-old homosexual murderer of Houston Texas. When he was finally shot dead by a 17-year-old accomplice, Elmer Henley, Corll had tortured and murdered around 30 young men.

Corll's method was to invite the youths —usually hitchhikers—to his house for a party, wait until they passed out (from liquor or drugs), then tie them to a "torture board". He often tortured and raped his victims for days before killing them. From the details that have been made public it is immediately clear that this was no straightforward case of a "sex maniac".

This was some kind of insane ego-assertion, bound up with a deep-rooted immaturity. (One photograph shows Corll cuddling a toy dog.) Compared with Corll, the rape murders of John Christie, the sex killer of London's Notting Hill, are easy to understand.

However, the criminals who make the headlines are usually untypical of the majority of murderers. Jack the Ripper, Neill Cream, and George Chapman were all multiple killers of women, who committed their crimes towards the turn of the century; but they were untypical: the age of the sex criminal still lay a quarter of a century in the future. Again, the crime of Leopold and Loeb—who battered to death a young boy to prove they were "supermen"—was completely untypical of its period—1924; but it is thoroughly typical of our own period.

It is always the strange criminals, the "outsiders", who fill the case history books and set the pattern for the future – while the majority of criminals commit the crimes that *are* representative of the age. So although the most notorious criminals of our own time are egomaniacs, driven by a passport for self-assertion, it is still rape and other forms of sexual offence that dominate the crime statistics.

This explains why so many of the worst sex criminals in the past few decades have *not* been rapists. The Scottish killer Peter Manuel was executed in 1958 for eight murders. Six of these were women. The body of 17-year-old Ann Knielands was without knickers; but she had not been raped. Another 17-year-old schoolgirl, Isobel Cooke, was strangled and stripped almost naked – but not raped.

In a house in East Kilbride, Manuel shot three women – Margaret Brown, her sister Mrs. Watt, and her daughter Vivienne. Mrs. Watt's nightdress was around her waist, and the pyjama trousers of the other two women had been pulled off – but there was no rape. Manuel himself was an egoist who, in the middle of his trial, insisted on conducting his own defence, convinced that he was cleverer than any mere lawyer.

Seduction

Again, in July 1966, sailor Richard Speck entered a hostel for student nurses in East 100 Street, Chicago, tied up nine of them, and then took them into the next room one by one and murdered eight of the nine. (One escaped by hiding under a bed.) None of the girls had been raped. Speck and Manuel were completely unlike the prototype rapist—bemused and slightly apologetic. A few months after the Speck murders, 18-year-old Robert Smith, a college student, walked into a beauty parlour in Mesa, Arizona, forced seven people to lie on the floor, then shot them all in the back of the head.

He explained: "I wanted to get known —to get myself a name." It is the same impulse that can be sensed in the personalities of Manuel and Speck that means that they cannot be classified as sex criminals.

But all this leaves one interesting question unexplored: the psychology of the genuine sex criminal—as distinguished from the apologetic rapist and self-esteem killer. The real sex killer falls somewhere between the two. He differs from the average rapist in being violent and ruthless, and often possesses a touch of sadism. His intelligence ranges from very low to normal—but not above.

An intelligent man generally tends not to commit violent rape, no matter how powerful his desires. Usually, if he possesses the normal social skills, he goes in for seduction – which carries no legal penalty. If he lacks these skills he may frequent prostitutes or use pornography to satisfy his sexual needs. The majority of sex killers are men who are psychologically inadequate.

The simplest way to illustrate this is through case histories. In the United States, the era of sex crime that followed World War I may be said to have begun with Earle Nelson, the so-called "Gorilla Murderer", who terrorized the North American continent for almost two years. Nelson undoubtedly belongs to the type of the physically impaired, as his photographs show. Nine months after his brith (in 1897), his 20-year-old mother died of a venereal disease contracted from his father. At the age of ten, he was knocked down by a street car, which made a hole in his head; he was unconscious for six days. For the rest of his life he suffered from pains and acute headaches. In 1918, he was charged with a sexual assault on a child, and sent to a lunatic asylum.

Prospective lodger

Nelson's criminal history was continued in February 1926 when a young man called on his aunt, Miss Clara Newman, in San Francisco; she owned a large house and let rooms, mostly to male lodgers. Unable to locate her, he pushed open the lavatory door—and found the naked body of the 60-year-old woman, the eyes wide open, propped on the seat. Medical examination revealed that she had been violently beaten and assaulted before being killed. (In that sense, Nelson was not a "normal" rapist; there was a sadistic element in most of his crimes.) The "To Let" card, which had disappeared from the front window, suggested that her murderer had been a prospective lodger.

A week later, on March 2, it became clear that the killer-rapist found his victims by knocking on the doors of houses with "Room to Let" signs. Mrs. Laura Beale, aged 60, of San José, was found strangled and violated under circumstances strikingly similar to those of the previous murder. Alarm spread throughout the Bay area; the newspapers began to refer to the killer as "The Dark Stranger" or "The Phantom".

EGOMANIAC Peter Manuel, who slew eight women, sketched the self-portrait (above) two months before his arrest.

2412 | Rape

His next victim was Mrs. Lilian St. Mary, 63, of San Francisco; her naked and brutally violated body was found under a bed in her rooming house. It seemed obvious that the killer knocked on the door, asked to see the advertised room, made sure he was alone in the house with his victim, then raped and strangled her. The strength and ferocity of the killings led some newspapers to dub him "The Gorilla Murderer".

The method seemed to be foolproof. Before the end of 1926, the number of victims had risen to 15 — among them an eight-month-old baby, who was throttled with a piece of rag after his mother, 28-year-old Germania Harpin, had been raped and strangled. In October, Nelson increased his pace and committed three murders on three consecutive days. The only description of the killer came from some old ladies who rented a room to him in South Portland; they said he seemed a polite, pleasant young man. His gallantry included selling them some jewellery stolen from one of the victims.

By the time the police interviewed his "customers", the killer had moved eastwards, first to Iowa, then Kansas City. In April, he killed a 60-year-old woman in Philadelphia, then moved from Buffalo to Detroit, and on to Chicago — bringing his death roll to 20. Then Nelson made his big mistake; he travelled north into Canada. In Winnipeg, he found a job as a builder's labourer and a room. Again his landlady found him quiet and likeable; he told her he was highly religious.

The next day, when Nelson had gone out — apparently to work — a 14-year-old girl, Lola Cowan, was reported to be missing. In the afternoon, a man named Patterson returned home and was puzzled by his wife's absence. Late that evening, kneeling down to pray, he found her violated body under the bed. Not long after this, Lola Cowan's body was discovered beneath a bed in the house where Nelson had taken a room; she had been treated so sadistically that the police refused to reveal the details.

These were Nelson's last murders. A few days afterwards he was arrested — having been recognized by a shopkeeper from his description given in the newspapers. He managed to escape from jail by picking the lock; but 12 hours later he was caught. Nelson was tried for his two **Winnipeg** murders, and hanged on January 13, 1928, despite his pleas of insanity and innocence.

"Lustful"

Nelson — the killer who hid corpses under beds — was mentally subnormal. The subnormality had the effect of removing the inhibitions that held his sex urge in check. Sexually speaking, Nelson may not have been more "lustful" than most healthy men in their twenties — almost any dominant young male would be happy to spend his life sleeping with a

YELLOW automobile rapist James Juricic thought that his forays in search of victims was a worthwhile risk. He got a life sentence.

different girl every night. A judge in an American rape case made the penetrating comment that nature has provided man with a sexual urge that is far stronger than it needs to be for the mere propagation of the species. Possibly civilization is to blame; animals living close to nature are altogether less interested in sex. Nelson is an example of what happens when a man with a powerful libido feels he has nothing to lose.

Against this, there are numerous cases in which a reasonably intelligent man has decided that he can "get away with it", and committed a series of rapes. In Peoria, Illinois, in 1934, a young man named Gerald Thompson made a habit of driving around until he saw a girl walking alone. He then knocked her unconscious and raped her in the back of his car—taking photographs of his victim naked. He silenced the girls by warning them that the photographs would be sent to their friends if they laid any complaints. His career as a rapist was highly successful until he killed Mildred Hallmark—probably because she knew his identity. Skilful detective work then led to his arrest, and officers found a large collection of photographs in his room. He was executed in 1935—before which more than 50 women had come forward in response to a police appeal for previous victims of the Peoria rapist.

Thompson, an after-dark motorist, preyed on his victims at night. Another rapist, James Juricic, drove about openly by daylight. He lived alone in a house outside Western Springs, near Chicago—his wife preferred to live in Alabama. He owned a conspicuous large yellow car, and the first of his rapes in the Chicago area took place on April 4, 1970, when he pulled up alongside a 15-year-old girl on her way home from an evening class.

Calculated risk

She was ordered into the car at gunpoint and made to lie on the floor, face down. Later they drove into a garage, and the doors closed electronically. The man blindfolded her and led her into a bedroom. There she was made to strip item by item, and the man raped her. He was recording the "love sounds" they made on tape—and she thought there was an automatic camera rigged up, filming the scene. He then made her dress, and drove her back to the place where he had picked her up; he removed the blindfold and speeded away. After this, there were a series of rapes—in one case, two teenage girls were kidnapped at once. (The rapist told the second one that she was his 56th victim.)

It was clear to the police that the perpetrator must live within a certain area, since the car journeys were usually brief. One victim was able to supply the first five digits of the car licence number; others helped construct an Identikit picture. In May 1970, a patrolling police

2414 | Rape

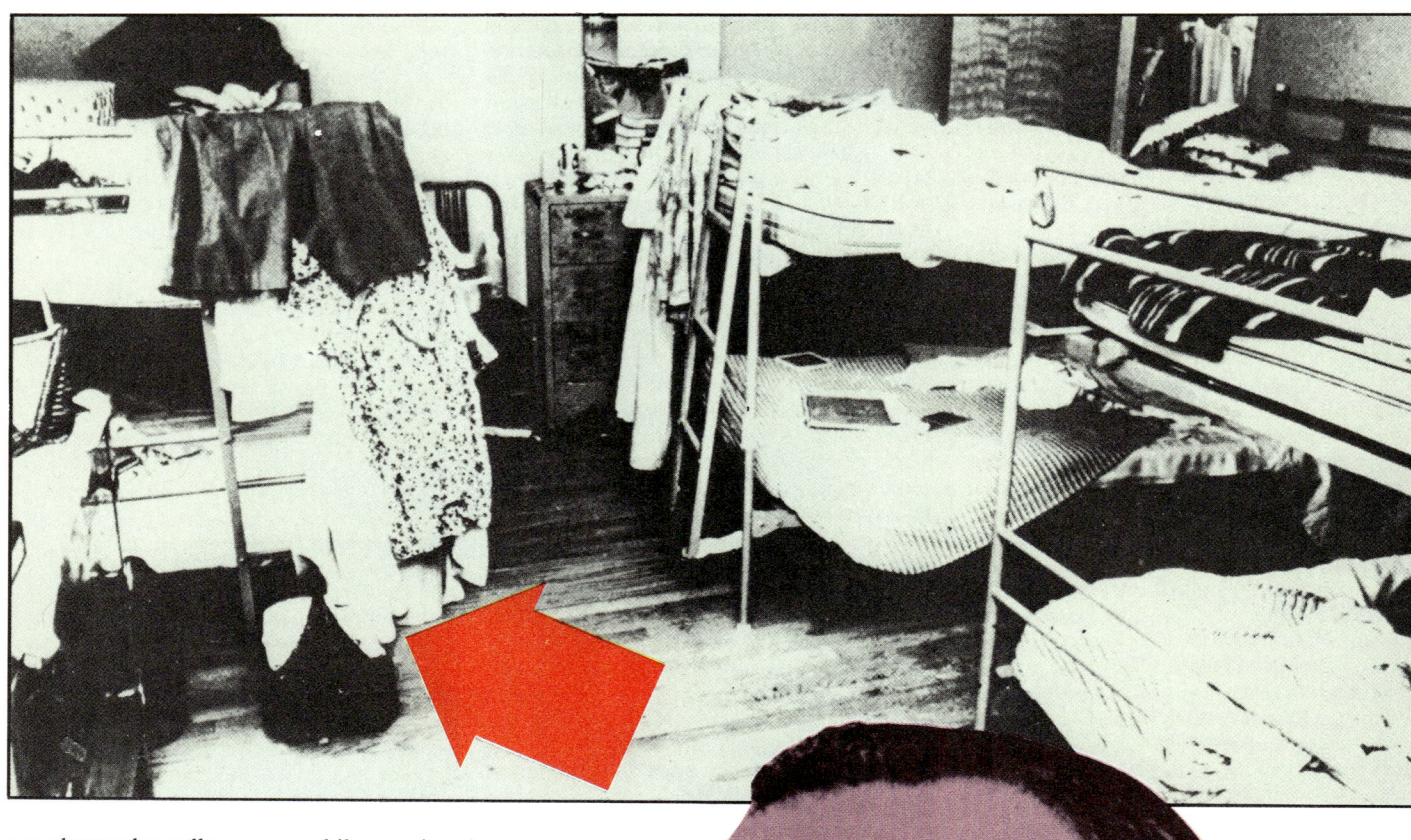

car observed a yellow automobile weaving in and out of the busy traffic. An officer in the police vehicle ran a check and found that the first five numbers corresponded with those of the rapist's licence plate, James Juricic, a 38-year-old research worker at Boeing, was arrested. Victims identified him, and he was sentenced to life imprisonment. The interesting point to note here is that Juricic was not a moronic pervert, like Nelson – but an intelligent man who calculated the risk.

Sociologists and psychologists have frequently tried to link the rate of sex crimes with permissiveness in society, but have consistently failed to prove a simple cause and effect – perhaps society is just too complex. At the same time geneticists and neurologists have been striving to find a physiological explanation for the sex killer, but so far have had only limited success.

Whatever the cause, violent sex crimes will continue to hit the headlines for the foreseeable future: sex killers like homosexual murderers Jeffrey Dahmer in America and Dennis Nilson in Britain, who killed and butchered seventeen and fifteen young men respectively; and serial murderer Henry Lee Lucas, who in 1983 confessed to the sex killing of 350 women, of which 157 were subsequently confirmed.

HIDING under the bed (arrowed above) saved student nurse Corazon Amarau from killer Richard Speck. Earle Nelson (right), whose strength and ferocity earned him the name of the "Gorilla Murderer".

RAPE EVIDENCE

WHAT IS RAPE?

A JUDGE'S DAUGHTER is found brutally murdered. She has been stabbed 37 times and dumped near her home at the spot arrowed below. But had Patricia Curran been sexually assaulted too? And how do scientists solve rape cases?

RAPE is rape, nearly all the world over, bringing a moment of unimaginable terror to the poor victim and sometimes destroying her mind.

Only in the United States is rape split into two different categories by lawyers, police and criminalists: *forcible* rape is the carnal knowledge of a female through the use or threat of force, while *statutory* rape is usually in a lesser category, implying unlawful sexual intercourse with a female without her consent, but with ravishment which does not involve excessive force or violence.

The difference is one which involves the courts in lengthy, costly, hair-splitting forensic debates, because almost all sexual intercourse involves force on the part of one or other of the parties. Very

Rape Evidence

often it has to be left to the forensic pathologist to produce the evidence on which will hang the verdict:

Did she want it, or didn't she? Did she struggle violently or was she attacked? Was she the completely uncooperating and unwilling victim of forcible raping, or after a show of force did she acquiesce out of genuine fear of injury, or from peer group pressure, to avoid embarrassment and ridicule as in "date rape".

One of the last official duties of L. Patrick Gray before he was politically ousted from his post as Acting Director of the FBI, was to give his Bureau's view on certain aspects of forcible rape — which caused forensic science laboratories in most countries to be extremely busy in close association with psychiatric investigators.

In Mr. Gray's final year (1971) 72 per cent of all offences reported in this crime class were actual rapes by force, while the remainder were attempts or assaults to commit forcible rape.

"This offence," he pointed out, "is a violent crime against the person, and of all Crime Index offences, law-enforcement administrators recognize this is probably one of the most under-reported crimes — due primarily to fear and/or embarrassment on the part of the victims.

"As a national average" (this, in the United States), "18 per cent of all forcible rapes reported to the police were determined by investigation to be unfounded. This is caused primarily due to the question of the use of force or the threat of force frequently complicated by a prior relationship between victim and offender..."

Human passion

On the other hand the British forensic student might feel the position is legally less complex in the United Kingdom, where the law (the Sexual Offences Act, 1956) is stated bluntly: *"It is felony for a man to rape a woman."*

This goes back to the Offences Against the Person Act, 1861, and might seem to stop any hair-splitting between statutory rape and forcible rape. But as every lawyer knows, there are dozens of additions and sub-sections: and human passions being what they are, there are many shades of rape — from violation of a girl by her half-brother, to rape of a wife by her husband when they are living apart under a legal separation order!

The "forcible" part of the act is usually covered in English law by some allied act of "GBH" (grievous bodily harm), and punishment for this may be additional to the imprisonment for life for the rape itself, or seven years for an attempt.

Professor Keith Simpson MA, MD, FRCP, Britain's most celebrated post-war forensic pathologist, once stated bluntly that "The police surgeon at the scene should keep his eyes open, his hands in his pockets and his mouth shut." This is true, but when directing the production of evidence which may show if a rape is forcible, statutory or imaginary, the criminalist may have to be even more realistic. He may have to try putting himself in the place of the attacker, and frankly ask himself such questions as:

TROOPS with mine detectors (below) help police hunting for clues to the killer of Patricia Curran. Pathologist George Wells (right) also helped detectives.

Rape Evidence

"If *I* had wanted to try raping that girl in these surroundings, would I have pleaded and argued first, would I have had my trousers undone, and would I have tried to get her tights down or her panties off before knifing her?"

Such brutal questions must have been in the mind of the forensic investigator Dr. J. B. Firth, CBE, FRIC, when he was Director of the North Western Forensic Science Laboratory of the Home Office, and when the murder was first reported in Co. Antrim (Northern Ireland) of young Patricia, daughter of Lord Justice Curran.

This case, which opened in 1952, became a *cause célèbre* lasting for ten years, involving a long campaign by a Sunday newspaper and political appeals to the then Northern Ireland Minister of Home Affairs.

Patricia's body was found in the grounds of her home at Whiteabbey, with 37 stab wounds including superficial face and neck injuries. There were deep cuts penetrating to the liver, but the limited amount of blood on the leaves of bushes suggested that the body had been dragged to the spot after the attack, and perhaps after the cuts on the face. The positions of her handbag, books and shoes also led the forensic investigator to believe they had deliberately been put there near the body, and not discarded in a struggle.

The post-mortem was conducted by Dr. A. M. Wells of Queen's University, Belfast, and Alan Thompson, a senior member of the North Western forensic laboratory staff started the examination until Dr. Firth could be flown across from Glasgow. It was decided that the attack was made with a narrow-bladed knife, and that face and neck injuries were received while the girl was standing up.

Tuft of fibres

In his subsequent report, made in conjunction with T. Alstead Cooper and his colleague Arthur Brooks, Dr. Firth talked of the girl's yellow wool cap.

"I removed a small tuft of fibres from the top of the outside of this... I found that it included a number of bright red fibres which, when put under the microscope, appeared to be composed of acetate rayon.

"Entwined in the red fibres were three wool fibres which were dyed an olive-green shade. There were a few wool fibres dyed bright yellow, which showed close agreement with the wool fibres of the cap, but the red and green fibres were not represented in the material of any garments worn by the girl..."

This kind of routine evidence, coupled with work by the Royal Air Force Special Investigation Branch, eventually led to the arrest, trial and conviction of Leading Aircraftsman Ian Hay Gordon. It took the jury only two hours to consider their verdict, and they found Gordon guilty but insane.

If there had been a sexual attack, what was the gravity of it? In his report Dr. Firth stated:

"I made copious notes on the condition of each garment, but the only facts of any significance concerned the girl's panties. I found recent tears all along the outer seam of the right leg, including the frilly edging in the region of the crutch. The back seam of the right leg was also torn for a distance of $4\frac{1}{2}$ inches, beginning an inch below the waistband.

"There were heavy bloodstains on the lower portion of the panties, mainly at the back of the crutch. The dispersal of blood indicated that the seams were torn *before* any blood reached the bloodstained zone—in other words, the results were consistent with the panties having been torn before the bodily injuries were inflicted, or at least very shortly afterwards.

"The elastic waistband was intact. It could be deduced from these facts that a determined effort had been made to remove the panties, and that it had not been successful, partly because the elastic waistband had remained intact, assisted no doubt by the additional protection of the girl's underslip and outer garments...."

Under English law, penetration of the vagina by the penis has to be established, not necessarily the emission of semen. It was, of course, not necessary to establish this with Gordon, who was being tried for murder. The psychiatrist Dr. Rossiter Lewis said that in his opinion Gordon had been suffering from schizophrenia and hypoglycemia on the night the girl was killed, and that he did not have the full sexual inclination—"as we know it".

R. Heber (American Association on Mental Deficiency), W. C. Sullivan (*Crime in Relation to Congenital Mental Deficiency*) and Britain's D. J. Power have all researched into aspects of subnormality and crime, with relation to epilepsy and aggravated subnormality of the mind, incidentally probing the mental pressures which result in rape, grievous bodily harm, forcible rape and even sexual murder.

That is why males accused of rape are not only physically examined for body fluids, such as seminal smears and saliva, for blood grouping and DNA fingerprinting, but may be asked to take the "WAIS" (Wechsler Adult Intelligence Scale) tests—a battery of ten tests, in fact, comprising arithmetical reasoning, digit symbol tests, perceptual ability and memory-span.

Mental illness

It may affect a subsequent verdict of Diminished Responsibility on the grounds of subnormality and/or mental illness in the form of reactive depression, and is not so isolated from forcible rape as it may seem.

While the layman might take it for granted that an essential element of forcible rape is the male attacker's overwhelming desire for an orgasm, this is not always the case. Indeed, it might be said to be one essential forensic difference between statutory and forcible rape.

The male's natural desire for intercourse is kept normally within bounds by self-pride, affection and our many

Belfast Telegraph

social disciplines; only where extreme temptations and circumstances allow does an irresistible erection and desire for orgasm take place.

Forcible rape by subnormals presents far more complex problems, and there may even be schizoid elements in the attacker's personality urging him to derive a perverted satisfaction from the knowledge that he has a new *power* — the power that he alone can decide how much the victim is to suffer in injury, or even in death, quite apart from the sexual assault.

Grave injuries may be inflicted before penetration, and the struggles may actually prevent emission and complete orgasm, because most women struggle frenziedly.

Whichever way it goes, the forensic worker is likely to be faced with identifying seminal stains; and one assumes it is now almost common knowledge that in the majority of cases such stains are uniquely identifiable through DNA fingerprinting.

Laboratory methods

As the stains dry out on a victim's clothing they tend to desiccate, and it becomes harder to find intact sperms. With current laboratory methods this is not always important, and we have certainly advanced since the early work of Alfred Swaine Taylor, one of the fathers of forensic research.

Citing a case of forcible rape tried at Edinburgh, Scotland, on November 27, 1843, Dr. Taylor recorded: "A man labouring at that time under gonorrhoea was charged with a criminal assault on a child. The shift worn by the prosecutrix, with other articles belonging to the prisoner, were submitted for examination. Some of the stains on the linen were of a yellow colour, and were believed to be those of gonorrhoea; others, characterized by a faint colour and a peculiar odour, were considered to be stains caused by the spermatic secretion.

"Digested in water, they yielded a turbid solution of a peculiar odour, and when submitted to a powerful microscope, spermatozoa were detected.

The stains were similar on the linen of the prisoner and the prosecutrix. I believe this to be a solitary instance of the use of the microscope for such a purpose in this country...."

Some 75 years after Taylor, forensic laboratories all the way from those of the FBI and the British Home Office were making an initial quick check — as one must in cases of alleged forcible rape — by taking garments of both parties and fluorescing them under filtered UV (ultraviolet) light. Speed is essential, for stains tend to dry out and it becomes increasingly difficult to separate vaginal discharge, semen, urine, soil staining, and grass (chlorophyll) likely to be found

UNDER ARREST... Ian Hay Gordon, the man who murdered Patricia Curran. Doctors were called before the court to say if he raped her as well...

when a victim alleges forcible rape in the open.

Fortunately the AP reaction can now be used as a routine in semen tests. Chemists discovered in the 1950's, that in certain substances acid-phosphatase occurs.

The acid-phosphatase found in the human body is an acid medium, and in forensic tests for semen a complex substance is broken down into parts and a test solution produced which, if semen is present, exhibits a bright purple colour.

The stain itself is not destroyed, and as several tests may need to be made by interested legal parties in cases of alleged forcible rape, this is most helpful.

The clinical work in the forensic laboratory is, of course, almost at the end of the evidence-getting story. But the criminalist would not be human if he were not moved to pity by the sight he sometimes faces at the start of a rape case.

MURDER CASEBOOK

BODIES IN THE UNDERGROWTH

Courtesy of Gannett Rochester

As a young man, Arthur Shawcross killed two children. He served his time then settled down to a quiet life in Rochester, New York, apparently content and rehabilitated. Soon, however, there was a string of prostitute murders in the town, their mutilated corpses turning up in the rough country Shawcross loved.

ONE DOUBLE MURDER

Jack's Buddy

Between May and September 1972 a quiet, upstate New York town was rocked by the disappearance of two young children. One woman claimed to know who was responsible – but the police would not listen to her.

From the moment 10-year-old Jack Blake disappeared from home in Watertown, New York, on Sunday, 7 May 1972, his mother suspected that a man named Art had something to do with it. But nobody would believe her.

Art had been known to go fishing with the mischievous Jack and a younger brother. He had told them scary stories about the Vietnam War, and – so the boys said – shown them pictures of 'naked women'.

Allen and Mary Blake ordered their sons to stay away from this Art (they did not know his other name), so when Jack was late for dinner, and one of his playmates remembered having seen him earlier in the day with Art, they were worried. Worry turned to alarm when Mrs Blake checked in the backyard shed and discovered that Jack's precious box of worms was missing. The boy must have gone fishing again. With Art?

Distraught

The night wore on, and calls to the homes of all Jack's friends proved fruitless, so the Blakes decided it was time to call in the police. Then Mary and her eldest daughter set out in the rain for the Cloverdale housing development, where they had heard that Art lived.

It was 3.30 a.m. when a squad car drew up beside the distraught pair. The police had identified Art as Arthur Shawcross, and had found out his address. The lights in 233 Cloverdale Apartments were out, but Shawcross appeared at the door fully dressed. He was a slim six-footer with long sideburns, prominent features, and a deeply cleft chin. His wife, Penny, was by his side, wearing a dressing gown.

Art Shawcross was understanding. Yes, he confirmed in a kindly, soft voice, he had seen the boy Jack playing with a pal named Jimmy. He was sorry, but that was all he knew. The Blakes were driven home, too weary to think any more.

In the morning, Art knocked on their door and offered to help look for Jack. 'We don't need your kind of help,' Allen Blake brusquely told him. The Blakes had traced the pal, Jimmy Knight, and Jimmy had told them that he had overheard Jack offer to supply the worms if Art would take him fishing. Jimmy had not seen Jack after that.

Next day, Art changed his story.

The wooded area where the body of Jack Blake, Shawcross' first victim, was discovered. From the evidence, detectives reconstructed the ten-year-old's ordeal. Jack had been lured into the woods, punched ferociously on the mouth and forced out of his pants. He tried to flee and managed to dash 40 yards through the bushes before being hurled to the ground at the spot where his remains were found. The boy's bones were partially covered by bark torn from a tree. Scattered about were a green jacket, blue sneakers and a grey T-shirt featuring a distinctive printed motif.

He told police he had taken Jack as far as the local school swimming pool, then gone fishing on his own. This brought the Blakes to his doorstep once more. 'I want to know where my Jackie is – right now!' Mary Blake blustered. Art lost some of his affability. 'I dropped your f—ing son off at Starbuck School!' he told her.

Jack Blake was wearing a green jacket and his favourite T-shirt – the grey one with the printed slogan that made him feel grown up: *'I act different because I am different'*. Among dozens of phone tips, the police received one from a caller who claimed to have seen a boy in a grey T-shirt being led into a wood by a man in his mid-twenties. Shawcross was 27. Mary Blake felt certain Shawcross was the man.

The police decided otherwise. Art Shawcross was known to be kind to kids, always ready with an ice cream or fishing advice. Besides, he had just married. Three days after the boy disappeared, the police declared that Mrs Blake's suspicions were 'unfounded'. 'We have questioned the man, and there is nothing to the story,' remarked police chief Joseph Loftus.

Police suspicion instead turned on the Blakes themselves – they were a big, poor, boisterous family who had been in scrapes with the law. After searching the Blake home on Water Street from attic to cellar, and requesting that the couple take lie-detector tests, detectives privately concluded that the boy was a runaway.

The state police were called in, and so was the army, thanks in part to an emotional phone call from Mary Blake to the commander of nearby Fort Drum military base. Soldiers joined boy scouts and scores of volunteers, including a group organized over citizens' band radio. A human chain made a dragnet of the woods and creeks, railway tracks and abandoned buildings, and all along the banks of the Black River, then in full spring flood. When this failed, the Blakes appealed for help from a clairvoyant, then issued a 'Jackie come home' appeal, just in case the local police were right.

Court reprimand

Jack Blake had been gone 11 days when Art Shawcross found himself in trouble over another young boy. Cloverdale residents saw him stuff grass cuttings down the shirt and shorts of a six-year-old, then put the boy down on the ground and spank him. Someone reported the incident, and Shawcross got a $10 fine and a reprimand from the City Court.

Over the following month, the search for Jack Blake petered out as it spread further afield. In June, the boy's picture was distributed around an area well to the east, where various sightings were claimed.

Mother knows best

Watertown settled into its summer slumber, and the police had the consolation of an official commendation for their efforts, though not one from Mary Blake. 'I think they stink,' she said. She instructed her children to keep a close eye on Art Shawcross.

It was a beautiful, clear Saturday afternoon in September when another young child went missing. Eight-year-old Karen Ann Hill had

> **If they [the police] had done their job, the little girl would have lived**
> PAUL BROWNE, Watertown journalist

Murder Casebook | 2421

MAY - OCT 72

7. 5.72	Jack Blake disappears
10. 5.72	Shawcross cleared by police
2. 9.72	Karen Ann Hill strangled
6. 9.72	Blake's remains found
17.10.72	Shawcross convicted

KEY DATES

DOUBLE MURDER

been playing on a front lawn on Pearl Street, not far from the Cloverdale Apartments. 'One moment she was there and the next she was gone,' mother Helene Hill told the police. The response this time was immediate, with city, county, and state police launching a full-scale search, and a description flashed on radio and television.

Witness

By 9 p.m. the police had found a witness who had seen a blonde child with an adult male wheeling a white bicycle in the vicinity of the Pearl Street steel bridge. This was an industrial area normally deserted at the weekend. The teenage witness could not name the man, but said he knew him by sight.

THE VICTIMS

HELPLESS PREY

Jack Blake, 10, came from a large family. He had a special place in his parents' affections, being the first boy after five girls.

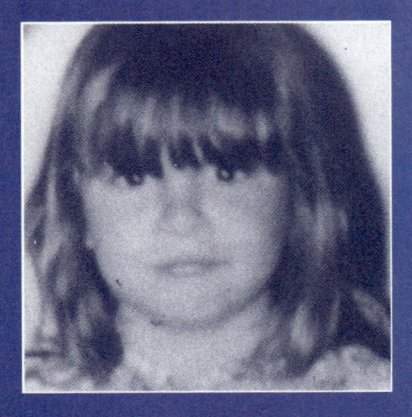

Karen Ann Hill, 8, was staying temporarily in Watertown because the family home had been destroyed by fire.

An hour later, the beam of a police torch probing the water beneath the bridge caught a flash of gold from a mop of hair. A search party clambered down and shifted stone slabs and debris to reveal the child's crumpled body. The small corpse lay face down, and was unclothed below the waist. Dirt was stuffed into the mouth and nostrils. Karen Ann Hill had been raped and strangled.

On Water Street, whoops from Jack Blake's sisters greeted the broadcast description of a white bicycle with brown mudguards. They knew that Art Shawcross had recently bought just such a bicycle. The Blakes wasted no time in reminding the police of Shawcross' address.

On the scent

Next morning, bloodhounds were brought to the crime scene. Pausing only occasionally to sniff a patch of pavement or a fence, the very first dog trotted across the bridge, up Pearl Street to Starbuck Avenue, and directly to 233 Cloverdale Apartments.

Art Shawcross was brought to police headquarters, and four girls picked him out of an identification parade as the man they had seen clamber over a fence by the bridge on the afternoon of the killing. After hours of interrogation, he told detectives that he 'could' have killed Karen Ann. Eventually he admitted: 'I must have done it, but I don't actually recall doing it.' He must have blacked out, he suggested.

Search

Three days later, after an intense search of a patch of dense woods two miles from the Blake home, police found the skeleton of a boy. The suggestion of where to look had come from Shawcross, in the course of the Hill interrogation.

Next day, the boy's blue dungarees were found with the underpants still inside. Beside the dungarees, almost lost in a thick bed of damp and blackened leaves, was a tooth.

District Attorney William McClusky had a problem. He was under pressure to close the embarrassing case as quickly as possible, but Shawcross continued to deny killing the Blake boy, and he now pleaded Not Guilty to the Hill murder as well. This meant a jury trial, when Shawcross' mental state was

Courtesy of Gannett Rochester Newspapers

BACKGROUND

WATERTOWN, NEW YORK

'Welcome To Watertown, The City Of The Future', the road sign declared, although few among its 30,000 inhabitants could explain precisely why, as it has long suffered from chronic unemployment.

Watertown is the last major stop before the Canadian border, and has a harsh winter climate. It manufactures paper and paper-making machinery, and is also the centre of a dairy farming region. It has a main square featuring a fountain topped by a nymph, which little Karen Ann Hill loved to watch.

The Watertown community is close-knit, and when an event of major importance happens, everyone feels involved. The Shawcross case 'just overwhelmed the town,' recalls Paul Browne, who covered it for the *Watertown Daily Times*.

certain to become a complicating issue, and the Watertown police were likely to face a number of awkward questions.

So a deal was struck between the two counsels whereby Shawcross agreed to plead guilty to the lesser charge of first-degree manslaughter, and at the same time to acknowledge he was responsible for both killings.

Unsympathetic

The morning proceedings before Jefferson County Judge Milton Wiltse on 17 October 1972 lasted only 18 minutes. The judge was unsympathetic to defence lawyer Paul Dierdorf's plea for psychiatric treatment rather than a long prison term. He imposed the maximum 25-year sentence, telling Shawcross, 'I trust that you will get some assistance in your difficulties during that period.' Shawcross showed no reaction.

By 8.48 a.m. it was all over. Shawcross was hustled off to the notorious Attica prison shackled to a beefy deputy, with eight other lawmen forming a protective shield from vengeance-seekers.

Art Shawcross (right, in glasses) is arrested the morning after police discovered Karen Ann Hill's body wedged next to an industrial sewage pipe in the grimy water beneath Pearl Street steel bridge (above). The eight-year-old had been raped and strangled. Once in prison, Shawcross was diagnosed as a 'psychosexual maniac'. Crime magazines seized upon the story and spread his notoriety with headlines such as 'Karen's Corpse Was The Key To Jackie's Grave' and 'The Kid's Friend Was A Killer'.

EARLY DAYS

PLAYING WITH FIRE

Art was no model child; his favourite pastimes were setting things on fire, bullying smaller children and tormenting animals. As a young adult his behaviour was no better. He was morose, awkward and short-tempered.

This 1960 yearbook photograph shows Shawcross (second from left, top row) in the 7th grade at General Brown High School.

The Watertown police knew a lot about Art Shawcross when Jack Blake went missing. Their fatal mistake was to presume that they knew everything.

Shawcross was a convicted arsonist with the peculiar trait of starting fires and then telling people about them. Art was 'a nut', they told Jack's mother – but harmless, except when he started flicking lighted cigarettes around.

The Shawcrosses were a local family – 'nice people, good, solid people,' is the description of Gerard Hoard, the principal at General Brown High School, who remembers Art as a thin, black-haired pupil who 'wasn't academically inclined', and who had to repeat a year.

Arthur Shawcross senior had served with the US Marines in the Pacific in the Second World War and then married his hometown sweetheart. Arthur junior was born in June 1945, the eldest of four children. They were raised in Brownville, a small rural community just outside Watertown.

Bully-boy

Art began brightly at Brownville Elementary School, but suddenly regressed in a way that perplexed his teachers. He became sullen and full of 'displaced hostility', according to a May 1953 report, written about the time he scared classmates on the school bus by brandishing an iron pipe.

He seemed to take pleasure in hurting small animals and sometimes he talked to himself in a high-pitched voice.

When he was 18, police found him one night cowering on a shelf in the basement of a Sears Roebuck department store. He had broken a pane of glass to get in, but had

Both pictures: Courtesy of Gannett Rochester Newspapers

panicked when he tripped a burglar alarm.

He married at 19, and had a child, but the relationship did not last long. His first wife, Sarah Chatterton, recalls nothing unusual about their life together, except that he was 'very immature' and would fake injuries to get out of going to work.

At the age of 20, he was arrested for assaulting a 13-year-old boy when a snowball fight got out of hand. Art had become enraged, and when the boy ran away, he chased him all the way into his home.

He was highly accident-prone as well as short-tempered. In the snowball fracas, he had injured a shoulder, and the following year he suffered head and other injuries when he stepped in front of a truck.

Army and divorce

Shawcross was 22 when the Vietnam War caught up with him. He was drafted into the army and, after basic training at Fort Benning, Georgia, attended quartermaster school at Fort Lee, Virginia. He also found the time to obtain a Mexican divorce, and married a second wife, Linda Henry.

Private First Class Shawcross served the customary one-year tour of duty in Vietnam, from September 1967 to September 1968. He was not in a combat unit, according to army records.

Demobilized in April 1969, he took a job in a Watertown paper factory, which very soon suffered

Art's second wife, Linda Henry (right), reported later that her husband was often depressed and once knocked her unconscious. The marriage was doomed.

$280,000 damage from a fire. It was Shawcross who raised the alarm. Four months later, he was again on hand to raise the alarm when a barn filled with hay caught fire. He was by then working in a milk plant, and three days after the barn went up, so did the milk plant, with Shawcross as usual on the spot to report the fire.

Shawcross then broadened his repertoire of crime and took part in a bungled service station break-in. Arrested, he owned up to everything, including the fact that he had been starting fires with cigarettes. He told Detective Sergeant Irving Angel that he had been nervous and talking to himself, and that 'something' had told him to start fires. Angel thought that he had marital problems.

Shawcross was brought before Judge Wiltse – the same judge he would face in 1972. He got five years, but was freed on parole after two. He had the usual ex-convict's trouble getting work, but the county used him on its 'grass gang', pushing a mower in summer and shovelling snow in winter. By December 1971 he had a regular job tending the unloading of refuse at the city dump at the end of Water Street.

Long afterwards, he was remembered for the way he sometimes pulled children's toys out of the piles of rubbish, and played with them. 'It seemed like he had a child's mind,' says Richard Gebo, his supervisor from that time.

On 22 April 1972, Art married wife number three, Penny Sherbino, and the pair set up home at 233 Cloverdale Apartments. It was her apartment and her first marriage. They had been wed only a fortnight when he took Jack Blake fishing for the last time.

TWO FREEDOM

Starting Over

Released on parole after fourteen years in jail, Art Shawcross drifted through small-town America, unable to settle because of public outrage at his past. When he finally found anonymity in the town of Rochester, a period of stability followed. But how long would it be before his urge to kill resurfaced?

Art was a model prisoner. He stayed out of trouble, gained his high-school equivalency certificate, and qualified in woodworking. Transferred to Stormville, in rugged hill country about 30 miles north of New York City, he even became a recreational counsellor in a mental unit.

Although he contacted his mother from time to time, she never came to visit him. However Art found a new friend on the outside – a kindly nurse named Rosemary Walley, who happily agreed to become his pen pal.

Social outcast

From the very first year, he had been applying for parole: he applied eight times in all. After 14 ½ years, it was granted. He emerged, aged almost 42, grey-haired and much bulkier, on 30 April 1987. Parole officers found accommodation for him in the medium-sized town of Binghamton, the county seat of Broome County, New York State. However, a local newspaper learned of his presence and there was an outcry.

Shawcross went to live with pen-pal Rose in a retreat in the Catskill Mountains but the local police chief objected. So did some of Rose's relatives. After four weeks, the pair were evicted. Much the same happened when they moved to an even more remote community.

Art thought about dyeing his hair and changing his name, but his parole officer encouraged him to try Rochester, New York, a major urban centre where he could hope to vanish in the crowd. He disliked cities, but at least this one had the Genesee River running through it. He found a job preparing vegetables for a produce stall in a suburban market. Rose nursed invalids. She worried about Art only when he spoke with his mother on the phone. Afterwards, he would fly into a rage, and storm out the door.

Art had been free for about a year when young Rochester women began to disappear. Their bodies would turn up some time later in out-of-the-way places, usually near fishing spots.

Dorothy 'Dotsie' Blackburn was the first. The 27-year-old vanished after lunching with her sister at Roncone's Grill in the city. Nine days later she was found floating face-down in Salmon Creek, a stream that meanders its way through woods and farmland on Rochester's eastern fringe. Dotsie had been strangled.

Ticked off

Police stopped Art the very next day for a traffic offence. He had a small child with him, which was a violation of his parole conditions, but that fact was somehow overlooked. All he received was a $25 dollar fine for failing to have a proper restraining seat for the child. He was also ticked off for not possessing a valid driving licence.

Six months later, a man searching the Genesee gorge for discarded bottles and cans checked what looked like a bundle of refuse, and found 'bones with a pair of jeans on it'. The

The Volunteers of America home in Binghamton where Shawcross lived after being granted parole in 1987. A local newspaper alerted neighbours to Shawcross' identity and he was forced to leave town.

badly decomposed body of a young woman, Anna Marie Steffen, was lying on its left side, crouched in a semi-foetal position, with the jeans down around the right ankle and the left hand clutching a T-shirt. As in the case of Dotsie Blackburn, the

APR 87 – NOV 89

30.4.87	Shawcross paroled
29.6.87	Arrives in Rochester
15.10.87	Rents apartment with Rose Walley
24.3.88	Body of Dorothy Blackburn found in Salmon Creek
11.9.88	Body of Anna Marie Steffen found in Genesee Gorge
21.10.89	Skeleton found in gorge
27.10.89	Body of Patty Ives found near gorge
11.11.89	Body of Frances Brown found in gorge
23.11.89	Body of June Stott found in lower gorge
27.11.89	Body of Elizabeth Gibson found

KEY DATES

FREEDOM

BACKGROUND

KILLING GROUND

Conservative, cautious, sometimes dubbed 'Smugtown USA', Rochester owes its existence to the fast-flowing Genesee River, that Nathaniel Rochester harnessed to power his flour mills in the early 19th century.

The Genesee tumbles over a cataract that is a smaller version of the Niagara Falls, 80 miles to the west. Then it bores through a deep gorge on its way to Lake Ontario. Despite being affected by industrial pollution, the gorge still manages to provide a leafy sanctuary for anglers and lovers.

At the end of the 1980s, this became the killing ground of the most dangerous predator to stalk these parts since the ferocious Seneca Indians fought to retain their domain 300 years before.

police had no suspects, and could discover no leads.

Art and Rose were making the best of city life. They had a neat, modest apartment in an old building near the heart of the city, close to Genesee Hospital, where many of Rose's clients received treatment, and an easy bike ride to good fishing in the river gorge. Art now rode a metallic-brown Schwinn Suburban, a woman's model with three baskets, one in front and two straddling the rear wheel, in which to stow his fishing gear.

The Shawcross apartment at 241 Alexander Street was on the ground floor next to the foyer, which was how Art liked it. He liked to know everybody's business, and he made some curious friends. He particularly charmed Clara Neal, a nursing home cook he met through Rose.

Clara was 58, and had ten children and 17 grandchildren. She became Art's mistress, and through her he had a choice of cars to borrow – a grey Chevrolet or a blue Dodge Omni. Trusting Rose assumed that they were just good friends. Clara's large family did likewise.

Tall tales

Art was as full of Vietnam War stories as ever – tall tales that had his workmates shaking their heads in wry disbelief. His employers, the Brognia brothers, knew that he was on parole for manslaughter, but nothing more. He told Fred Brognia that a drunken driver had killed his wife and child while he was in Vietnam, and that he had killed the driver in revenge. He told Tony Brognia he had been a Mafia hit man.

It was while living at 241 Alexander Street (left) with his fourth wife Rose that Shawcross met two of his victims – June Stott, a mentally disturbed drifter, and Dorothy Keeler, a homeless tramp.

The brothers did not care – he was a good worker – until May 1988, when state police tipped them off to the truth. 'Holy shit,' they gasped in unison.

Forced to leave, Art turned to selling hot dogs on Main Street, then he landed a permanent job as a salad maker for G & G Food Services, a catering firm supplying hospitals and schools. He worked nights and was paid $6.25 an hour.

In September 1989, Art proposed, and Rose became the fourth Mrs Shawcross. The relationship with Clara continued as before.

A macabre touch

The following month, a salmon fisherman found the fully-clothed skeleton of a woman under some shrubbery on an island in the gorge. As a macabre touch, police found a brown wig tied in a pony tail, but no skull. The only other clues were a blue 'Handi-Wipe' towel and a pair of white socks rolled up together.

A week later, children hunting a lost ball saw a foot protruding from a heap of cardboard lying under a large maple tree near the eastern lip of the river gorge. Police removed the cardboard to reveal the body of Patty Ives, a young prostitute.

Murder gorge

About this time, Art Shawcross was wearing a plaster cast. He told neighbours he had hurt himself in a fall along the Genesee gorge. A week after the discovery of Ives, a pretty brunette named Maria Welch was reported missing by her boyfriend, and that same week the gorge gave up yet another body.

It was a cool, drizzly Saturday afternoon when anglers Michael Bassford and Charles Hair spotted what they took to be a dress shop mannequin, with the buttocks sticking jauntily from undergrowth about 50 feet below them. Bassford scrambled down the precipitous slope, curious, half-fearful.

Police retrieve the body of 25-year-old prostitute Patty Ives (right). Ives' head had been thrust into a hole dug beneath a rusty fence and was covered by a swarm of bees.

Courtesy of Gannett Rochester Newspapers

SYSTEM FAILURES — IN CONTEXT

Shawcross was freed by a three-member panel of the state parole board after two state psychiatrists had examined him.

'He did a comfortable adjustment to parole,' said Edward Elwin, director of the state Division of Parole. 'We hate it when one of our people goes sour.'

A notorious previous case of system failure was that of Charles Yukl, a talented musician with a choirboy's face and a problem with women. Yukl coached aspiring nightclub singers. In 1968, he strangled one of them, and dragged her body on to the roof of his Manhattan apartment building. Eight years later, when another corpse was found in identical circumstances, investigators could think only of Yukl. They were startled to find that he had been freed after serving only five years. Convicted a second time, Yukl committed suicide in prison.

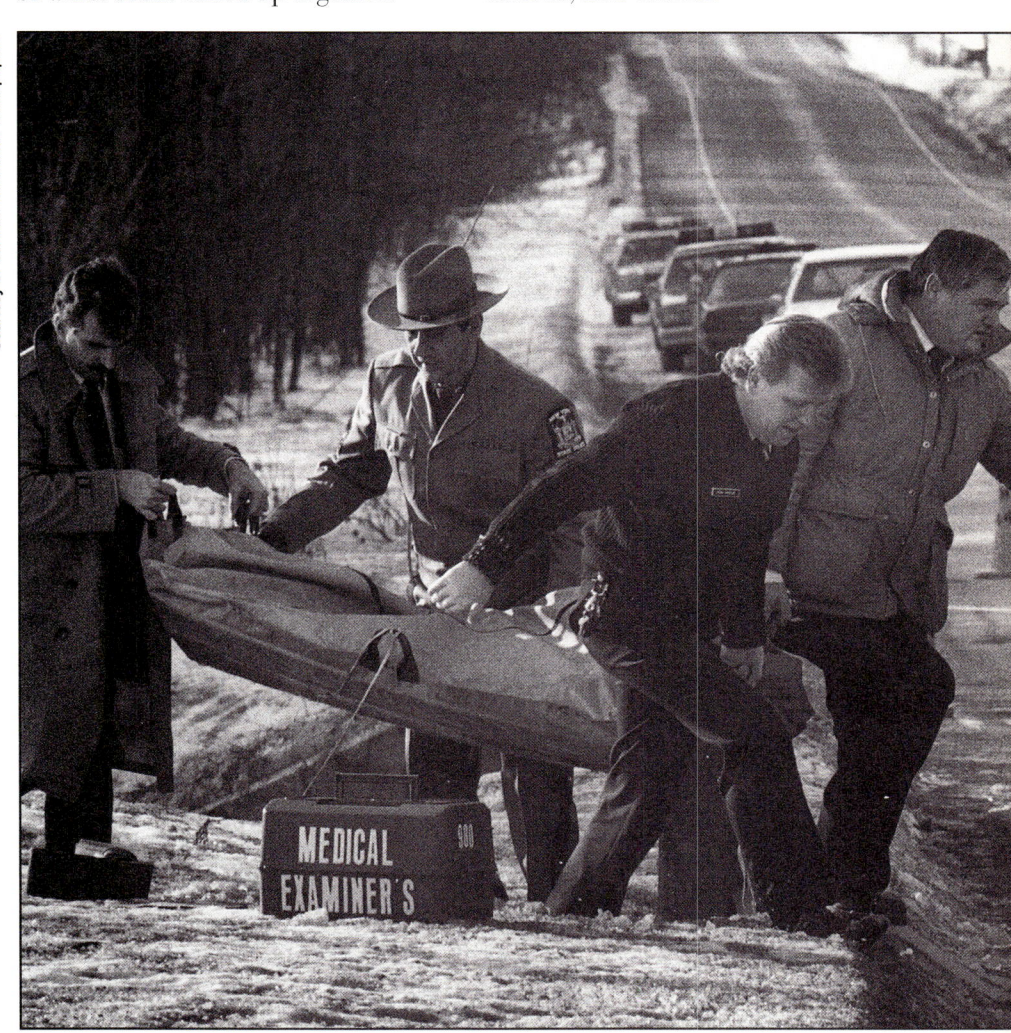

Murder Casebook | 2429

FREEDOM

THE VICTIMS

STREET SLAUGHTER

Most of Arthur Shawcross' victims were prostitutes and met their deaths as a result of some sort of sexual encounter with him.

DOROTHY BLACKBURN had two convictions for loitering in 1985, but was trying to get off the streets.

ANNA MARIE STEFFEN, 28, turned to drugs when her paralyzed sister died.

MARIA WELCH, contrary to the popular image of the prostitute, had a very loving, close relationship with her mother and boyfriend.

PATRICIA IVES, 25, was a school drop-out and heavily into drugs. She had a baby boy, who was placed in foster care. Then followed a series of prostitution convictions and three jail sentences.

FRANCES BROWN, 22, had a baby girl when she was 18 and soon after became hooked on drugs.

JUNE STOTT, 30, was the youngest of eight children, and slightly retarded.

LIZ GIBSON married the day she left school. She was described as 'very bright' but became addicted to coccaine and started passing bad cheques to get money for her habit.

DOROTHY BLACKBURN  *ANNA MARIE STEFFEN*
MARIA WELCH  *PATRICIA IVES* 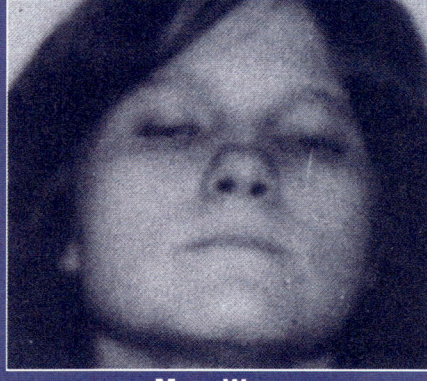
FRANCES BROWN 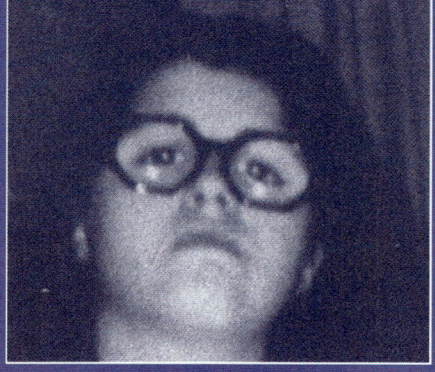 *JUNE STOTT*  *ELIZABETH GIBSON* 

'Oh, no!' he gasped as the dummy proved to be real. She was naked, with blonde hair tumbling over her shoulders. On one buttock, there was an amateurish tattoo.

'Kiss It Off,' it said.

Police assumed that it was Maria Welch, who was known to have a tattoo. When the fingerprints did not match, 'a gong went off like Big Ben' at police headquarters, Deputy Police Chief Terrence Rickard was to recall. That night – 11 November 1989 – the Rochester police faced up to the fact that they were dealing with a serial killer. The blonde was identified as 22-year-old Frances Brown, who had been chatting with a neighbour only hours before.

Art Shawcross was by now taking a lively, concerned interest in the killings. He took to dropping into Dunkin' Donuts, an all-night pastry shop round the corner from his apartment, for a snack and gossip with local police who also frequented the place.

Rickard had been put in charge of a task force operating out of the fourth floor of police headquarters in what was dubbed the 'War Room'. A notice taped outside warned: 'Serial Investigators Only.' The walls inside became filled with the photographs and data on murdered or missing women.

Rickard dispatched squads with dogs to comb the Genesee gorge, while state police helicopters conducted aerial surveillance, SWAT teams rappeled down the gorge's steep walls, and divers checked the river and lake shore.

Despite this, it took a man walking his dog to find the next body, this time much further along the gorge, amid reeds and rusted river barges. Mark Stetzel noticed an ice-covered

All pictures: Courtesy of Gannett Rochester Newspapers

Art Shawcross with his 58-year-old mistress, Clara Neal, (far left) and one of her ten children (right). He carried on this relationship even after marrying his fourth wife Rose Walley in September 1989. It was only when the body of 22-year-old Frances Brown was discovered (below) that police faced up to the fact the they were dealing with a serial killer. Shawcross was by now taking a lively interest in the killings, and even warned Clara to stay off the streets of Rochester and keep her doors locked.

object that had been dragged into a clump of tall cat's-tail reeds.

It was a piece of frozen carpet. A glance at what was underneath and Stetzel beat a retreat. 'I didn't feel like losing my stomach,' he told police, who were able to identify the badly decomposed body as the remains of June Stott, Shawcross' mentally-disturbed friend. A few feet away, hanging from a four-foot cat's-tail stalk, was another Handi-Wipe cloth, this time bloodstained.

Four days later, one-time beauty queen Elizabeth Gibson was found by a deer hunter in woods ten miles to the east of Rochester. She had been suffocated. Police found tyre impressions and blue paint chips where a

> **By God's help, wherever he goes, I'll be there**
> CLARA NEAL, Shawcross' mistress

vehicle had scraped a tree.

Art Shawcross turned up for work with a big bruise on his head and several scratches on his face. He drew sympathetic chuckles from his colleagues when he explained that he had got hurt trying to break up a violent argument between one of his hunting buddies and the buddy's mother-in-law.

He had been punctilious in seeing his parole officer twice a month, and never missed his weekly group counselling session at a mental health centre. He was, the authorities felt, coming along nicely.

IN FOCUS

AMERICA'S APOCALYPSE

By the time the USA withdrew its troops from Vietnam in 1973, more than 40,000 Americans had died there. The war scarred a whole generation.

To the very end, Rose Shawcross chose to believe that what happened was not her husband's fault. It was Vietnam, she reassured him, and Agent Orange ...

Vietnam was America's ugliest war, and the men who fought it returned to suffer the contempt that America reserves for losers. The most enduring image was of Lt William Calley and his crazed platoon of Charlie Company butchering 347 women, children and old men in a hamlet called My Lai.

Lone survivor

Art Shawcross came back a braggart, full of fanciful tales about having 39 confirmed kills with his M-16 rifle, and being the lone survivor of an encircled battalion, but none of his gross descriptions of exploding babies and women tied to trees and being ripped apart were worse than what actually happened at My Lai and many other places.

A pile of dead bodies (left) was an everyday sight in the Vietnam War. The sniper (below) takes up position amid domestic debris, the doll a symbol of shattered homes and ruined lives.

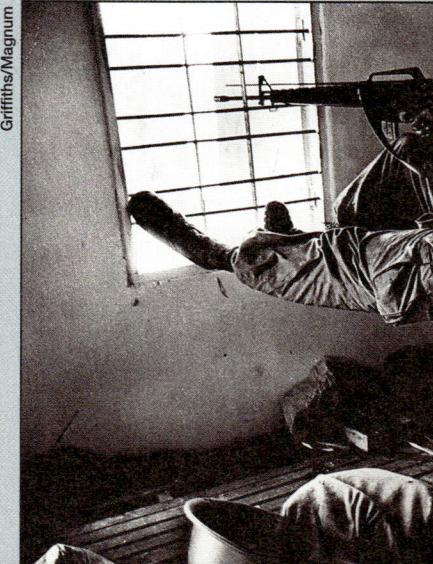

Jobs were as scarce as victory parades for the returning warriors, and a quarter of a million of them found no work at all. As many as 100,000 were drug addicts, and the anguish and disaffection of certain men gave rise to a new medical term – post-traumatic stress disorder, or PTSD. Homely old phrases like 'shell shock' and 'combat fatigue' were inadequate for describing the mental condition of some minds exposed to the totality of this war.

The other enduring legacy of Vietnam was a lethal defoliant known as Agent Orange, actually a grey vapour, squirted by the ton from aircraft to strip the jungle bare. By the late '70s, hundreds of veterans were complaining of all sorts of ailments, psychological as well as physical, that came to be attributed to exposure to a dioxin contained in Agent Orange.

A wounded American soldier, grimacing with pain, is dragged by his comrades to the safety of a makeshift bunker (above).

US air power played a highly important part in the Vietnam War. Cowed Viet Cong prisoners wait to be taken away in helicopters for interrogation and incarceration. (above). The horrifying effects of defoliation agents such as Agent Orange are clearly visible in this devastated landscape (left).

Violent deaths

In 1987, the Center for Disease Control reported that the Vietnam veterans were dying at a rate 45 per cent higher than a control sample of those who had served in the US Army at the same time but in other places. Vietnam vets also had a 72 per cent higher suicide rate, and a comparably higher incidence of 'violent deaths', including homicides.

Shawcross could have been speaking for men more normal than himself when he maintained that 'Vietnam messed up my whole life . . . it taught me how to kill; and it didn't teach me how not to.'

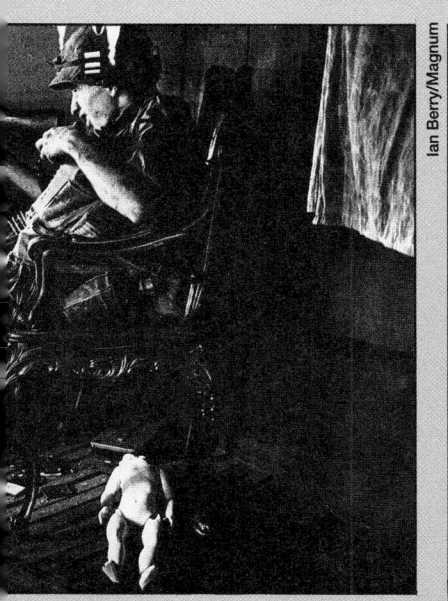

THREE
CAPTURE

As prostitutes continued to fall prey to the serial killer, panic and desperation seized the city of Rochester. Police had no real leads, but a breakthrough came by chance and a seemingly harmless man emerged as the chief suspect.

On the last day of November 1989, the Police Department acknowledged publicly that a serial killer was at work, preying upon women whose lifestyles exposed them to danger. Many prostitutes fled. Tentatively, at first grudgingly, a spirit of co-operation began to develop between those who remained and the police.

Callers offering advice and tips clogged police lines. They included cranks, like the man who announced that Batman would soon apprehend the killer. Another caller told the police that he knew the identity of the murderer, and intended to kill him at 5 p.m. The caller was arrested.

More than 100 phoney leads were apparently motivated by spurned lovers and women who wanted to harass their spouses or boyfriends. Other tips were too vague; in one, a nervous prostitute identified the man only as 'Gordo', a name that unfortunately meant nothing to the police.

Church leaders appealed for help and understanding. Feminists seized upon the issue of violence against

KEY DATES
DEC 89 - JAN 90

17.12.89	June Cicero disappears
23.12.89	Darlene Trippi disappears
31.12.89	Felicia Stephens' belongings found
3.1.90	Body of June Cicero found
4.1.90	Body of Felicia Stephens found; Shawcross arrested; he leads police to bodies of Maria Welch and Darlene Trippi

Under The Ice

Rochester Deputy Police Chief Terence Rickard (above) headed the investigation into the series of prostitute killings. Police scuba divers (left) join in the search for evidence near where Maria Welch's body was found.

women, and they organized a 'Take Back the Night' march through the danger zone.

Multi-coloured ribbons bearing victims' names were woven around a straw wreath at a service for their families. Maria Welch's boyfriend Jim Miller was there with their baby on his lap. Jim had become the county morgue's most regular visitor, summoned each time an unidentified victim was brought in. He had had a dream that Maria would return on Christmas Eve.

On Alexander Street, Art Shawcross was caught up in the Christmas spirit, fussing over presents to give his lady friends ... a coffee-maker, a set of steak knives, candies, even bags of potatoes filched from work. He baked pies and cakes.

On 17 December, one of Rochester's most hardened and street-wise prostitutes went missing. June Cicero was known to the police as a 'wildcat'. If Cicero had fallen prey to the killer, no-one was safe.

On 23 December, Darlene Trippi disappeared without trace. She was a petite brunette: just the sort the killer seemed to savour most. On 31 December, a pair of boots and black jeans were found by a roadside not far from Salmon Creek. A Social Security identification card was in the pocket. It belonged to Felicia Stephens, a prostitute like the others, but out of pattern, for she was black. Deputy Police Chief Rickard feared that the killer might be entering a new, even more frenzied phase.

That night, a crowd of 25,000 braved the freezing weather to link hands and see in the 1990s with a riverside firework display that lit up central Rochester. One of Rose's patients threw a party for the Shawcrosses. Art arrived slightly dishevelled. He confided to a fellow guest that he had run a friend's car into a ditch on a country road.

The snow melts

State and city police gave up their New Year celebrations to search the woods, fields and swamps around Salmon Creek, looking for Stephens. By Wednesday, 3 January, eight square miles had been systematically searched without result, but hopes rose as the sun broke through and blanketing snow began to melt.

Later that morning, a state police helicopter with Senior Investigator John McCaffrey aboard was churning along Salmon Creek at tree-top level when McCaffrey spotted a body lying face down in the ice. It was about two

CAPTURE

miles from where Stephens' pants were found, and half a mile from where Dorothy Blackburn's body was discovered in 1988. A grey Chevrolet was parked on a bridge overlooking the spot, with the passenger door open. A man was leaning out, apparently urinating.

McCaffrey trained his binoculars on the odd spectacle, and radioed word to the ground. State troopers trailed the Chevrolet for six miles to the Wedgewood Nursing Home in Spencerport, where they questioned the man. It was Art Shawcross. He explained that he had stopped for lunch by the creek while on his way to pick up his girlfriend at the nursing home. Clara Neal was due off at 1 p.m., and until then he chatted amiably with the troopers in the nursing home car park.

At Rochester police headquarters, Task Force chief Rickard was never to forget the way 'all hell broke loose' when a routine identity check revealed the record of the man on the

All pictures:Courtesy of Gannett Rochester Newspapers

A state trooper picks up a boot that was found to belong to missing prostitute Felicia Stephens. Other clothes and personal belongings were found nearby.

WOMEN OF THE STREETS

THE VICTIMS

JUNE CICERO, aged 34, arrived from Brooklyn, New York, in 1973 and had been a fixture on the Rochester streets for 16 years. She was a strong character and something of a mother figure to several of the young girls who operated in her area. Like so many women in her profession, she had a drug problem and often spoke of seeking a cure.

DARLENE TRIPPI was 32 years old. Arthur Shawcross knew her well enough to bring her a Christmas present. She also had fond relatives who tried to forget the sordid side of her life. A married sister recalled their last chance meeting at a street corner in Rochester, and how 'the kids made a big fuss over her'. Four days later, Darlene was dead.

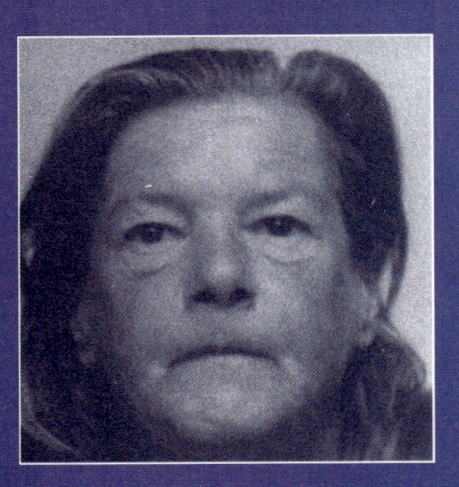

DOROTHY KEELER, aged 59, was a drifter with a drink problem. She distrusted strangers and had no use for men – 'she shunned them like the plague,' said Doris Cohen, a cook at the Blessed Sacrament homeless shelter, where she spent her winters. Shawcross won her confidence with little kindnesses. Her remains were unidentified until he confessed.

bridge. The Chevrolet was impounded, and Shawcross and Clara Neal were questioned separately.

The body in the creek was not Stephens, but Cicero. It was naked except for a white sweater and white socks, and a single small earring with a distinctive pink stone. The genital area had been mutilated, and the stomach and face marked some time after death. Beside it was an empty salad container, identified by Shawcross as one he dropped from the bridge.

At 9 p.m. Neal was released, and went home to do some laundry. Shawcross accompanied the detectives to a diner, where he was treated to apple pie and black coffee. He talked about his childhood, his marriage, and how much he loved to fish. Then he was driven home. The police had no grounds to hold him, but they decided to take the precaution of keeping him under surveillance.

On 20 November 1989, a memorial service was held for the prostitutes who had been murdered in the Rochester area over the previous two years. The total number of victims was then put at ten, and altar-boy Jim Pacheco (right), extinguished ten candles that had been lit for them. Jim Miller, the father of Maria Welch's baby son Brad (together below) was among the mourners.

That night, Shawcross phoned the Neal household, sounding 'unusually cool', according to the son who answered. When he was asked what was happening, he explained briefly, and casually commented: 'Oh well, that's the way it goes.'

Police showed Shawcross' photograph around Lyell Avenue, Rochester's red-light district. He was quickly identified as a regular customer of prostitutes, who knew him by the streetnames of 'Gordo', or 'Mitch'. Detectives also learned that Shawcross had called at Darlene Trippi's home with a Christmas present of venison a few days before she had disappeared. While there, he had discussed the serial killings with one of Trippi's friends.

A frozen body

By midnight, the police were back knocking on Clara Neal's door. In Art's Chevrolet they had found a pink earring matching the one discovered in June Cicero's ear. They asked Mrs. Neal to show them where Shawcross fished, and through the pre-dawn hours, she took them on a tour of the Genesee gorge and other favourite haunts. He had never taken her to Salmon Creek, she said.

Shortly after 7 a.m, on Thursday, a deer hunter found Stephens' frozen body in a derelict farm house only 300 yards from where her jeans and

CAPTURE

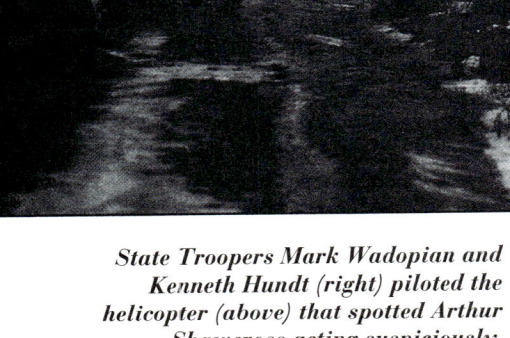

State Troopers Mark Wadopian and Kenneth Hundt (right) piloted the helicopter (above) that spotted Arthur Shawcross acting suspiciously, leading to his arrest on grounds of possible murder soon afterwards.

boots had been discovered. Like Cicero, she had been strangled.

At 10.15 a.m., Rickard ordered his men to arrest Shawcross. The salad-maker was stopped while he was wheeling his bicycle in the heart of the city. For several hours, Shawcross held a team of interrogators at bay. Initially he denied everything. He even insisted that he had never patronized prostitutes – he didn't want to get AIDS, he said.

'I had to hurt her'

The breakthrough came at 4.40 p.m., after wife Rose was taken to him. He had been asking for his wife, but she had taken a patient to a doctor's office and tracing her took time. They hugged and kissed, and she told him that she loved him, and would always stand by him. He told her that he had 'hurt a girl ...'

'Remember the day I came home with scratches on my face? I had to hurt her.'

Rose was allowed to remain only a few minutes. When she had gone, the circle of interrogators closed on their quarry. He told them: 'Give me the pictures.' Then: 'Give me a map.'

Shawcross flipped through the photographs of murdered or missing women as though dealing a deck of cards. Some he rejected; most he acknowledged as his victims. He admitted to 11 murders, and described each in vivid detail. Afterwards, he saw his wife again, and begged her not to let his mother find out.

Night had fallen when Shawcross and three detectives piled into an unmarked police car. He directed them to a remote spot near the Lake Ontario shoreline. Holding a flashlight with his manacled hands, he led the way through a thicket, then brought the party to a halt. 'There she is,' he said. The three-month search for Maria Welch was over.

The body hunters proceeded to a culvert about five miles beyond Salmon Creek, where Trippi's corpse was recovered in the same way. Shawcross also admitted responsibility for the headless skeleton discovered in October. It was all that was left of Dorothy Keeler. He later explained that he had thrown the skull in the river.

Clara Neal had two minutes alone with Shawcross in the interrogation

All pictures: Courtesy of Gannett Rochester Newspapers

room before he was formally charged with murder. 'Why, hon, did you do this?' she asked him. He told her, 'I don't know.'

Many people now claimed to have been aware of a 'weird' man fitting Shawcross's description. 'Every night since June, I've seen him sitting in his car,' said Mrs Janice Dukes, a close friend of Maria Welch. A male neighbour described Shawcross as 'a slimy guy' who did favours to ingratiate himself – 'he was overly friendly; just the kind of person you would stay away from.' Yet those who thought that they knew Arthur Shawcross best were stunned by the news of his arrest. One neighbour even wept. 'He was such a good guy,' she sobbed.

Baptism and funeral

Clara Neal seemed bemused. 'I don't know nothing bad about him,' she said. 'He may have done wrong, but he treated me better, and with more respect, than my children's father ever did.'

Welch's baby son, Brad, was baptized next day at the Holy Rosary Church. A day later, her funeral was held there also. Police officials did their awkward best by inviting victims' families for what was termed a 'support-group' session. That night, police arrested 22 women in a sweep necessitated by what Rickard described as an 'excessive' flow of prostitutes back on to the streets.

In Brownville, Shawcross's mother spoke of the son she had not seen for 17 years. He was 'sick', she said, and had not received proper help in prison: 'They should never have released him. Never.'

Helene Hill only discovered that she had been living near her daughter's killer when she saw the scruffy, handcuffed man on television. For years, she had fantasized about finding him and running him down with her car. Now that she found him staring at her from the screen, all she could do was cry. 'I feel like running, just running,' she said. 'Maybe if I run fast enough, and far enough, I'll forget.'

In Watertown, Mary Blake was dry-eyed. 'I'm not shedding any tears because I've got none left,' she said.

On 5 January 1990, the day after Shawcross' arrest, the Rochester Chief of Police, Gordon Urlacher, was able to announce at a press conference (below) that a suspect had been charged with murder.

THEY ESCAPED
IN CONTEXT

A prostitute named Joanne Van Nostrand 'played dead' for Shawcross at the height of the killings, and lived to tell the tale. She described for police how Shawcross had asked her to lie down and pretend that she was dead. She was scared, she said, but she complied, and it seemed to excite him.

Barbara Mae Dodson 'dated' Shawcross twice at a time when she was probably the only prostitute in Rochester who actually hoped to encounter the killer. Her plan was simple – to wait for him to make his move, then to stab him 'as much as I could'.

But Shawcross made no move, and she suspected nothing. 'I remember he had rough hands,' she said. 'He wasn't weird, he wasn't rude, he meant nothing to me.'

Dodson, who got into prostitution to support a $600-a-day cocaine habit, admitted: 'It's a miracle I'm still alive. I'm just crazy, that's all.'

TALKING POINT

HI-TECH DETECTION

Up to a hundred serial killers may currently be at large in the USA. To try to combat this horrific wave of murder, the FBI has enlisted the aid of computers.

Shawcross goes into the FBI computer as the first serial killer to be caught when in the act of urinating into a Pepsi-Cola bottle. That, at least, is what he insists he was doing, and he had the bottle to prove it.

The FBI's new computerized approach to the serial killer menace is a match for even this situation. Interested parties need only tap into item 134 in the Crime Analysis Report on Shawcross. Item 134 of the standard 186-part questionnaire is reserved for instances where there is 'evidence to suggest [that] a deliberate or unusual ritual/act/thing had been performed on, with, or near the victim (such as an orderly formation of rocks, burnt candles, dead animals, defecation etc.)'.

By marrying such exhaustive data to the latest computer technology, analysts attached to the FBI's Behavioral Science Unit's Violent Criminal Apprehension Program (VICAP) hope one day to make 'template pattern matching' and similar techniques so sophisticated that slaying sprees will become all but impossible.

Misplaced pride

Some criminologists suggest that a national task force armed with comprehensive computerized reports could clear up two-thirds of America's unsolved murders in a month. But for now, misplaced pride, the fragmentation of the police system, and territorial rivalries contribute to make America a congenial place for the killer with a compulsion to roam.

VICAP is the brainchild of Pierce Brooks, a Los Angeles homicide detective who started with only newspaper cuttings in 1958. Brooks had no luck selling his idea to police chiefs around the country until called in as a consultant during the Atlanta Child Murders of the late 1970s. When the epidemic of serial killing showed no sign of abating, and the Reagan Adminstration began to agitate for action, the FBI turned to him for help.

Instead of relying upon gut instinct, Brooks' unit

Pierce R. Brooks (right) pioneered VICAP (Violent Criminal Apprehension Program). VICAP is based in Quantico, Virginia, but the mainframe computer which outputs VICAP information is located at the FBI headquarters in Washington DC (above).

tries to get inside the murky mind of the serial killer, through psychological profiling and a study of their behaviour patterns.

The FBI estimates that there are between 35 and 100 serial killers currently active in the United States, and the number is rising. There are four in New York City alone. They have been called 'mutants from hell,' but the reason for the phenomenon is not clearly understood. Brooks has

Murder Casebook | 2441

suggested increased alienation: 'We are becoming more of a society of strangers,' he says.

VICAP had little opportunity to prove its worth with Shawcross, since the Rochester police did not turn to the FBI until things were getting desperate in December 1989. The profile provided by VICAP 'somewhat' fitted Arthur Shawcross, Rochester's task force commander Terence Rickard allowed, but he played down its significance. VICAP had termed the killer a 'transparent' personality - one who blended totally with his environment.

Art Shawcross fulfilled most, if not all, the criteria established by the FBI behavioural unit. Yet he was not among 50 suspects the police pulled in for polygraph testing, and he was never questioned. A slightly ludicrous figure wobbling around town on a girl's bicycle at all hours, being nice to old ladies, and munching donuts with his police pals, he might have been Mary Poppins for all they knew. 'There was no reason to believe he was the guy we were looking for,' said Police Chief Urlacher. 'I personally never knew he was here at all.'

The Rochester police received official notification of Shawcross' presence and crimes on 14 July 1987, two weeks after his arrival. The rest is lost in a muddle involving various police and law enforcement agencies.

It is known that shortly after the Dotsie Blackburn slaying, the county sheriff's office contacted the parole board looking for likely suspects, and that several agencies, including a state police agency, obtained pictures of Shawcross from May 1988 onwards, but for what reason is not clear.

THE MAN IN THE MORGUE

Arthur Shawcross was such an efficient killer that most of his victims died without a struggle, leaving only a few marks on the neck. Dr Nicholas Forbes, the county medical examiner, was first to conclude that a serial killer was at work because of the spate of throttled bodies that arrived in his morgue. The uncommon manner of death became the common thread, says Dr Forbes, who would normally expect to deal with only one or two asphyxia deaths a year.

Shawcross' secret was his powerful hands, but Dr Forbes – a South African from Cape Town – looked for evidence that the killer carried a syringe, or a chloroform pad, or even a stun gun to enable him to subdue his victims before killing them. However he found none.

Courtesy of Gannett Rochester Newspapers

He was ruled out as a suspect early on, because he did not own a car, and he was deemed the wrong kind of offender. It was Watertown all over again. 'He killed two children; that's a whole different psychology,' said Rickard.

Luck intervenes

Once luck intervened, and the state troopers had Shawcross bottled up, the Rochester police leapt into action, using state of the art forensic technology to prove conclusively that he was indeed the murderer.

'State police got the bear. We made bear soup,' boasted Rickard, and more than 50 officers crowded the dais at a celebratory press conference. Only the Medical Examiner, closest to the carnage, stayed away.

Above:Topham;right:Pierce Brooks

FOUR
CONFESSION

The Casual Killer

Most of Shawcross' victims were murdered after some sort of sexual encounter with him. He claimed to be 'in a daze' during these attacks, but later described, in a matter-of-fact tone, each killing in detail – including his mutilation of some victims.

Art had an explanation for every single murder. It was all there in his 47-page signed confession.

Take Frances Brown, the blonde with the saucy tattoo on her bottom. She incurred a death sentence when her foot got caught by the gear lever, while entangled with her $30 'date'. The gear knob snapped off.

'I got pissed off and just kept hitting her in the throat,' the suspect told his various interrogators – five city detectives together with two from the state police.

Frances Brown had nothing on but her socks when she died. Shawcross took those off, too, and dropped all her clothing into a nearby skip. With the naked body propped by his side in the front passenger seat, he drove around Rochester in the blue Dodge Omni, and eventually parked by the river gorge, near one of his favourite fishing spots.

There they sat for an hour, Art and the body, listening to country and western music on the radio. Then he opened the car door and 'rolled her over the cliff side.'

Fatal shove

Another victim, Anna Marie Steffen, surprised Shawcross with a display of joyous abandon down by the river on a hot summer night. 'You know, she took off all her clothes and started swimming in the river.' Art joined her, and they 'got to fooling around'. They were on the river bank when Steffen made the fatal mistake of playfully shoving him back into the water. He clambered out, and retaliated with a shove that knocked her to the ground, hurting her. She begged him to be more careful, as she was pregnant. At this, his rage exploded. 'I hollered, "Why the hell did you come down here fooling around, right, and in this condition, right?" She threatened to call the police.'

'So what happened, Art?'

'I strangled her.'

Dorothy Keeler was next. He suspected her of stealing during her visits to his apartment, and when he complained, she threatened to tell his wife that they were having an affair. He took her on a fishing trip down in the gorge.

'We didn't get no fishing done,' he recalled. He picked up a log and hit her hard. 'I think it broke her neck.'

Patty Ives died because she was being too noisy, and Art panicked at the thought that some children playing nearby might hear them together. 'I put my hand over her mouth and held her nose.' When she continued to struggle, 'I used my forearm on her neck and she shut up.' Afterwards, he went for a walk.

June Stott was killed for insisting that she was a virgin. They had gone for a drive, Shawcross said, and were sitting on the grass by the river when she told him she had never had sex, and would appreciate some instruction. Shawcross told the police that he obliged, but became suspicious: 'I said, "You ain't no virgin".' Stott then started 'screaming and hollering' that she was going to tell on him, so he suffocated her.

Mutilation

He kept Stott's pocket knife, and three days later he returned and cut open the body from throat to crotch. He did not know why, he said at first, but then he told the police that he

UPI/Bettmann

happened ... she just quit breathing.'

For some reason, he felt concern this time: 'I tried to revive her, and then I gave her mouth to mouth, and that didn't work.' He told the detectives that he wept a little, then he dumped the body in nearby woods and drove back to the city, dropping off Gibson's clothes along the way, and pausing for a while at a scenic spot by Lake Ontario.

Darlene Trippi, another prostitute,

> **S**he was giving me oral sex, and she got carried away ... so I choked her
> SHAWCROSS, on the murder of Dorothy Blackburn

died because she called Shawcross 'hopeless' after an unsuccessful sex session. He got mad, he said, and crushed her face against the car door until she died.

Shawcross became bold enough to kill Felicia Stephens a block and a half from police headquarters, after she stuck her head in the car passenger window and propositioned him. He trapped her by the neck by activating the automatic window, then reached over and choked her before hauling her into the car.

Art Shawcross (above) was charged with eight counts of murder in Rochester City Court. The defence plea of 'not guilty by reason of insanity' resulted in the most expensive trial in local history.

had done it to hasten decomposition. It was a trick he had learned from 'Uncle Sam', he said, in a reference to his war service in Vietnam. Asked why he did not simply drop the body in the river, he replied that he 'kind of liked June'.

Wallet complex

He suspected Maria Welch of stealing money from his wallet, so 'when I got done ... I grabbed her and choked her.' Elizabeth Gibson also fell foul of his wallet complex. She put up a fight, grabbing at his eyes and digging in her nails. Then – 'something

'SO I STRANGLED HER ...'

One of Shawcross' victims confronted him with the truth about himself. Here he describes what happened with June Cicero in the early hours of 17 December 1990.

DETECTIVE: *This is the one with the earring in your car, do you remember? Where did you pick her up?*
SHAWCROSS: City Mattress on Lyell.
OK, what happened?
I didn't enjoy it.
Why not? What happened?
She called me a wimp.
Was she laughing at you?
She said I was no better than a faggot.
This is while you were trying to have intercourse?
No, afterwards. We was sitting up there with no clothes on. The car was all steamed up.
What happened then?
I smacked her on the mouth and she said, I am going to call the cops, right. Then she says, I think I know who you are anyway. I said, well, you ain't going to tell anybody.
What do you think she meant?
The guy that killed all the other ... all the girls.
What did you do with her?
Strangled her.
What did you do then?
I drove out somewhere ... I opened the car door, right, and she went right over the guard rail.
And after you dropped her off, where did you go?
I went down to Dunkin' Donuts.

EVIDENCE?

CONFESSION

Stephens was the only black woman he admitted killing, and he did so reluctantly. 'I don't do black girls; never even talk to them,' he insisted. After hours of interrogation, and being confronted by incontrovertible forensic evidence, he admitted making an exception in Stephens' case, but he still denied having sex with her. When police asked him why her body was found naked, his explanation was that he 'just wanted to look at her'.

In retrospect, Shawcross wished he had disposed of the bodies differently. 'He had thought about finding a big hole, so that they would be in one place,' the police reported.

The police concluded their efforts with a 62-page report featuring an admission from Shawcross that 'if he was ever released, he would kill again.' Chilling and conclusive as it seemed, it was only the start.

Shawcross pleaded not guilty by reason of insanity. Nobody could recall an insanity defence prevailing against a murder charge in Monroe County, and there was a clear public desire to keep it that way.

Ten counts

The Gibson killing became a separate case because the body was found in adjoining Wayne County. That left prosecutor Charles 'Chuck' Siragusa seeking a conviction on ten counts of murder.

Both sides armed themselves with a big name in criminal psychiatry. The defence hired Dr Dorothy Lewis, a professor at New York Medical School, celebrated for her study into Death Row inmates. The prosecution hired Dr Park Dietz, a top consultant to the FBI and the CIA.

Motive for murder

The rival psychiatrists set to work, burrowing into the mind and motives of Shawcross. Their taped interviews and examinations began in the spring and continued all summer.

The trial was put back twice, and still Dr Lewis was so late with her final report that the judge threatened to bar her testimony. The prosecution was stunned to discover that she had used hypnosis to extract revelations about Shawcross' past.

Jury selection was on the same grand scale as the rest of the enterprise. From a pool of 3,000 potential jurors, a panel of ten men and two women was selected through an exhausting nine-day inquisition, in which the defence subjected candidates to a graphic preview of what was in store, with horrifying descriptions of torture, incest, and genital cannibalism.

Blood stains

The northern woods were in their full autumn splendour when the trial finally got under way. Siragusa took three weeks to put his case. He called more than 60 witnesses, and capped their testimony with forensic evidence. The broken gear lever, a blood-stained car door panel, and the automatic window system from the Chevrolet lent an additional, convincing sense of realism to the sheaves of gruesome colour photographs and pathology reports.

Occasionally, the jury was remind-

At the start of the Shawcross trial, prosecutor Charles 'Chuck' Siragusa (above) had an unbroken string of 40 successful murder prosecutions behind him. The defence team – David Murante (right) and Thomas Cocuzzi – were experienced in cases involving gunmen and mass rapists.

All pictures: Courtesy of Gannett Rochester Newspapers

Murder Casebook | 2445

Police retrieve the frozen body of Darlene Trippi, a 32-year-old prostitute. Trippi had refused to give Shawcross his money back after an unsuccessful sex session.

ed that some of the victims, at least, had been loved and were deeply missed. When Maria Welch's clothing tumbled from evidence bags, her boyfriend James Miller blurted out, his body heaving with emotion, 'I done the laundry every week.'

Expressionless

Shawcross had gained 3½ stones while awaiting trial. He sat expressionless at the defence table, hands clasped around his distended belly, seemingly oblivious of the events unfolding around him. He was quite alone. His family had disowned him, and neither his wife nor his mistress would attend his trial.

Clara Neal had had second thoughts about the man whose ring she still wore on the third finger of her left hand. 'That guy in the courtroom isn't the guy I know,' she said. 'He's got a split personality.'

IN CONTEXT

VICE SQUAD VICE

At the height of the Shawcross trial, Rochester police chief Gordon Urlacher (left) was arrested by the FBI. Four of his inner circle of top officers were suspended – among them 44 year-old Deputy Chief Terence Rickard, the man who led the hunt for Shawcross.

Urlacher was accused of stealing more than $150,000 from his own Police Department's vice-squad evidence fund, using most of it to make undercover drug purchases. The embezzlement charge carried a maximum penalty of ten years and a $250,000 fine. Urlacher pleaded not guilty, but he was fired by Rochester Mayor Thomas Ryan.

According to the aide who turned informant, money skimmed from the vice-squad evidence fund was frittered away on good living — plane trips, drinks, restaurant meals, a golf tournament, and tickets to Broadway shows like *Phantom of the Opera*.

MURDER IN MIND

KILLER UNDER THE MICROSCOPE

Psychiatrists probing the sick mind of Arthur Shawcross unearthed a 'killer cocktail' of violent emotions. But were these the result of being physically and mentally abused as a child and in Vietnam – or the product of an inherently evil nature?

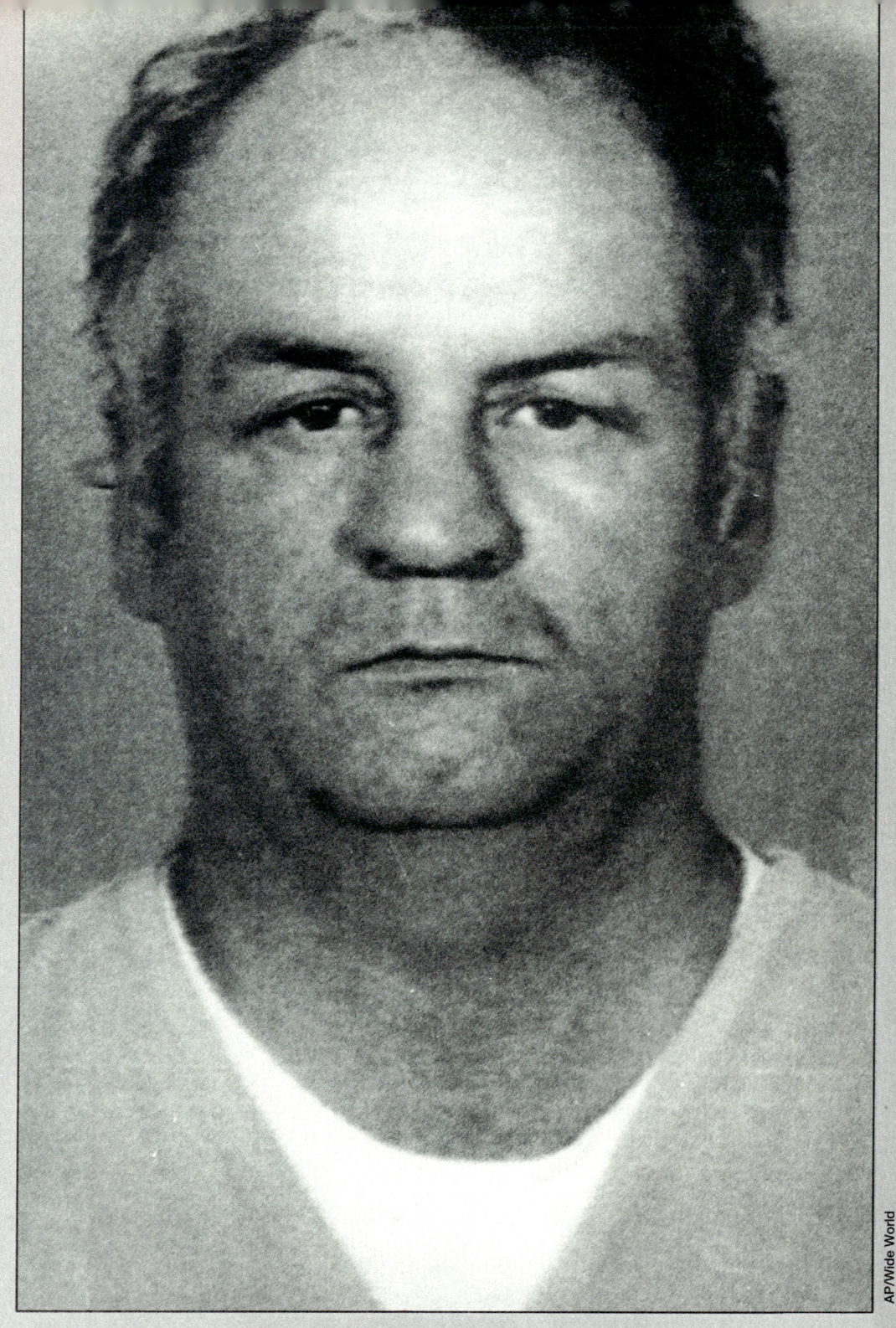

Since the 1980s, psychiatrists and criminologists have been trying to understand and isolate the serial killer syndrome.

A new branch of neuro-psychiatric theory sets out to pinpoint all the physical, psychological and environmental elements that combine to trigger the rage to kill and kill again. Dr Dorothy Otnow Lewis believed in the theory. In 1986, she caused a stir with a study which found that a majority of Death Row inmates had a history of head injury.

Lewis thought she detected gaps and inconsistencies as she talked Shawcross through his

Shawcross told psychiatrists that most of his victims reminded him of his mother or younger sister.

murders. So on five occasions between March and August 1990, she propped his feet on a chair in the Monroe County Jail and eased him into a hypnotic trance. In doing so, Lewis opened up a hell's kitchen of horrors. Shawcross took on multiple personalities, and through them appeared to relive vile and traumatic past experiences.

Punishment

In one session, he regressed to boyhood and screamed as he described a broom handle being thrust up his rectum by his mother, seemingly as punishment for engaging in an incestuous act with a sister. At other times he became his mother, who would whip him with straps and rods, and once burnt his fingers on a stove when she caught him masturbating.

He even conjured up a cannibal ancestor and mentor from 13th-century England named Aramus or Ariemes and provided stomach-turning descriptions of torture, decapitation, and cannibalism. Particularly repugnant was his description of how he cut out and ate the genitalia of two of his Rochester victims and the Blake boy.

Confirmation was hard to come by. 'We loved him as a child,' Bessie Shawcross insisted in a tearful interview. 'He had a normal life, just like the rest of the kids.' But she did list several head injuries, including a blow from a discus in his schooldays. None of the Vietnam anecdotes could be verified, and he had no combat record. Mutilation of two or three victims was confirmed, but cannibalism could not be proved.

The prosecution's expert, Dr Park Dietz, used traditional interview techniques, as Shawcross gave him a rambling but vivid account of his experiences as a GI in Vietnam.

Shawcross compared his crimes with those of Ted Bundy, the most charismatic of all serial killers. He told Dietz he was usually in a 'daze' when he killed, and did not understand why he drove around with some of the dead bodies propped next to him, or revisited the corpses days afterwards, sometimes falling asleep next to them for hours.

Shawcross told Dietz that he was having problems becoming sexually aroused, but thinking of incest helped. Karen Ann Hill had strongly reminded him of his sister as a child.

Dr Lewis thought it possible that Shawcross was suffering from post-traumatic stress disorder, the mental condition first diagnosed among Vietnam veterans, and also observed among persons violently abused as children.

Malingerer

But Dr Dietz saw only a clever malingerer making up stories. His diagnosis was anti-social personality disorder, a catch-all phrase used to describe the absence of moral scruple and feeling for others that often marks the behaviour of criminals.

With the trial well under way, Lewis was still not done. She created courtroom turmoil by announcing the discovery of lesions on a magnetic image of Shawcross' brain. She also pointed to genetic studies that concluded he had an 'X-X-Y syndrome' – a combination of sex chromosomes sometimes associated with unusual aggression and violent behaviour.

In such a pathological state – Dr Lewis claimed – uncontrollable explosions of rage could take the form of seizures, followed by dizziness, some memory loss, and an urge to sleep.

The exploration of Arthur Shawcross' brain was suddenly terminated at this point by the trial judge, who refused to permit a recess so that Shawcross could have a PET scan (Positron Emission Topography) – the ultimate test for brain damage. The nearest of these $5.5 million machines was 400 miles away on Long Island.

'This is not a research project; this is a trial,' he instructed.

Defence psychiatrist Dr Dorothy Otnow Lewis (above) tried to prove that Shawcross' violent behaviour was a result of brain damage and of being abused as a child. The jury watched a video of Shawcross (left) in an hypnotic trance, during which he took on multiple personalities.

FIVE
THE TRIAL

Trial By Television

There was no doubt that Arthur Shawcross had killed again and again. The defence pinned their hopes on a psychiatrist's ability to convince the court that the accused was legally insane. But how would the expert stand up to cross-examination by the wily prosecutor?

On 24 October 1990, the video tapes rolled and the flickering image of Art Shawcross under hypnosis – writhing, groaning, screaming – filled the teak-panelled courtroom.

It seemed like a real-life enactment of the classic Alfred Hitchcock horror film *Psycho*.

Seeming to become possessed by the spirit of his mother, Bessie, he/she took responsibility for the killings in a shrill, feminine voice. 'I love my son,' the voice piped. 'Noboby comes between me and him [so] I hurt all them girls.'

At other times, Shawcross became himself as a child, suffering his mother's abuse. 'Mommy's hurting me ... Oh, she's crazy,' he cried, his face contorted in apparent pain. 'No. No.

No.' Suddenly, the voice and manner switched, and he was Bessie again, shouting, 'You little bastard.'

On another occasion, he was his sister Jeannie, pining over his departure for Vietnam. 'I didn't want Artie to go,' he sobbed, and wiped tears from his eyes.

The jurors read along from transcripts that helped them keep track of the personality jumps. When it came to Ariemes, his cannibal mentor from the 13th century, the Shawcross voice lost its nasal twang. 'I take him out, show him a good time,' the Ariemes character declared in a stately tone. 'I take him out to meet girls.'

The tapes became especially graphic when describing mutilation and cannibalism. In the case of June Stott, Shawcross described how he lay down and slept by her body after strangling her, but when he began to describe the act of eating Stott's genitals, he spoke as his mother:

'I showed it to him, I said, "If you want to eat something like this, eat it now."'

Then ... 'He's sitting there crying. He ate it, then he threw it up.'

The tapes rolled for three days, and all that time the subject himself sat slumped between his lawyers, staring at the floor. The jury did not blanch, though some began to complain of sleeplessness and nightmares.

The prosecution set out to convince them that Shawcross was a

KEY DATES

OCT 90 - FEB 91

1.10.90	Trial begins
23.10.90	Court starts viewing video testimony
28.11.90	Prosecution charges Shawcross with faking mental illness
13.12.90	Shawcross found Guilty
1.2.91	Shawcross sentenced

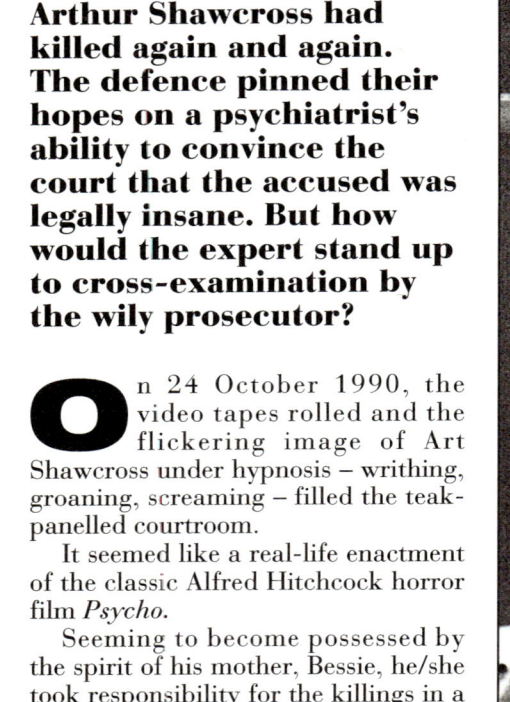

Murder Casebook | 2449

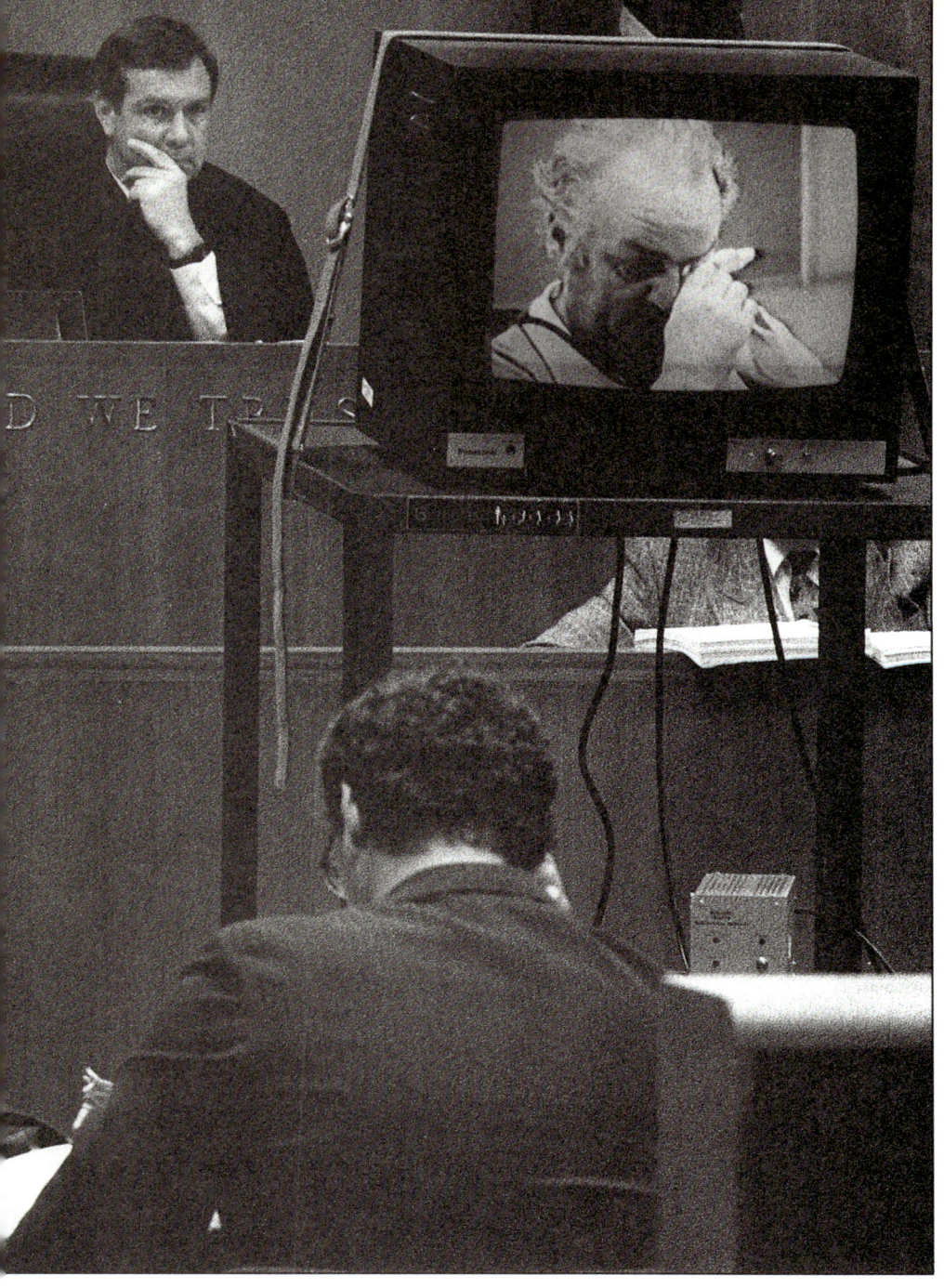

'fake and a fraud' trying to play-act his way out of prison and into mental hospital. Under relentless cross-examination, psychiatrist Dr Dorothy Otnow Lewis admitted she was not an expert in hypnosis, and that the technique was 'very controversial'.

Prosecutor Siragusa's target was the defence expert's major weakness – her rambling, disorganized presentation. 'The more she talked, the worse it got,' jury foreman Robert Edwards commented afterwards.

Dr Lewis sat with a pile of papers perched precariously on her lap. As time went by, the papers became more and more crumpled; the prosecutor seemed to delight in making her dig out details that were difficult for her to locate easily.

> **Brand him a murderer, cold and remorseless, for whom killing was 'business as usual'**
> PROSECUTOR CHARLES SIRAGUSA

Then he would stop his usual pacing before the jury box, and sit behind his table to emphasize the time she took to find the document. Once, in asking for a particular transcript, he coaxed her, 'that would be one of the bigger ones, one of the heavier ones,' in a manner more appropriate to addressing a child.

The mockery was taken up by the Rochester public. A radio station broadcast a parody of the Lewis testimony, set to the music of a Coasters' hit record of the 1960s, 'Dorothy's Back...Yackety Yak'.

After six days of cross-examination, Dorothy appeared to crack, and in an outburst that startled the jury she complained of being 'lied to repeatedly' by her own defence team. 'Witnesses have gotten flustered before,' Judge Donald Wisner dryly remarked when the demoralized defence tried to make this grounds for a mistrial.

Dr Park Dietz, the prosecution expert, dismissed the Lewis diagnosis of Shawcross as 'so improbable as to be absurd'. He was unconvinced that Shawcross had been abused as a

Arthur Shawcross' trial was dramatic by any standards. The bulky defendant sits impassively (back to camera) as the court watches a videotape of his emotional testimony under hypnosis, in which he delved back into his childhood. The jury had to decide if he was mentally ill or just cleverly faking. Dr Jacqueline Martin (left) gave evidence about the autopsies on murder victims June Cicero and Darlene Trippi.

Both pictures:Courtesy of Gannett Rochester Newspapers

THE TRIAL

child, or that he had eaten anybody. Talk of fantasies did not impress Dr Dietz. 'My son sometimes thinks he's a Ninja Turtle,' he told the court.

Siragusa produced letters that Shawcross had written from jail to his mistress Clara Neal. Referring to the results of his last brain scan, Shawcross wrote that 'there better be something there, otherwise my ass is cooked, fried and roasted.' Reviewing his chances, he confided to her that 'I prefer mental hospital [because] I may be able to get back out.'

Laughter in court

Siragusa had also acquired a 37-page statement that Shawcross had written for another psychiatrist months before. In it, Shawcross claimed that as a child he engaged in oral sex with his mother, two sisters, a cousin, two neighbours, and one of his kindergarten teachers. He also maintained that during his adult life, he was raped by five men in Attica prison, and by five men while fishing in Rochester.

Shawcross also mentioned sexual activity with a chicken, a cow, a dog, and a horse.

'He said he did it with a chicken and the chicken died,' Siragusa told the jury, who broke up in laughter.

As a final touch, Prosecutor Siragusa called a local neuropsychiatrist, Dr Eric Caine to give evidence. He had the court chuckling over what he called 'Shawcross's Law ... the more you talk to psychiatrists, the more bizarre the story gets.'

The final argument began on 5 December. 'Climb into his mind,' defence lawyer David A. Murante urged the jury. 'It's a sick mind that is operating here.'

Siragusa responded with silence – 30 seconds of silence, ticked off on his wristwatch as he stood before the jury box, and the packed courtroom held its collective breath.

When the half-minute was over, the prosecutor made his point. It took 30 seconds to strangle a person to death – in other words, it was something that required a strong effort of will, not an act that could be attributed to a sudden impulse. Then, pointing a finger at Shawcross, he urged the jury: 'Brand him a murderer – cold, calculating and remorseless, for whom killing was not an emotional disturbance, but in the defendant's own words, "business as usual".'

The jury deliberated for six-and-a-half hours, with an overnight hotel break. The families of the victims sat quietly, some tearful, some holding hands, as the jury foreman stood at 10.57 a.m. on Thursday, 13

Dr Dorothy Lewis (right) was the psychiatrist on whom the defence attorneys rested their hopes. In court, however, she was out of her depth and was comprehensively outclassed by the highly experienced prosecutor Chuck Siragusa. Her comic expression and throwaway gesture show that she took her cross-examination in good humour, however.

Shawcross sits between his lawyers and listens calmly as the Guilty verdict is announced by the head juror. His detached expression never changed throughout the trial.

December 1990 to deliver the verdict. When the foreman appeared to indicate a conviction for manslaughter, Siragusa clenched his teeth and winced, and several jurors yelled 'No.' Edwards, looking flustered and turning as purple as his tie, hastily proceeded to clarify the verdict. Shawcross, he proclaimed, was guilty of murder, ten times over.

The jury's verdict on Shawcross was immediately flashed on the police radio frequency: 'All cars be advised. The verdict is in. All ten counts guilty. Murder second.'

No reaction

Shawcross showed no more reaction to the verdict than he had throughout the trial. But on his way back to the county jail, he sobbed a little.

Outside the courtroom, a tearful Helene Hill seized and hugged Charles Siragusa. He consoled her, 'Hopefully, he will never see the light of day again.'

The mother of Karen Ann Hill had fainted during a pre-trial hearing in June. Now, she said, her 18 years of anguish were at last over. She went shopping for a Christmas tree.

'It's for my daughter,' she said. 'She's still 8, you know. She always will be.'

Flurries of snow were sweeping in from Lake Ontario and, thousands of miles away in the Persian Gulf, the final onslaught of the Allies' Operation Desert Storm was getting under way, when Shawcross at last came up for sentencing.

The packed courtroom was in dead silence as Siragusa read a statement from the mother of Maria Welch: 'I see her murdered in my nightmares. I see her fighting, trying to get free. I hear her screams. I feel her fear.'

Judge Wisner had Shawcross stand before him. 'Mr. Shawcross, this is your opportunity to speak,' he urged. 'All of us wish to understand what it is that happened.' Ears strained to catch the reply.

'No comment at this time,' mumbled Arthur Shawcross imperturbably, and he continued to stare blankly as Wisner pronounced ten consecutive sentences of 25 years to life – 250 years in all.

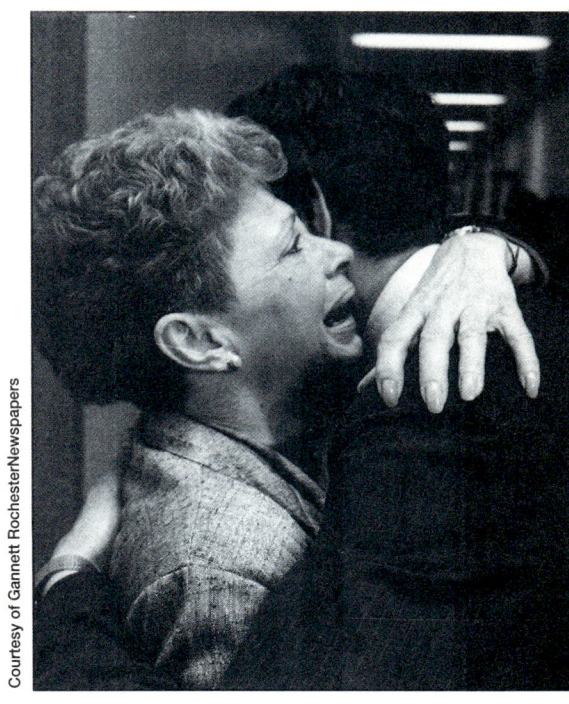

The mother of Karen Ann Hill, Shawcross' 8 year-old murder victim in 1972, tearfully embraces prosecutor Charles Siragusa after the Guilty verdict is announced.

AFTERMATH

■ Shawcross pleaded guilty to an 11th murder – of Elizabeth Gibson – following a deal which saved neighbouring Wayne County the expense of a further trial, and did not affect his appeal prospects.

■ He was sentenced on 8 May 1991 to a further 25-year term, to run concurrently with the 250 years. 'This was not justice done,' protested the victim's father, Bruno Stanisci. 'This man is not going to serve more time for killing my daughter.'

■ The appeal process could take years. As well as bringing up the accusation of sabotage by their own star witness, the defence contended that the judge erred when he denied a request for additional neurological tests, and that the jury had been tainted by the intense media publicity surrounding the trial. Also disputed were the police methods in obtaining Shawcross' confession. The defence said they were unethical.

■ Prosecutor Chuck Siragusa received an avalanche of congratulatory mail. Well-wishers sent him pumpkin bread, nuts, candy and other gifts. A fan in England sent him hair tonic.

■ Dr Dorothy Otnow Lewis, the defence psychiatrist, was the target of 'hate mail' from Rochester. 'It was frightening,' she said, 'but you have to be prepared for that kind of reaction.' She said she was not surprised by the jury's failure to accept her analysis of Shawcross's condition, because 'it's a phenomenon that's very hard to believe.'

■ The man who guarded Shawcross throughout the trial claimed that the stories of childhood abuse were made up. 'He said it never happened,' said Deputy Sheriff David Gerew.

Shawcross is brought to the Wayne County courthouse in Lyons for a hearing in connection with his 11th victim.

The binding of this book is the Skin of the murderer William Corder taken from his body and tanned by myself in the year 1828

George Creed
Surgeon to the Suffolk Hospital

RED BARN MURDER

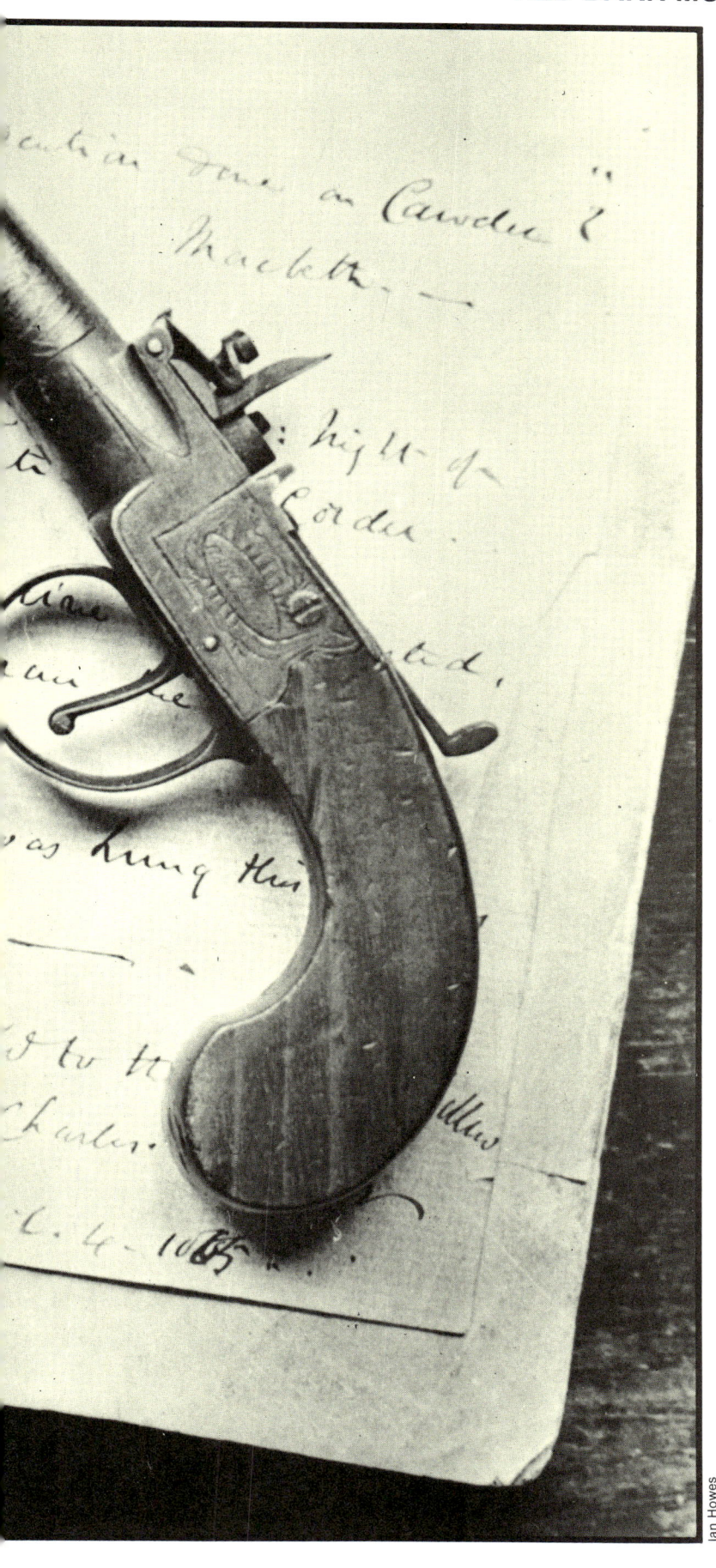

THE MYSTERY OF MARIA MARTEN

Georgian England turned Maria Marten into an innocent murder victim, defiled by a cruel landowner who met justice on the gallows. Her half-naked body was found rotting in a shallow grave, with a sack as a shroud. After his execution, killer William Corder's scalp (far left) was preserved and his skin was used to bind the book, pictured left with the gun he used to kill Maria. But was Corder the villain he was made out to be? Or was he a weak-natured man, driven to kill . . .

Red Barn Murder

SHOOTING Maria Marten (below) was William Corder's desperate way of escaping marriage. The Red Barn, left, became famous as the murder scene.

THE FIRST night that middle-aged Mrs. Anne Marten awoke screaming in her east of England cottage was printed indelibly on the memory of her farm labourer husband Thomas. "I dreamed of our Maria," sobbed Mrs. Marten when her husband had done his best to soothe her. "I dreamed she was murdered and buried underneath the right-hand bay of the Red Barn."

Thomas Marten, who all his life had been a realist and had never gained marks for imagination, then settled for the first thing that came into his head. "I'll make you a warm drink," he said. "You'll probably sleep better after that."

For the remainder of that night Anne Marten did sleep. But each successive night throughout the rest of that week, in April 1828, she woke violently, shaking her husband and forcing him to sit up and listen to her. "For God's sake, Tom, go to the Red Barn and look. She's there; I saw the ground open and show her body before it closed again."

Thomas Marten went to the small window of the bedroom. In the distance he could see the Corders' barn, outlined against a dawn sky where the last stars blinked. A year had passed since their daughter Maria had gone off with Corder's son William – a year noteworthy for the complete absence of letters or news from either of them.

Had something terrible happened to his daughter? Or was his wife, driven by despair, now teetering on the brink of madness?

In the next few days Thomas Marten made up his mind about these two things. Unless he went to Corder's barn and looked around for himself, his wife would know no peace. And if he did that, he would have to do it surreptitiously, for if the villagers learned the reason for his inquiries, they would surely declare Anne Marten insane.

Eerie scene

Thomas did not have far to go. Although the farm stretched across 300 prosperous Suffolk acres, his farmhouse, a large black and white Tudor-style building, was in the centre of the tiny village of Polstead, not far from the village pond.

In the grounds immediately behind it was a collection of agricultural outbuildings, one of them a barn so positioned that, when the evening sun lit the meadows around Corder Farm, it cast upon the barn a vivid reddish hue which, according to an onlooker's disposition, might be described as romantic or eerie.

The reason he wanted to look inside the Red Barn, Thomas told Mr. Pryke, the Corders' bailiff, was that he thought his daughter might have left some of her clothes there on the day she went off with young William Corder. When Pryke opened the barn door, Thomas went straight towards the right hand bay and scratched in desultory fashion with a stick at the loose hay. Suddenly the stick sank into soft earth.

"There may be something buried here," Thomas said. "I'm going to dig."

Feverishly now, he thrust his spade into the earth. At the second strike the spade hit something in a sack. Helped by Mr. Pryke and the light of the lantern they had brought, he scraped back the earth and the sacking. There, gazing up at him ghoulishly in the half light, was the putrifying, half-clothed body of a girl, bent almost double like an embryo.

If Thomas Marten had any doubts about identity they were dismissed at once on sight of a pair of earrings adhering to the rotted, shrunken skin. They belonged to his missing daughter Maria, and this corpse, lying in a hole a foot below the ground, was all that was left of her. Thomas dropped his spade and started back in horror. Pryke, who had shrunk mutely from the opened hole, was the first to recover his wits. Followed by the distraught Marten, he hurried out of the barn and ran across the fields to the constable's cottage.

Small-time thieving

Then, as soon as the primitive communications system of Georgian England permitted it, the hunt was on for William Corder, third son of Farmer John Corder, sometime farm manager, sometime writer, and altogether something of a mystery man. Indeed, while history has been at pains to take affectionate care of the female star of the Red Barn murder, Corder could justifiably complain that he, who dreamed of fame, has been virtually forgotten.

At the Polstead village school which he attended, William's thin talent for writing had served only to isolate him from his fellow pupils, the local sons of the land, who called him "Foxy". It had the same effect on his father, who had made William the butt of his ill will almost from the day the boy was born.

For his other three sons, Thomas, John, and James, Mr. Corder had made it clear that there would be a substantial inheritance; for William there would be nothing. Also there was no question of William becoming a teacher or a writer. He would be a farmer, working for, and not with his three brothers.

William had bitten his lip and retired to his room with his dreams and his collection of books. Later, when he was older and his duties on the farm allowed it, he would take the coach to London and join the disciples of some of the capital's literary lions – including the artist, forger and murderer Thomas Griffiths Wainewright. Sometimes, to get his own back, he would do a bit of small-time thieving from the family. Once he sold one of his father's pigs and pocketed the cash. Certainly he looked more like a petty thief than the notorious murderer he was to become. He was short and thin, and the hours of midnight reading had made him myopic. He walked habitually with a stoop and according to a friend was given to making "Napoleonic gestures".

Despite all this, William had a way with him. His big eyes and high cheekbones helped with the illusion, noted by Polstead folk, that he was always smiling. This was the smile that one day caught the attention of Maria Marten.

To examine the real facts about Maria Marten and compare them with the Victorian heroine of the Red Barn murder melodrama, it is difficult to believe that they are the same woman. To the Victorians, Maria was rustic innocence brutally defiled – an innocent maiden peach-skinned, blue-eyed and beautiful, robbed of her cherished virginity by a vicious seducer who then, tiring of her, savagely slew her and buried her pathetic, lifeless body in the Red Barn grave.

In fact, by the age of 24, when she caught the eye of William Corder, who was two years her junior in age and light years her inferior in experience, Maria Marten was already the unmarried mother of three bastard children. She was currently being sought by the police on an immorality charge, and was known by half the adventurous young men of Suffolk as one of the "easiest" girls in the county, as long as you had the money to pay.

Among the lovers whose child she had borne was Thomas Corder, brother of William. And when she finally disappeared from Polstead village, the only people living there who thought she had not gone off to her one true calling as a London whore, were her own devoted parents.

Notable attraction

For Maria, the farm labourer's teenage daughter, the four Corder sons of the village's most prosperous farmer, were a notable attraction. Not long after she produced a child by Thomas, the eldest, the unfortunate father was drowned in an accident in Polstead village pond.

Two more of the brothers, James and John, then rapidly succumbed to the dreaded twin killers of nineteenth-century England, typhus and tuberculosis. When they had joined Mr. Corder senior in the village graveyard, the fortunes of William took a sudden turn for the better.

William, however, was unable to rise to his inheritance. It irritated him, for it curtailed his "literary" excursions to London. He sought solace in the company of Maria, whom he had met through his brothers, and fathered her next child.

STILL standing, the Corder farmhouse and Marten cottage, with William and Maria inset.

ensnared and lacked the courage to get out?

The questions are relevant in the light of the remarkable events that happened on Friday, May 18, 1827. At eleven o'clock that morning William had a date with Maria; he was to call for her at her parents' cottage. He arrived an hour late, but that didn't matter to Maria, for his very arrival annulled some fleeting thoughts in her mind: there had been some bad quarrels lately and she was so much in love...

Unmoved

She rushed to the door to greet him as he walked up the garden path. "Bill!" she cried, embracing him tightly about the neck. "You're here at last!" Nothing seemed to matter, the time or the waiting, now that he was with her, now that he still cared.

Unmoved, William detached her slim white arms from his neck. "We're going to get married," he said. "This morning. Get ready—we haven't much time."

Maria recoiled as if she had been hit. "But they'll arrest me!" she said. She was referring to the charge of immorality pending against her.

"I've brought you some clothes—men's clothes," William replied. "They belonged to my brother James. You can put them on as a disguise. I'll take you up to the Red Barn; you can wait there till it gets dark, then I'll come for you."

He thrust a jacket and a pair of trousers at her. "It's what you've always wanted, to get married," he said.

Suspicious

A little while later, when Maria came down from her bedroom wearing the odd outfit, she might, at a short distance, have been mistaken for a man.

What is certain is that Mrs. Marten was in her kitchen a few minutes after she heard the front door close behind her daughter and William. Looking out of the window she saw, some hundred yards away, two figures dressed in male clothing, one of whom she recognized as Corder. They were walking along the path that led to the Red Barn. That was the last time that Maria Marten was ever seen alive.

In the next few weeks William Corder made no attempt to absent himself from Polstead. When Mrs. Marten asked him about Maria he was never evasive. "She is in Ipswich, waiting for the marriage licence to come through and doing some shopping meanwhile... She says to tell you she's well and she sends you her love."

Somehow Corder maintained his plausibility throughout that summer of 1827. Significantly, though, Mrs. Marten was beginning to find flaws in the flow of

The baby, born in the spring of 1827, lived for only two weeks. Its burial was a mystery, for there was no funeral, and it was believed that William and Maria secretly buried the little corpse in a field outside the village. If that were so, it gives rise to speculation on how the baby died. Was its death accelerated by one or both of its parents, to whom it was clearly an embarrassment?

The question, which was to be frequently asked in Polstead village during the next two years, was never answered. What everyone was soon to know, however, was that both William and Maria were people little affected by qualms of conscience.

Certainly the disappearance of the baby's body had no adverse effect on William's acceptibility by the Marten family. While the child was still warm in its makeshift grave, old Thomas Marten and his wife eagerly discussed plans with William for his wedding to their daughter. Sometimes Maria would join in and there would be an argument. The Martens began to notice that the arguments between the lovers were becoming more frequent.

By the middle of May a pattern of disagreement was emerging. William had already put off one suggested wedding day that month, and Maria was now siding with her parents and fretting for a quick marriage. Perhaps her enthusiasm could be interpreted as nagging, and perhaps it made William anxious. Did he begin to see his dreams of a literary life receding under the onslaught of a shrewish wife? Did he feel that he was already gossip and information that Corder supplied her about Maria. She began to notice things—like the time Corder turned up at a funeral carrying Maria's green umbrella—and she pigeon-holed them in her memory.

It was this talent for observation that later was to make Mrs. Marten the principal and highly effective witness against Corder.

By harvest time that year Corder was beginning to realize that he had started something bigger than he could maintain. He would go to Ipswich, he said, get married to Maria, and return to the village. He packed his bags and, as soon as he was out of sight of Polstead, he turned towards London.

There, in fact, he did get married. His bride, however, was not the turbulent Maria but Miss Kathleen Moore, who was as different in upbringing and character from Maria as is iron from water.

They had met some time previously when Corder made a trip to the Sussex coast, and in London Corder lost no time in renewing the friendship. Miss Moore, a schoolmistress of great virtue, gentleness, and intelligence, returned his ardour and married him at St. Andrew's Church in Holborn.

A century and a half ago the London suburb of Ealing was "in the country", and it was in this rural village that the newly-wed Corders set up Kathleen's new school. For William, it was paradise attained. Each day he came into the classroom, wearing glasses and carrying books.

Fearful urge

Thus went winter, and when spring's blossom covered the Suffolk countryside in the following year, 1828, William Corder and Maria Marten had, as far as Polstead villagers were concerned, passed into history. Except, that is, in the mind of one villager—Mrs. Anne Marten.

Each night, as she busied herself in her cottage, Mrs. Marten gazed out of her little window at the vivid reddish hue which fell from the setting sun upon Farmer Corder's barn. The restless, fearful urge to cry out that something was wrong, that Maria was horribly dead, that her daughter's blood demanded vengeance, swelled within her. Finally, in April, in her nightmare, she saw it all, and told her husband where to find the body.

Tracking down the suspect in his old "literary" haunts in London fell to the lot of Police Constable Jonas Lea, of Lambeth, who diligently followed the trail to the Ealing school. When he knocked on the Corder's door one April morning William Corder was half way through his breakfast.

"I've never heard of a girl called Maria Marten," he said, peering bookishly over his spectacles at the policeman.

Nearly four months went by before Corder entered the dock at Bury St. Edmunds Assizes, Suffolk, to face a murder charge—and the damning evidence of the lynx-eyed Mrs. Marten. Those four months saw the genesis of the Maria Marten myth—the fiction of the innocent maid ravished and then slain by a wealthy, unprincipled scoundrel—that the Victorians were to turn into their favourite after-dinner melodrama.

The plot began to take shape in church pulpits, where ministers ranted against loose girls who met their "dark end" at the hands of people like Corder. Impressed by this hell-raising, travelling showmen demonstrated puppets that re-enacted the murder in the Red Barn. In fairground booths the grisly details quickly became a permanent sideshow. And with each new development in the story line, Maria became more and more pure and Corder more and more vile.

The reason why is not difficult to understand. As every nineteenth-century novelist and dramatist knew, the Georgians and Victorians simply preferred stories about the despoilation of an innocent virgin to stories about hardened female seducers—particularly when the heroine

TRUTH AND FICTION: A handsome and dashing Corder according to a film of the tragedy made in 1928, but, inset, a drawing made while the landowner was in Bury jail. Opposite, plays such as this gave a twisted idea of the tragedy.

THEATRE, LINCOLN.

BY DESIRE OF
G. E. WELBY, Esq. M.P. & C. FURNOR, Esq.
THE STEWARDS OF THE STUFF BALL.

On WEDNESDAY Evening, OCTOBER 27th, 1830,

Will be presented, the celebrated drama of

Sweethearts and Wives.

Admiral Franklin, ... Mr. SHIELD. Charles Franklin, ... Mr. SIMMS.
Sandford, ... Mr. CULLENFORD. Curtis, ... Mr. HODGSON.
Billy Lackaday, ... Mr. GURNER.
Mrs. Bell, ... Mrs. DANBY. Susan, ... Mrs. GURNER.
Eugenia, ... Mrs. W. ROBERTSON. Laura, ... Miss STEWART SMITH.

A COMIC SONG ...... by ...... Mr. HODGSON.

With (for the **LAST TIME**,) the new Tragic Melo Drama, in 4 Acts, founded on Fact, called the

RED BARN;
OR, THE PROPHETIC DREAM.
THE MUSIC SELECTED AND ARRANGED BY MR. STANNARD

WITH NEW SCENERY PAINTED FOR THE OCCASION BY MR. SIMMS.

Mr. ROBERTSON is induced to bring forward this piece, not only from the unprecedented success it has been received with at the various Theatres in the Kingdom, but as a moral lesson, that Murder, however for the time concealed, will speak with most miraculous organ. Every one must be aware of the Incidents on which the Piece is founded, but the Dramatist has avoided the real names of the parties, still blending all the principal Incidents, with an effect at once awful and instructive.

Cordel, a young Farmer, ... Mr. HAMILTON.
Mr. Delamere, a Magistrate, ... Mr. BRUNTON.
Wilton, a Gipsy Confederate of Cordel, ... Mr. TALBOT.
Marlin, a labouring Farmer in the vale of years, ... Mr. STYLES.
Robin, a Factotum to Chatteral, ... Mr. SIMMS.
Peter Christopher Chatteral, a Barber, Beadle, &c. .... Mr. GURNER.
Nell Hatfield, a Gipsy, .. Mrs. W. ROBERTSON. Anna Hatfield, her daughter, .. Mrs. GURNER.
Dame Marlin, ... Mrs. DANBY. Mrs Cordel, ... Mrs. HAMILTON.
Maria Marlin, ... Miss STEWART SMITH.

A Brief Sketch of the Incidents:
CORDEL for his numerous Crimes receives the **CURSE** of the GIPSY CHIEF.
CORDEL'S FIRST MEETING WITH MARIA MARLIN.
His promise to marry her—The anguish of old Marlin and his Dame at parting with her—His proposition to meet her at the RED BARN disguised in Man's Apparel—Her joy at the thoughts of Marriage.
AWFUL MEETING AT THE RED BARN,
WHERE THE DEED IS PERPETRATED.
THE APPEARANCE OF MARIA TO HER MOTHER IN A DREAM.
The Interior of the Barn where the Body is discovered.
CORDEL's Marriage in London.—His living in splendour when the GIPSY's CURSE is fulfilled.
CORDEL'S APPREHENSION AND CONFESSION,
And the appearance of the Shade of Maria Marlin in Cordel's Dream, which produces the denouement.
Among the minor Incidents to give effect to the serious part of the Melo-drama, some Comic Parts are introduced which must set gravity at defiance.

Red Barn Murder

was as pretty as Maria Marten. It was an age of high emotions and grand gestures, and given the stuff of the Red Barn murder, dramatists and showmen projected an ideal image of Maria that no mortal woman could live up to.

Against this kind of pantomime played out at fever pitch up and down the land, what possible chance, William Corder's defence counsel demanded to know, had the prisoner of getting a fair trial? Mr. Justice Alexander concurred; he deplored the goings-on, but declined to halt the trial.

Testifying against Corder, a witness remembered seeing him walking towards the Red Barn during the late afternoon on the day of Maria's disappearance carrying a pick-axe. Another witness revealed that Corder had borrowed a spade from him about the same time and returned it later the same day. A long knife and a pair of pistols were produced; one of these was the murder weapon.

Corder's defence was pathetically weak. There had been a quarrel in the barn, he said, and he had walked off in a pique, leaving Maria there. He had gone only a yard or two when he heard a shot; hurrying back, he found Maria lying dead on the barn floor. There was a pistol beside her and picking it up he realized with horror that it was his own.

"She must have taken it from my bedroom," Corder said. "I decided to bury her in the best way I could, thinking that suspicion would surely fall upon me."

His story, however, failed to allay that suspicion, for the jury took only 30 minutes to find him guilty. Corder accepted the verdict philosophically and had nothing more to say until a few hours before his execution. Then, in a rush of words, he decided to tell all.

What had happened, he said, was that there had been a quarrel in the Red Barn and then a scuffle. In the struggle he took his pistol from his pocket and shot Maria in the side.

On the scaffold, nineteenth-century murderers died hard. As a crowd of thousands watched, Corder stepped on to the platform erected outside Bury St. Edmunds' Jail and declared contritely, "I deserve my fate."

A mask was put over his head and the body dropped. The hangman then increased the weight on the rope by pulling on the twitching victim. Despite this primitive act of "mercy", it took nearly ten minutes for the Polstead farmer, and would-be man of letters, to die.

EVEN in her final grave (right) Maria could not escape the Red Barn. Below, Corder's death mask, and the crowd that turned out for his execution.

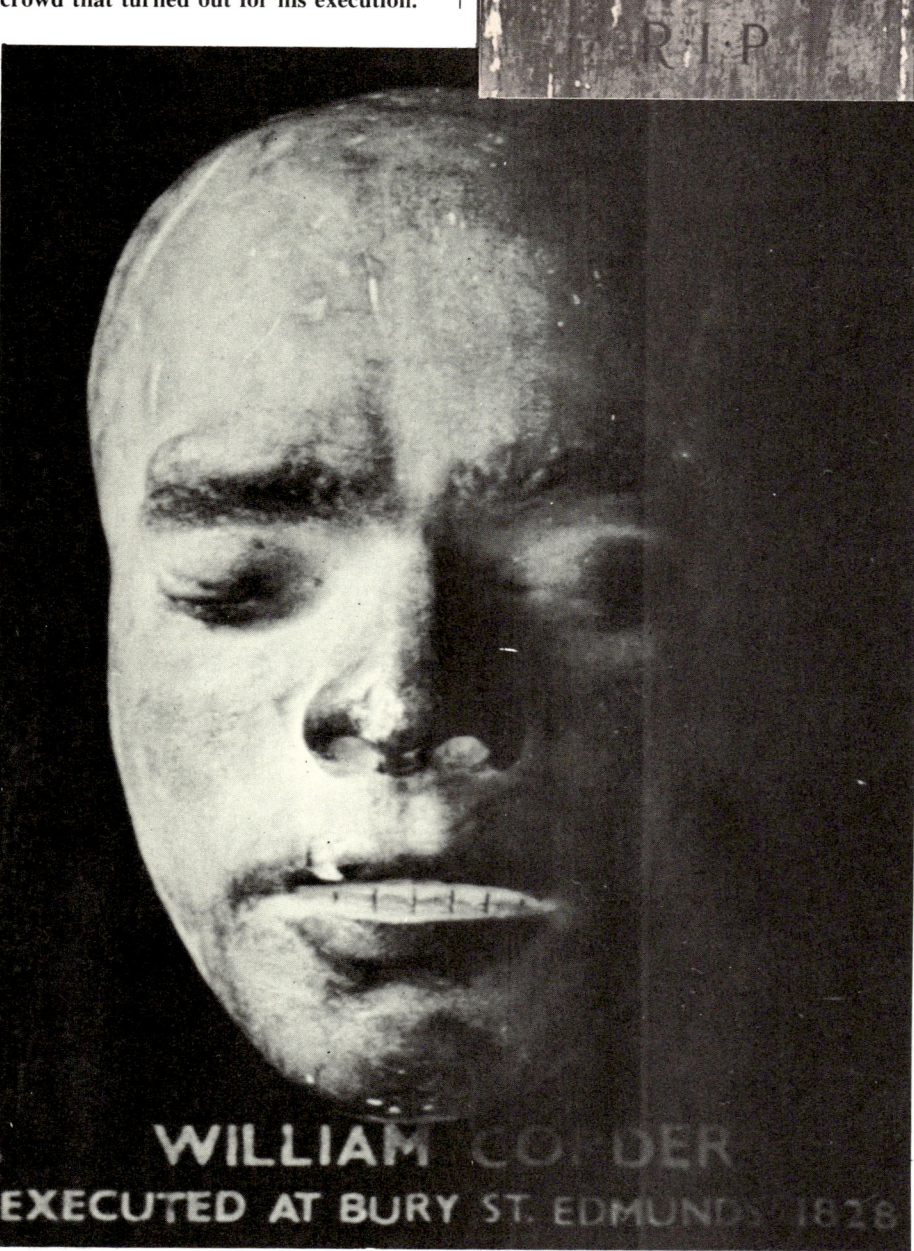

RED LIGHT BANDIT

CARYL CHESSMAN

SMALL-TIME crook Chessman always denied the crimes which brought him the death sentence. And for 12 years he fought for life from his cell.

2462 Red Light Bandit

execution. For 12 years he had been waging a relentless battle to survive – a battle whose theatres of combat were the state and federal courts of the United States: a battle that had few parallels in the judicial history of the United States.

For 12 years Chessman lived in the shadow of death. In his time he had seen nearly a hundred men pass by his cell – cell 2455 – on their way to the green, octagonal-shaped gas chamber, referred to as the "time machine" by the inmates. He had seen those who had gone bravely to their extinction, keeping up the charade, the bravado of insolence; he had seen young "innocents" uncomprehendingly being dragged to their date with death. He had seen and sympathized, but he was determined that there was one man who would never be "sucker enough" to walk down that corridor – himself.

At Chessman's trial Judge Fricke had asked the traditional question: "Is there

HAPPY FAMILY . . . Chessman the boy with his mother (left). But Chessman the man was to live a life of crime. He was arrested (centre, below) and sentenced to death for kidnapping. He died 12 years later in San Quentin (right).

THE NOTE was a simple one, somewhat brusque but efficient – like any business letter. "Dear Sir: On this date I received . . .," it began, possibly an overdue bill presented for settlement. In a way it was – except that the creditors were not businessmen, but the state; the recipient not a householder, but a Death Row detainee; the note not an overdue bill, but notification of an execution date.

With cold objectivity, the note continued: "On this date I received Death Warrant in your case, issued January 25, 1952, by the Honorable Charles W. Fricke, Judge of the Superior Court of the State of California, in and for the County of Los Angeles, fixing date for Friday, March 28, 1952. Very truly yours, H. O. Teets, Warden." The condemned man was Caryl Chessman, the "criminal genius" of San Quentin.

For the majority of inmates of Death Row their first notification was also their last. Yet by the spring of 1960 Chessman had received nine notices of his imminent

any legal cause why sentence should not now be pronounced?" Chessman was quick to retort: "The defendant is absolutely innocent of these charges." To which the judge dryly remarked that declaration of innocence is not a legal cause but "merely an assertion".

Chessman had received his first lesson in jurisprudence. To survive he would have to do more than claim innocence or bemoan his fate. He would have to accept the only weapons offered him – not the guns he was used to, but textbooks of law.

Chessman accepted the challenge, accepted not because he believed in the law – the law was "their" weapon – but in order to show them that he could take whatever they gave him, take it and throw it right back in their faces.

The Chessman who entered Death Row at San Quentin in the spring of 1948 was a bitter young man psychopathically driven to commit crime. Yet, remarkably, in the struggle to survive, under the necessity of having to come to grips with the law, he was transformed from a hardened criminal to a sensitive and creative person who engendered warmth, trust, and friendship. A person who inspired love and who gave love to his friends and to the lost souls of Condemned Row.

Chessman's story began in the second decade of the twentieth-century. Baptized Carol, he later changed his name to Caryl to escape the effeminate implication of his name. He was born into a poor, lower-middle-class family. His mother, Hallie, was a quiet woman whom Chessman called "a dreamer, at heart a poetess"; his father, Serl, was a weak person who never quite succeeded in any of the ventures he set his hand to — carpentry, poultry farming, repairing Venetian blinds. A sense of helplessness in the face of the world exuded from the Chessman family, and fate, ever ready to oblige misfortune, reinforced that feeling.

A world of terror

When Carol was nine his mother was severely injured in a car crash – she became paralyzed and was never to walk again. Meanwhile Carol himself suffered a series of debilitating illnesses — including bronchial asthma and rheumatic fever — which isolated him from his fellow playmates. Sickly, weak, and alone, he created a world of his own – a world of fantasy and terror. For the young Carol carried within himself an insufferable burden of guilt – guilt for this family's poverty, guilt for his mother's crippled state.

His mother and father were so good and so kind that obviously God was punishing the Chessman family for his, Carol's, inborn wickedness. That seemed to be the only explanation. For how could he admit to himself that his mother and father were failures?

As Chessman grew so did his guilt. To stifle the screaming, accusing voice in his head he would do anything; he would become fearless. Let God do his worst – he didn't care; he would show Him; he would flaunt his bold villainy in His face.

At the age of 16 Carol was pilfering from shops and developing a taste for the "highs" of criminal life – for the first time he felt himself respected. His exploits were gaining him friends, women, and money. By his late teens Chessman was a well-known figure in the Californian underworld. A punk, maybe, but smart!

Yet never quite smart enough. Crime to Chessman was not a business proposition, the cautious undertaking of the professional, but a pathological drive, an obsessive need constantly to prove his toughness and his cunning. However, his

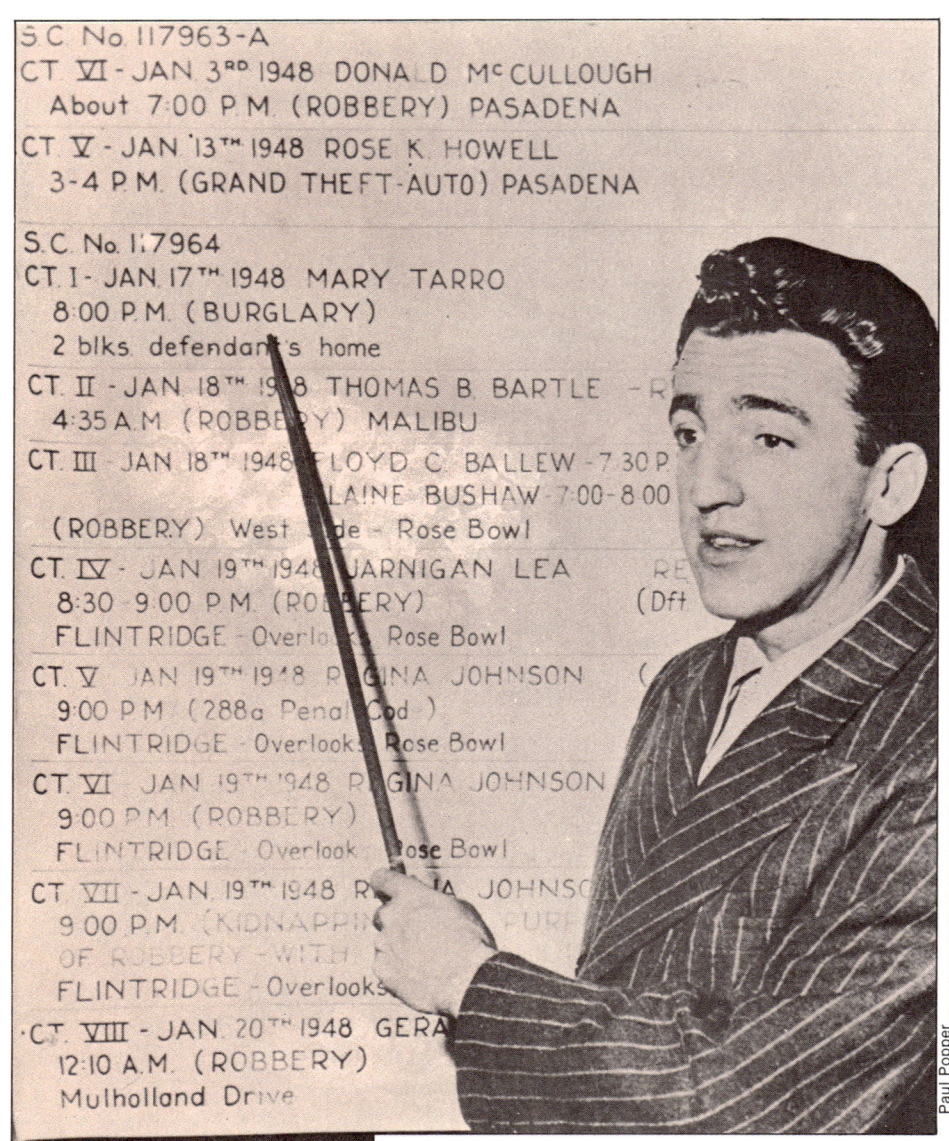

Red Light Bandit

bold arrogance inevitably led to capture and imprisonment.

On December 8, 1947 Chessman was out on parole again. Six weeks later he was back in custody accused of being the notorious "Red Light Bandit". This time, however, he would not obtain a ready release by assuring a gullible judge of his "sense of repulsion against all things criminal—including myself for having become ensnared in their brutal grip during my formative years". A train of events was set in motion which radically altered Caryl Chessman, the law, and a nation's awareness of those condemned to die. Caryl Chessman was about to begin his longest journey.

For weeks before that the various lovers' lanes of Los Angeles had been terrorized by a bandit driving a grey Ford coupe. He sought out necking couples and approached them flashing a red spotlight at them, copying the manoeuvres of patrolling policemen. Then at gunpoint he would rob his victims.

On two occasions he had forced the women to accompany him back to his car and perform fellatio—oral intercourse. One of the victims, a young girl of 17, Mary Alice Meza, was, in addition, forced to strip and then was criminally assaulted by the dull-speaking, stone-faced criminal.

Chessman had been picked up in January of 1948 after a mad, Keystone Cops chase through the streets of the city. He had been driving a Ford coupe that closely resembled descriptions of the Red Light Bandit's car. Inside the automobile police found a quantity of stolen clothing, a .45 automatic pistol, and a red bandana handkerchief which had been tied in such manner as to fit over the spotlight.

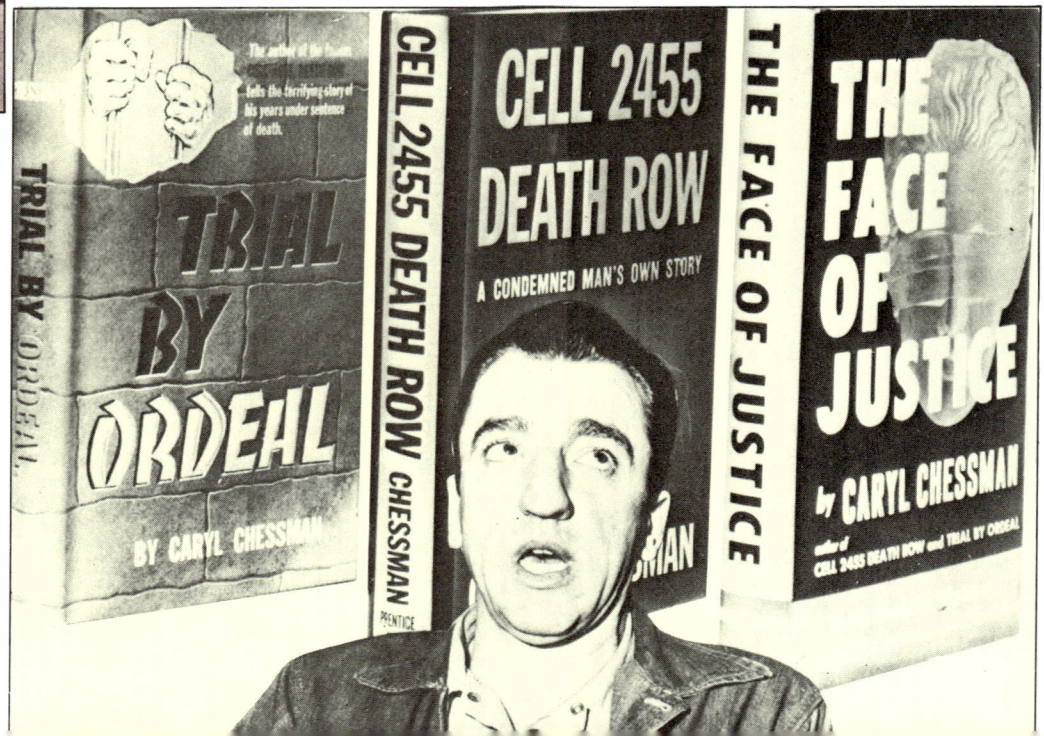

GUILTY... Chessman, pictured above during his trial, admitted a life of crime. All these offences were committed in a month. But in a series of books (right) he fought the death sentence for an offence he had always denied.

Chessman was indicted on 18 counts – including 3 counts of kidnapping with intent to commit robbery. The charge of "kidnapping with bodily harm with intent to commit robbery" was a capital offence in California. The charge was pressed under a peculiar law known as the "little Lindbergh Law", passed as a result of furious public reaction to the kidnapping of Colonel Charles Lindbergh's baby.

It was a little used law, but one which gave the police a powerful weapon in dealing with suspects. For by simply removing his victim a few inches the assailant could technically be charged under that law and thus face the death penalty.

Chessman's trial was loaded against him. He was faced with a hostile judge – Charles W. Fricke had the unique distinction of sending more men to their death than any other judge in the history of California. The prosecuting counsel, Deputy District Attorney J. Miller Leavy, stated that, "This young man is completely worthless," and obviously considered the accused to be beneath contempt. The jury thought him both foolish and arrogant for conducting his own defence.

A second chance

In view of all this, the outcome was startling only in one respect: Chessman was found guilty on 17 of the 18 counts, and sentenced to death not once, but twice! That Chessman did not die soon after, that he was given a second chance, is due to the extraordinary conduct of the trial judge in handling the court record.

The law required the record of a trial to be certified as a verbatim transcript by an official reporter. Judge Fricke had denied Chessman a daily transcript of the court proceedings as was Chessman's right. Two days before Chessman was sentenced, the official court shorthand reporter, Ernest R. Perry, dropped dead of a heart attack. Only one-third of the trial proceedings had been transcribed.

An attempt to move for a retrial on the grounds of an incomplete court record was denied. Judge Fricke ordered another reporter to finish Perry's job. The reporter chosen was Stanley Fraser, an alcoholic brother-in-law of the prosecuting attorney. Fraser received $10,000 to complete the task – more than twice the usual sum paid for such a job – and had the assistance of both Leavy and Fricke in compiling the transcript. The final version was approved before Judge Fricke, Deputy D. A. Leavy, Frazer, and one official court witness. It had neither been seen nor approved by the defendant – Caryl Chessman.

There lay Chessman's only hope. If he could show that his constitutional rights had been cancelled, if he could demonstrate that the due process of law had been contravened, then he would get his chance to prove the innocence he so volubly claimed. But first he had to turn to the law.

The District Attorney's office of the state of California did not take kindly to the idea of a new trial. They wanted Chessman executed as soon as possible. For every move that Chessman made they had a countermove; for every brief that Chessman submitted they filed an opposing one; for every stay of execution granted to Chessman they appealed for a reversal.

Every means possible was used to hasten Chessman to the gas chamber. Every lapsed execution date saw a statement issued from the D.A.'s office about "this perversion of justice".

Pleas for leniency on behalf of Chess-

THE PROTEST . . . Chessman supporters demonstrate outside San Quentin prison as he went to the gas chamber. But even as Chessman died, his lawyer was negotiating another reprieve . . .

man raised the righteous wrath of Judge Fricke who in an angry explosion of words claimed that "if we are going to grant leniency solely because a man who deserves the death penalty he got from the jury was able to write English and get a book published, we might as well throw criminal law into the ashcan."

Prosecutor J. Miller Leavy was ever quick to reiterate the judge's sentiments. He posed for pictures with Mrs. Ruth Meza, mother of Mary Alice – who had become schizophrenic following the Red Light Bandit's assault. Mrs. Meza was

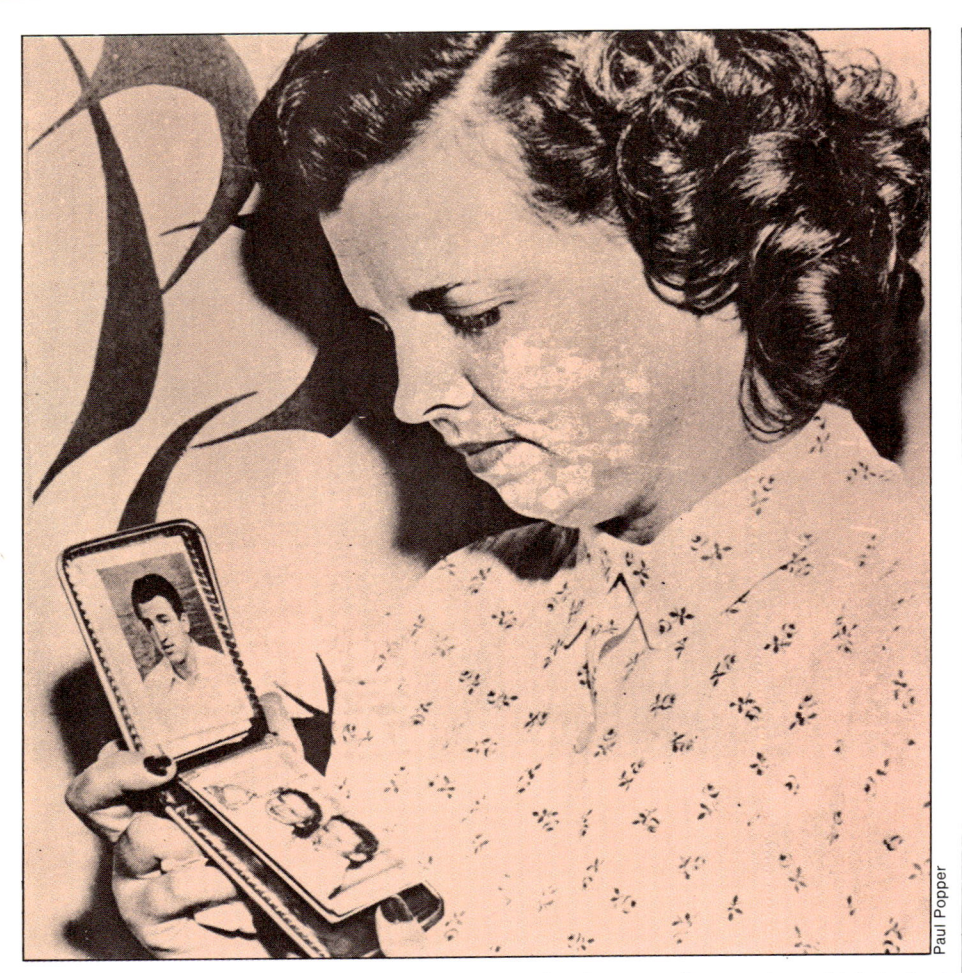

Red Light Bandit

WAITING... for her man: Chessman's fiancée, Frances Couturier (left).
Waiting... for death on May 2: Caryl Chessman in his cell (far right).
Waiting... for the execution: the San Quentin gas chamber (right).

quoted as saying: "The only way to restore Mary Alice's sanity is to tell her that Chessman is gone."

A vicious press clamoured for Chessman's death. "Reprieves for Rapist-Kidnapper Caryl Chessman are turning California justice into a light-hearted game of musical chairs with the able assistance of some members of the State judiciary" the Los Angeles *Mirror* asserted angrily—voicing an opinion that was echoed by the general public.

Chessman, however, would not accept the majority opinion. He established a "study" in one of the empty cells in Death Row. There, in his "legal den" under the harsh glare of the bare yellow light bulbs he produced the outflow of briefs, appeals, and the three bestselling books which were to gain him fame.

Chessman approached law from point zero. He immersed himself in a subject which to most people—much less a convicted criminal waiting to die in the tense atmosphere of a Death Row—is mysterious and incomprehensible. A secret, cabbalistic language open to initiates only after long and arduous years of training. Chessman mastered that language determined in his arrogance "to beat the rap".

For four years Chessman worked alone driven by fury and hate. Then in 1952 he received a stay of execution which he had not expected to come through.

Warden Teets dropped the envelope into his hands and stopped a moment. He looked at Chessman, puzzled by this convict, the "criminal genius" as the newspapers had typed him, capable of so much, yet so twisted. He looked at Chessman and let his question drop almost imperceptibly. "I wonder, Caryl, if you really wanted another chance?" What did he mean? asked the surly Chessman, ready to attack anyone who challenged him. The warden quietly replied: "You know very well what I mean."

But the warden did not stop there. He pushed Chessman, he asked questions which the criminal had never before considered. Did it not occur to Chessman that it also took guts to be honest, that it took guts to lead an honest, creative life?

"If you have the guts, Caryl," the warden concluded, "now you can make some sense out of your life and do something with it to repay Judge Stephens for the chance he's given you."

"Oh sure," Chessman replied, smiling faintly. "But what?"

"Figure it out for yourself," replied the soft-spoken warden, and with that he left the condemned man.

The warden left but his words would not. They buzzed ceaselessly in Chessman's mind. They were a spur forcing him to rethink his life, to reconsider all that he had done and all that he had lived by.

Why was he fighting so hard and so desperately—so that he could once again join the ranks of the criminal world? No, that was not the answer. Chessman began to search for himself, for the sensitive Caryl that had been smothered years before. The result of that quest was his first book, *Cell 2455, Death Row,* an international bestseller which brought Chessman's plight to the world.

Meanwhile the legal battles continued unabated. But now Chessman was not alone. His inner transformation had brought him friends, distinguished lawyers who offered him their services, the love of a gentle woman who only wished for Chessman to be a father of her two children. Chessman's days were as busy as ever in the narrow confines of Death Row—days that were now filled with love rather than hate. Chessman wanted a new chance, not to fight against society, but to contribute to it.

Tired of all the legal hassles and involvements in seeking vindication, eager to commence a new life in the outside world, Chessman petitioned the Governor of California, Goodwin Knight, for clemency. He had good reason to hope for a reprieve.

Technical charge

Six years had passed since he was first sentenced to death, not for murder but for a highly technical charge of kidnapping. The "little Lindbergh Law" had been subsequently changed by the California Legislature, and parole eligibility granted to everyone convicted under it except Chessman. And finally, the matter of the trial reporter's transcript had never been cleared up.

The clemency papers were filed with the Governor's office on April 12, 1954. Chessman's latest execution date had been set for May 14. He had just over a month to live. Once again Chessman was waiting. The days passed in hushed and restrained anticipation. His book had been published on April 19. Chessman was busy reading the reviews, listening to the comments raised by his work, preparing his next move in case his petition for clemency was denied.

The answer came on May 3, 11 days before he was due to die. NO. The Governor could find no grounds for clemency.

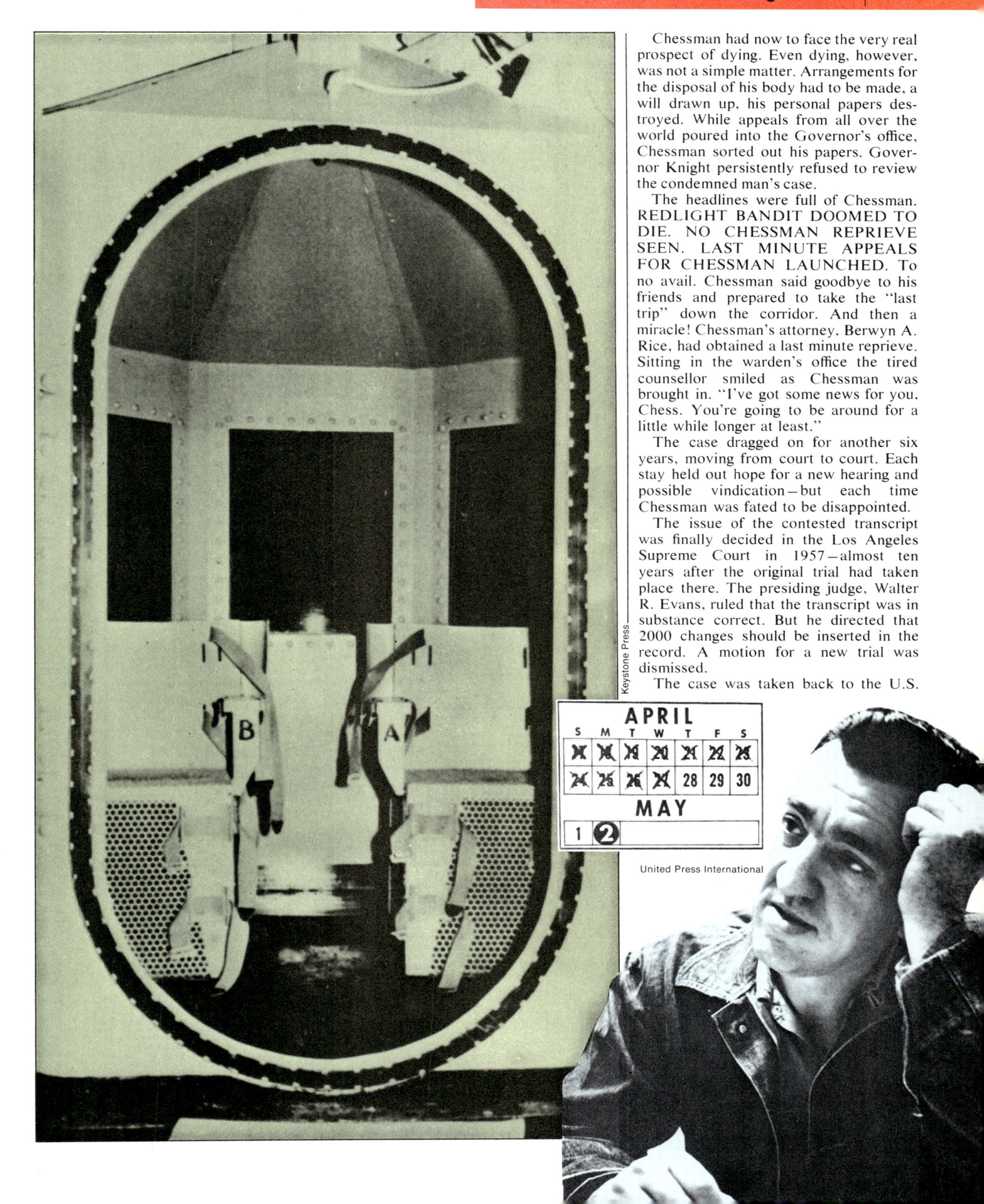

Chessman had now to face the very real prospect of dying. Even dying, however, was not a simple matter. Arrangements for the disposal of his body had to be made, a will drawn up, his personal papers destroyed. While appeals from all over the world poured into the Governor's office, Chessman sorted out his papers. Governor Knight persistently refused to review the condemned man's case.

The headlines were full of Chessman. REDLIGHT BANDIT DOOMED TO DIE. NO CHESSMAN REPRIEVE SEEN. LAST MINUTE APPEALS FOR CHESSMAN LAUNCHED. To no avail. Chessman said goodbye to his friends and prepared to take the "last trip" down the corridor. And then a miracle! Chessman's attorney, Berwyn A. Rice, had obtained a last minute reprieve. Sitting in the warden's office the tired counsellor smiled as Chessman was brought in. "I've got some news for you, Chess. You're going to be around for a little while longer at least."

The case dragged on for another six years, moving from court to court. Each stay held out hope for a new hearing and possible vindication – but each time Chessman was fated to be disappointed.

The issue of the contested transcript was finally decided in the Los Angeles Supreme Court in 1957 – almost ten years after the original trial had taken place there. The presiding judge, Walter R. Evans, ruled that the transcript was in substance correct. But he directed that 2000 changes should be inserted in the record. A motion for a new trial was dismissed.

The case was taken back to the U.S.

Red Light Bandit

Supreme Court—where Chessman obtained his seventh stay of execution in 1959. Two hours before the deadline for his next execution date, Governor Pat Brown granted Chessman a 60 day reprieve—his eighth and last. A new execution date was fixed for May 2, 1960. Time had run out for Chessman—though even as he breathed in the deadly fumes a last-minute, and desperate, attempt was made to bail him out.

As Chessman was being led to the gas chamber his attorney, George T. Davis, had prevailed upon Judge Goodman to grant a stay. The time was 10 a.m.—the exact moment that Chessman was being strapped into the chair. Judge Goodman turned to his clerk asking him to get San Quentin on the line.

The clerk relayed the instruction to the judge's secretary in the next room. She picked up the phone and dialled the number, GL4-1460.

"San Quentin prison?" she asked breathlessly as she heard the receiver being lifted at the other end. No, she had the wrong number. Precious moments elapsed while the number was verified and then quickly dialled again. This time correctly. The call was transferred to the Judge's chambers.

Judge Goodman listened for a few moments and then turned to Davis. "It's too late," he said. "The pellets have already been dropped." Then after a brief pause, he added, "You should have gotten here earlier."

In the end Chessman lost. He was

HERE HE DIED . . . San Quentin Prison, where Chessman went to the gas chamber. Next morning, London's newspapers told of the drama as he was executed.

strapped into the chair, the cyanide pellets were dropped, and he died. He died claiming his innocence and perhaps, more importantly, he died hoping that his life had not been lived in vain. Hoping that he had made a contribution to society. Hoping that his example would lead to the abolition of capital punishment.

Chessman had begun his long and dangerous struggle bitterly and defiantly—hating himself and hating society. When he died he was no longer fighting for mere survival, but something more precious—the humanization of man.

REINSCH TEST

A TRACE OF ARSENIC

The arsenic Dr. Taylor found in "bottle no. 21" almost ruined his reputation... and may have allowed an inept killer in the tradition of (insets, from top) Doctors Pritchard, Ruxton and Cream to escape.

Reinsch Test

> **COPY OF VERSES**
> ON THE
> **CHARGE OF WILFUL MURDER**
> Against Thomas Smethurst, for administering Poison to a Lady (whom the Prisoner had illegally married) at No. 10, Alma Villas, Richmond.
>
> Come all good people and pay attention,
> Unto these lines that I indite,
> A case of poisoning I will mention,
> This cruel deed has been brought to light.
> Remember the case of William Palmer,
> This one does all exceed,
> Upon an unoffending woman:
> It will make the stoutest heart to bleed.
>
> A married man is Doctor Smethurst,
> A man in whom the sickly put their trust;
> The common stabber will meet you fairly,
> The cruel poisoner he must be worse.
> A loving and confiding woman,
> Gave him her heart as we are told,
> But Dr. Smethurst, thy love was falsehood,
> Thy love was merely for her gold.
>
> A life interest of five thousand,
> And more besides by her father's will.
> To D'ctor Smethurst she got married,
> Yet his first wife was living still.
> The marriage day was scarcely over,
> When Elizabeth Banks was taken ill,
> With treacherous heart he waited on her,
> He beg'd of her to make her will.
>
> He attended on her in her sickness,
> No one else would the Dr. trust,
> He pretended to be all love and meekness,
> The poison then was doing its worst.
> He kissed her cheek — it was the kiss of …
> With false tears he the girl betray…
> The medicine himself he gave …
> The murderer is alway…
>
> 1859

A FICKLE PUBLIC agreed with the anonymous verses above: that Dr. Smethurst (right) was guilty of murder and "the day must come when he must die". But after successful prosecution by Mr. Serjeant Ballantine (facing page), public opinion — especially other doctors and scientists objecting to Dr. Taylor's inconclusive findings of arsenic — forced a last-minute stay of execution. The "murderer" served a year for bigamy.

THE medical man who takes to murder has, perhaps oddly, never been very successful. Palmer, Pritchard, Lamson, Cross, Cream, Crippen, Ruxton, Smethurst and Coppolino were all dealt with by the law; of them all only Cross, Lamson, Ruxton and Coppolino had professional quantification, and none of them, except perhaps Crippen, showed any real expertise.

One of the most curious cases was that of Thomas Smethurst, a "doctor" who obtained his degree through what would today be called "a diploma mill", in this case the University of Erlangen in Bavaria. It is certain Smethurst practised and, from somewhere, acquired a quite respectable medical knowledge.

He was born, according to some sources, in Lincolnshire in 1805. It is believed his father was a herbalist, and that he had two brothers and a sister. In 1827 he married a lady 20 years his senior, said to be a patient of his at the time. Mary Smethurst brought to him a very modest fortune, and this he put to good use for six years by running a hydropathic establishment at Moor Park in

Surrey, where Swift wrote *A Tale of a Tub*. This was a successful and profitable venture, for in 1852 Smethurst became a "gentleman of leisure".

The Smethursts seemed a pleasant and contented couple without any real roots, or children. In appearance he was a rather small and insignificant man, with thick reddish hair and a not very commanding presence which he managed to overcome with a slight pomposity, and the authority usual to medical men. In the autumn of 1858 the Smethursts were living in a boarding house in the better part of Bayswater, London, at 4 Rifle Terrace which was at the top of what is now Queensway, not far from Whiteley's Store.

In October a new lodger arrived at the house, Miss Isabella Bankes, a 43-year-old spinster of some means. She possessed £1800 in property and lived on the life interest of £5000 which, on her death, would revert to her family. There was an immediate attraction between Miss Bankes and the doctor. Smethurst managed to spend little time with his semi-invalid wife, but a great deal with Miss Bankes, and the affair became so marked to everyone except Mrs. Smethurst that the landlady, appalled at the boarding-house gossip, told Miss Bankes at the end of the first week in November that she would probably be more comfortable "elsewhere".

There was a quick exodus. Miss Bankes set up house in rooms at 37 Kildare Terrace, not far from Rifle Terrace, and there the "star cross'd lovers" — as a newspaper was to call them — were so enamoured of each other that they came together, Thomas Smethurst having calmly left his wife. The picture of Isabella Bankes that has survived does not suggest that she was a Victorian Helen of Troy, for she was "a gentle lady of quiet aspect, a bright eye and a kindly manner."

"United illegally"

But she was sufficiently attractive for Smethurst to bigamously "marry" her at Battersea Parish Church on December 9, 1858 — at his trial he was to excuse this action by claiming ". . . we united ourselves illegally, but it was for a permanency, and the marriage took place this way: At the request of Miss Bankes . . . she knew I was married — and in order that she should be protected from reproach hereafter, this marriage was preliminary to one at a future period, in the event of my wife dying — she is now 74 years of age".

"Dr. and Mrs." Smethurst now settled in rooms at 27 Old Palace Gardens, between The Green and the river Thames at Richmond. Here they lived peacefully — or, anyway, without attracting notice — until March 28, 1859, when Isabella was suddenly taken ill with symptoms resembling those of dysentery.

The illness did not clear up quickly and on April 3 Isabella was still so unwell that her lover did something that has always puzzled believers in his guilt. He sent for medical help, seeking the co-operation of Dr. Julius and Dr. Bird, who were at that time the most prominent medical men in Richmond; Dr. Julius, as the senior physician, obtained all his information about the medical history from Smethurst and from physical examinations of the sick woman.

Smethurst was always present at every visit to the sick-room, though neither of the doctors found any fault with his medical knowledge. The patient was diagnosed as suffering from diarrhoea and was given medicines which, however, failed to help. It was felt that healthier quarters, above river level, might help, and the couple moved to 10 Alma Villas, on Richmond Hill. The move was made on April 15, when the doctor supported his weak spouse in a cab which took them and their possessions to the new quarters on the first floor of a very charming house.

Smethurst wrote to Louisa Bankes, sister of Isabella, at her home in Maida Vale. She came at once to Richmond on April 19, but did not stay very long. The doctors now diagnosed poison of some sort, but certainly Smethurst did not act like a poisoner. He treated the invalid with the greatest kindness and patience, and her genuine affection for him was obvious, yet he never permitted anyone to see her unless he was also in the room.

Smethurst called in a third, very prominent, doctor to see what could be done, and then on April 30 summoned a solicitor. The solicitor was shown the draft of a will drawn up "by a London barrister" — despite the fact it was wholly in Smethurst's handwriting. It left all Isabella's property to her "friend". A final will was drawn up by the solicitor, in haste, and was signed quite willingly by Miss Bankes.

Over 200 bottles

Nevertheless this last action disturbed the two local physicians. They now became very suspicious, and decided to test the bodily evacuations of the patient; as a result of what they found they called the police, and Thomas Smethurst was promptly arrested. Over 20 bottles and containers holding, or having held, various medicines were removed from 10 Alma Villas. The unfortunate Miss Bankes appeared to have been only dimly aware of what was happening. Her doctors and her sister attended her, but in spite of every care she died on May 3.

The manifest suspicions of three well-known medical men, the arrest, and police evidence were not, just the same, sufficient to impress the Richmond magistrates. It was decided that Smethurst should be discharged on the basis of insufficient evidence; he went free, but only for a brief time.

The local coroner was less inclined to see the evidence and the suspicions in the same light. He considered the available facts and after various questions to witnesses issued a warrant for the re-arrest of Smethurst. It was not long before one of the greatest medical jurists of the time entered into the picture. This was Dr. Alfred Swaine Taylor, Professor of Chemistry at Guy's Hospital, who is remembered today as author of the classic *Taylor's Principles and Practice of Medical Jurisprudence* which, under succeeding editors, remains a cornerstone of forensic medicine.

As Government analyst, he gave evidence at the preliminary hearings to the effect that he found arsenic in vomit from the deceased. In one bottle of medicine — "No. 21" in the list of articles taken from Alma Villas — he also found arsenic. This naturally increased suspicion of Smethurst.

Dr. Taylor had arrived at his conclusions by using the analytical method known as the Reinsch Test, devised by a German chemist, Hugo Reinsch, in 1842 as a new method of detection of arsenic poisoning. The test was reasonably simple. Solutions suspected of containing arsenic were strongly acidified by the addition of hydrochloric acid. Pieces of copper foil were then introduced, and the liquid was heated to near boiling point. The presence of arsenic was shown by deposits on the copper. If present in any quantity, the poison showed as a lustrous black deposit, while a steel-grey coating indicated smaller quantities.

Remarkable contrasts

Dr. Taylor was satisfied after his investigations that arsenic was indeed present, but in the medicine bottle he examined he calculated that there must have been less than a quarter of a grain of arsenic mixed with the four ounces of matter in the bottle. Arsenic, he noted, presents remarkable contrasts, which tend to depend on the human body — adults have died from the ingestion of 0.12 grain, while others have tolerated, and overcome with medical help, as much as eight grains. However, Dr. Taylor's evidence at the preliminary hearing clinched the committal for trial.

Thomas Smethurst — still described as "Dr." in the newspapers — was taken to the Old Bailey's Central Criminal Court for his trial. Three years before, the Central Criminal Court Act of 1856 had been passed; Palmer, the Rugeley Poisoner, had been tried there through this Act by which an accused person could be tried for an offence outside the jurisdiction of the court, instead of at the local assizes, in order that he could receive a fair trial.

IRATE FURY — and an unduly harsh sentence on the bigamy charge — was the reaction of Lord Chief Justice Baron Pollock to Dr. Smethurst's reprieve.

The hearing was held on July 7, 1859, before the Lord Chief Justice Baron Pollock with the great Mr. Serjeant Ballantine prosecuting. One of the great sensations of that bitter legal contest was the evidence of Dr. Taylor, for though he stated that he had received no less than 28 articles from Alma Villas through the police for examination, only bottle No. 21 was of any importance, plus the vomit. He had to make an admission which more or less turned the case upside down.

He stated that though he had found arsenic according to the Reinsch Test, he came up against a factor that was to fault his findings, and this was the presence of possible impurities in the reagents used. In other words, both hydrochloric acid and metallic copper invariably contained minute quantities of arsenic, with the hydrochloric acid often containing the larger quantity of the impurity.

The copper had shown the steel-grey of minute quantity, but Dr Taylor's unhappy position in court was that he had to admit the arsenic may well have been in the reagents — the process of ensuring absolute purity is not a difficult one, but it is possible that either the doctor or, more probably, one of his assistants did not take the proper prior steps.

But medical opinion was on his side, in the shape of Professor Odling of Guy's Hospital, the Professor of Practical Chemistry, and others. The overall opinion was that there had been a continuous administration of some irritant poison, such as arsenic or antimony. Against this the defence put forth its own medical experts, who claimed that the dead woman had died not by slow arsenic poisoning, but by idiopathic dysentery. Just to play safe, it was also suggested that ordinary bismuth, which Miss Bankes had been given from time to time, almost always contained arsenic.

It was revealed in court that the deceased had been nearly two months pregnant. It was also suggested that she might have died from "gastric complications" following her condition, while Dr. Taylor proposed that the accused might have given the woman potassium chlorate after the arsenic, to eliminate its traces.

The judge in his summing-up clearly indicated that he thought Smethurst guilty; this the jury obviously accepted, for they took only 20 minutes to return a verdict of guilty. The sentence of death was passed, but as so often happens, the public, which had been anti-Smethurst, promptly switched sides on hearing the verdict, and there was a great outcry against it. Experts in law, medicine, toxicology and other spheres began to join the passionate discussion.

Hard labour

A medical journal venomously suggested that "we must now look upon Professor Taylor as having ended his career, and hope he will immediately withdraw into the obscurity of private life, not forgetting to carry with him his favourite arsenical copper". This tasteless attack was quite without result. Dr. Taylor went on from success to success, and in 1865 he published the book on medical jurisprudence that immortalized his name.

The Home Office was disturbed by the raging controversy and directed a leading London surgeon, Sir Benjamin Collins Brodie, to look into the matter and study the trial record, to the surprise of the medical profession and the irate fury of Lord Chief Justice Baron Pollock.

Brodie offered as his opinion that there was "not absolute and complete evidence" of Thomas Smethurst's guilt. The Home Secretary did not intervene until two days before the execution date, when the condemned man was reprieved and freed, to be at once arrested for bigamy. He served a year's hard labour, a more severe sentence than was usually passed in similar circumstances.

After his release he went to live in a house off Vauxhall Bridge Road and, though still a comfortably situated man, aroused sensation by suing for the legacy left to him by Isabella Bankes and, to the distress of her family, winning his case. Nothing is known of him after that except an item in a local paper referred to "Dr. and Mrs. Smethurst", which suggests that, after all his troubles, he at last returned to his true wife.

RICE, WILLIAM MARSH

AN OLD MAN'S MONEY

William Marsh Rice was a financial genius who, during his long life, accumulated vast wealth. Whenever a man does that he brings down upon his head the envy and greed of others less successful than himself. So it was that one lawyer carefully plotted the destitution and death of a millionaire.

OCCASIONALLY he licked his lips nervously; the jagged scars on his throat were a constant reminder of how, in his fear, he had tried to kill himself in prison. But his voice was clear and steady as he told the New York court about the night he murdered the benevolent multi-millionaire who had befriended him and given him a home. He described how, in September, 1900, he had crept furtively into the bedroom where the old man was sleeping and placed a towel containing a chloroform-soaked sponge over his face. He had then waited in a different part of the house for 30 minutes — long enough for his victim to die of lung congestion.

Not long after his arrest he had tried to lie his way out of any blame and, in his cell at the Tombs, had been so terrified that he had slashed his throat with a penknife. Now he was confidently telling the truth, for he no longer faced the threat of execution.

More evil

Charles F. Jones, 27, from Houston, Texas, had found sanctuary in a new role — as a prosecution witness. He had been given a guarantee of "some immunity" — and subsequent events showed that he had almost certainly been promised his freedom — if he would co-operate with the State. The People's Prosecutor explained to the jury: "If it were not for the fact that many criminals squeal on each other, many crimes would go unpunished."

The prosecutors considered that Jones, although he had actually done the killing, had merely been acting under the domination of a far more evil and dangerous man — a 41-year-old lawyer called Albert T. Patrick. So it was Patrick who had been indicted with the first-degree murder of the financial genius William Marsh Rice.

On March 26, 1902, the trial — which had lasted more than two months — was reaching its climax. The evidence against Patrick, particularly that given by medical experts, was so overwhelming that the jury had little hesitation in finding him guilty. Under New York law this made the death sentence mandatory. Patrick was condemned to die in the electric chair early in May, 1902.

Most people then thought that this was virtually the end of an amazing story of treachery and forgery, of greed and cold-blooded viciousness. But it was only the end of the first act. For Patrick, with all the scheming brilliance of his depraved mind, was still determined to cheat the executioner.

Exceptional flair

The amazing tangle of intrigue which culminated in the murder of 84-year-old William Marsh Rice was described by the Prosecutor, James Osborne, when he opened the trial in January, 1902. He explained to a crowded court how Rice had left his native New England in the early 1830s to seek his fortune in the frontier state of Texas. He was a man with an exceptional flair for making money. He speculated in oil and in land. He opened a chain of stores and hotels. He became a multi-millionaire.

Rice had married twice, but there had been no children. It was a will left by his second wife, Elizabeth, which had precipitated the events which eventually led to his death. Elizabeth Rice had died in 1896. In her will she tried to leave half his money—her share of it, as she considered—to her relatives. She claimed that this was correct, as they were both citizens of Texas—where the law treated man and wife as equal partners over money and property.

Plausible rogue

Rice considered this to be savagely unfair, and although he had spent comparatively little time in New York since 1865, he insisted that the city was his home. New York had no community-property law. He instituted a Federal Court suit against the executor of his wife's will—aiming to have it declared void. For he had very clear ideas about where he wanted the bulk of his money to go. Texas had been so good to him that he wanted the State to have a permanent memorial to him—a corporation which would not seek profits, but which would be dedicated to the advancement of science, literature and art. It was to be called the Rice Institute.

The issue over the will was therefore a straightforward one. If Rice was a citizen of Texas at the time of his wife's death, her relatives got half his money. If he was a citizen of New York, almost the entire estate would eventually go to the Rice Institute. It was this issue which brought Albert T. Patrick into the story.

Patrick, an impeccably dressed and fine-looking man with a neat ginger beard, shifted uncomfortably on his courtroom seat as Mr. Osborne, the Prosecutor, described his background for the benefit of the jury. Patrick, said Osborne, had been employed by the executor of Elizabeth Rice's will to defend the action being brought by Rice. He was a plausible rogue—a man of great charm who could inspire the confidence of others. But in Texas, where he had initially practised, he had won himself an unsavoury reputation as a sharp operator.

"The man Jones will tell you how Patrick made his acquaintance—and what transpired from there," said Mr. Osborne.

Charles F. Jones avoided looking at Patrick as he went to the witness box. He took the oath and explained how he had become the confidant and only companion of the multi-millionaire. He had been working as a storekeeper in a Texas

PLOTTER... Charles Jones (above) performed the murder but lacked the brains to plan it. The mastermind behind the slaying was Albert Patrick (previous page).

hotel owned by Rice. The old man had chatted to him there, and, taking a liking to him, had engaged him as his personal clerk. A year later, in 1897, he and Rice had moved together to New York City, where they shared an apartment in Madison Avenue. In their behaviour they were more like father and son than employer and employee.

"Now let us come to the month of November, 1899," said Mr. Osborne "Do you recall somebody coming to the apartment?"

Jones nodded towards Patrick. "He did."

"And what did he say to you?"

"Well, he didn't tell me his name, not his real name. He said he was called Smith and that he wanted to see Mr.

Rice about some cotton business."

"And did he see Mr. Rice?"

"No, Mr. Rice was in bed, and I didn't think it was right to disturb him."

Patrick returned to the apartment later—this time admitting his true identity—and told Jones he would make it worth his while to help clinch the business of the will. All Patrick needed was a letter, on Rice's stationery and apparently with Rice's signature, in which Rice admitted he was a citizen of Texas. Patrick offered to pay Jones $500 if he could provide that sort of letter.

Draft will

Jones, whose salary was $55 a month, was interested. He prepared the forged letter, but refused to hand it over to Patrick when Patrick would not give him the money. However, Patrick—with his charm and promises of rich rewards to come—stayed on friendly terms with Jones and soon learned all about Rice's business. Jones let him go through all Rice's private files and papers, and showed him a copy of a will which Rice had made in 1896.

"Was there any discussion between Patrick and yourself about a further will?" asked Mr. Osborne.

"Yes, in the February—or perhaps it was the March—of 1900," said Jones.

Patrick had shown him a draft of a will, arranging the disposal of all Rice's property, which had been drawn up by Patrick. All the friends and relatives who had been named in Rice's 1896 will were to receive bequests—more generous ones, in fact, than Rice had intended. The rest of the estate was to be divided between Patrick and the Rice Institute.

Too close

Patrick then persuaded him to copy the will on Rice's typewriter—putting his own name down as a witness. The 1896 will was not to be destroyed because, as Patrick pointed out, the relatives and friends would then see that they would do better under the later one—and be as eager to sustain it as he was himself. Jones was not named as a beneficiary.

"He told me I was too close to Mr. Rice and that someone might claim the will had been executed under duress," he told the court. "He said I would be well taken care of."

How would they get Rice to sign the forged will? That was a problem they discussed at length. Finally they decided to resort to forgery. But more than one copy of Rice's signature was needed. One went on a general assignment, purported to have been executed by Rice on September 7, 1900, which transferred all his property to Patrick. This document said that there were two conditions—Patrick was to pay Rice an income of $10,000 a year as long as Rice should live. After Rice's death, Patrick was to erect a monument costing not less than $5000 over his grave.

Another signature went on a will dated June 30, 1900—witnessed by two of Patrick's friends—in which Rice purported to leave nine-tenths of his property to Patrick. One more went on an assignment giving Patrick possession of all Rice's stocks, bonds, and other evidence of indebtedness in his safe-deposit boxes at two New York banks. This document also revoked an earlier order permitting Rice's own lawyer access to the boxes.

Meticulous care

Four cheques—the $250,000 total value of which would have exhausted the money Rice had in New York banks—also bore phoney signatures. Then there was a further signature—on a letter, apparently written by Rice to Patrick in the August, directing that his body after death should be cremated.

INCREDIBLE that Patrick, a lawyer of considerable experience, should think he could get away with forging a paper as inexplicably generous as this one . . .

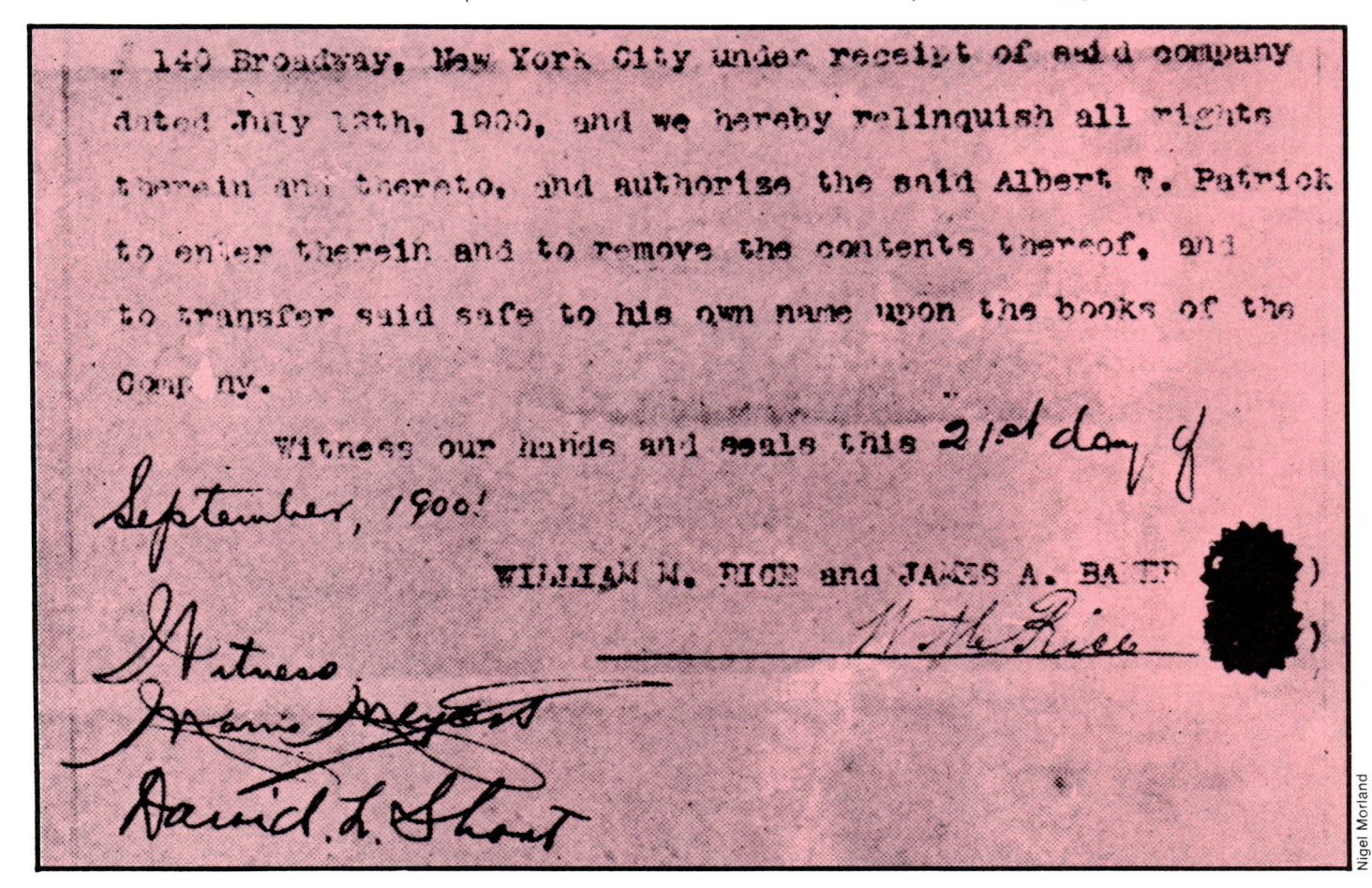

All these signatures, traced from genuine ones supplied by Jones, had been drawn with meticulous care. Patrick had even asked for a bottle of the ink used at the Madison Avenue apartment — pointing out that it would never do to use the wrong ink.

Cheques which Rice really had signed were also intercepted by Jones and forged ones for the same amounts were substituted. These forgeries were put through the banks in the normal way and paid. The reason behind this exercise was that Patrick anticipated that, if any of the forgeries putting money into his own pocket were suspected, the "genuine" forged cheques could be produced for comparison.

Agent and friend

But why should it be believed that Rice should wish to lavish so much generosity on a man like Patrick — a man who was employed to fight him over a will he resented so violently?

Again, Patrick had worked out the answers. The official story would be that he had met Rice while trying to settle the business of the Texas will, and had struck up a friendship with the old man. That was why he got Jones to type some 20 letters to Rice's business associates in which Rice apparently referred to Patrick as his lawyer, agent, and friend.

Also, to indicate that he carried on an active correspondence with Rice, he told Jones to send to him, at his office, a series of empty envelopes which had Rice's return address boldly on them. This was the mesh being drawn around the unsuspecting Mr. Rice who was still regarding Jones as his most trusted friend.

TOO ALIKE . . . this composite picture shows these two signatures are forged (above). Genuine signatures tend to vary slightly; these are almost identical. (Top) the missing "L" in "Abert" came between Patrick and Rice's vast wealth.

Undisguised contempt

There was one more character who, unwittingly, was to play an integral role in the murder — an ancient and doddery doctor called Walter Curry. Patrick, working through Jones, had arranged for Curry to become Rice's personal physician — for, although the doctor was honest and kind, Patrick was confident his eyesight and judgment were blurred enough to make him an unwitting accomplice.

While Jones was giving this evidence, Patrick regarded him through his clip-on nose spectacles with undisguised contempt. But the contempt gave way to anxiety as Prosecutor Osborne led Jones into a conversation which had taken place in August, 1900.

"About that time did you have a discussion with him about the state of health of the deceased?"

Jones hesitated. "Do you mean . . . ?"

"The question is a very simple one, Mr. Jones. Do you, or do you not, recall having any discussion in the early part of August about Mr. Rice's health?"

"Yes, sir, I do."

"Then please tell the court about it."

"Patrick asked me how Mr. Rice's health was, and I said he was better than he had been. Then he said: 'Don't you think Rice is living too long for our interest?'"

Mr. Osborne repeated the words. "'Living too long for our interest.' I see. And what was your reply to that?"

"I said: 'It does seem that way.'"

"And was any suggestion made about how this position might be . . . er . . . corrected?"

"Patrick said that, if I let him in one night, he would put Mr. Rice out of the way. I said that, if anything like that was to be done, Dr. Curry would have to do it, but he told me that Dr. Curry wouldn't do a thing of that kind."

There was a discussion about the use of chloroform, and they studied a magazine article, provided by Patrick, about the effects of chloroform. Patrick told Jones to obtain some and to find out casually from Dr. Curry if it would be difficult to tell if a person had died as a result of chloroform. Curry informed Jones that it would be hard to tell—particularly so if the heart were affected. Patrick also instructed Jones to start dosing Rice with mercury to "break him down". Jones, having persuaded Dr. Curry that he needed mercury tablets for himself, acquired a bottle of them.

Very sick

On September 1 Jones started giving Rice two tablets a day, assuring him that they were good for him, and Rice immediately started to suffer from diarrhoea. Patrick provided stronger mercury tablets, and Rice's condition worsened. Jones called Dr. Curry, but did not mention dosing Rice with the mercury.

About 10 days before Rice died on September 23, a friend of his, a Mrs. Van Alstyne, called and recommended that bananas were good for stomach troubles. Rice took her word and ate nine of them—making himself very sick and "clogging his stomach". Jones gave him an extra large dose of mercury "to clear him", and Patrick told him later: "It was silly to have given him the mercury pills. If he had been left alone he might have died from eating the bananas."

Specific instructions

The important thing was that they had now established with Dr. Curry that Rice was thoroughly unwell—and that was paving the way to the night of the murder. On that night, however, Patrick broke the news that he would not be doing the killing—but would be leaving it to Jones. At first, Jones refused. But, after "considerable persuasion", he agreed to "do the job"

Rice was already asleep when Jones returned to the Madison Avenue apartment after his meeting with Patrick. All Patrick's instructions were specific, and Jones knew exactly what to do. He made a "cone" out of a towel and dropped a sponge saturated with chloroform into it. "I put the cone by my own face to test it and got a very strong effect from it," he said.

He then poured a little more chloroform on to the sponge and crept into the bedroom of the sleeping man. Gently, so that he would not disturb him, he placed the cone over Rice's nose and mouth and then hurried from the room. Half an hour later he was able to telephone Patrick with the coded message: "Mr. Rice is very ill." That meant Rice was dead. Jones next called Dr. Curry and he arrived at the apartment at the same time as Patrick.

Dr. Curry then entered the witness stand, and he identified a death certificate he had signed. It said: "Cause of death—old age and weak heart; immediate causes—indigestion followed by collacratal diarrhoea with mental worry."

Cremated

He testified to having had an extensive experience in the use of chloroform, having attended more than 40,000 medical and surgical cases while a Confederate Army surgeon during the Civil War. He stated that its smell would have lingered in the room for four or five hours. He would certainly have noticed it if it had been used. There was no evidence of it either in the room atmosphere or on the body.

The next to be summoned to the murder scene were the undertaker, Charles Plowright, and the embalmer, John S. Potter. They both gave evidence that Patrick had insisted that the body was to be cremated "as soon as possible"—and Potter identified the forged "cremation letter" which Patrick had given him as an authorization to show to the officials at the crematorium.

So far the killers were completely in the clear. They would probably have remained in the clear—as far as any murder charge was concerned — if Patrick had not been so eager to get his greedy hands on William Rice's vast wealth as quickly as possible.

A little queer

If he had waited two days, his forged "cremation letter" would have ensured the disposal of Rice's body—and the final medical evidence would have rested on the safe opinion of Dr. Curry. But the very next morning a paying clerk at the private banking house of S. M. Swenson and Sons found there was a stranger at his window—presenting a cheque for $25,000 which had apparently been signed by Rice.

The old clerk studied the cheque carefully because of the large amount involved, and satisfied himself that it really was made out in the handwriting of Rice's secretary, Jones. He was familiar with Jones's writing and knew that he usually wrote Rice's cheques.

But, as he told the court, the signature "W. M. Rice" was, in his opinion, "a little queer". Then he noticed that the name of the payee on the face of the cheque was "A*b*ert T. Patrick", but the endorsement on the back was "A*l*bert T. Patrick".

Uneasy

He sought the advice of another clerk, Walter O. Weatherbee, and, after comparing the signature with genuine ones, they were not prepared to declare it was a forgery. But Weatherbee suggested that he should not accept the cheque because of the wrong endorsement. There would have to be a new endorsement which corresponded with the name of the payee on the face of the cheque. This was explained to the stranger, who left and returned later with a second endorsement on the cheque, "A*b*ert T. Patrick".

However, the clerks were still uneasy and showed the cheque to one of the bank's proprietors, Eric T. Swenson, who instructed them to telephone Mr. Rice and get his authority before accepting the cheque. Jones answered the telephone and assured them that everything was in order. Still Swenson was not satisfied. He wanted to speak personally to Rice.

For a while Jones hedged with him, saying that it was not possible for Mr. Rice to come to the telephone, before finally admitting that Rice was in fact dead. Swenson asked the stranger to identify himself, and he gave his name as David L. Short—"a friend of Mr. Patrick". This was the same David L. Short who had acted as a "witness" to Rice's signature on the forged documents held by Patrick.

Flame of suspicion

Soon Patrick, alerted by Jones, was telephoning the bank. But Swenson refused to discuss the matter over the telephone. Patrick hurried to the bank and told Swenson it was a pity that the bank had not seen fit to certify the cheque since it was Mr. Rice's intention that it should be paid.

Swenson replied that, as a lawyer, he should know the bank could not pay once it had knowledge of Rice's death. There would have to be an administration of Rice's affairs to establish to whom the money belonged. Patrick insisted that there would be no administration, for Rice had left no property in New York.

He also told Swenson that he had another of Rice's cheques on the bank for $65,000 and an assignment of all Rice's bonds and securities. Then, adding the final drop of fuel to Swenson's flame of suspicion, Patrick added that the body was being cremated the following day.

Curt telegram

As soon as Patrick left the bank, Swenson consulted his lawyers—suggesting that the business was so strange that it rated an urgent investigation. They called in the New York City Detective Bureau and the District Attorney.

None of Rice's relatives had been told about his death. However, with an official investigation starting, Jones began sending them telegrams—advising them that the cremation would take place at 10 o'clock the following morning. Rice's own lawyer heard the news and sent a curt telegram to Jones, ordering him to delay the funeral arrangements.

An autopsy showed that all Rice's organs were sound—except for his lungs. They showed a congestion "as though from some gas or vapour". On October 4 Patrick and Jones were arrested on charges of forgery and were locked in the Tombs. Three months later Patrick's family secured his release on bail—but he was immediately rearrested on a charge of murder.

Impartial

Patrick's "not guilty" plea was based on the argument that Jones was an "incredible liar" and that Rice had died a natural death. That was why Prosecutor Osborne had assembled a most impressive team of medical witnesses for the prosecution. The first was Dr. Hamilton Williams, coroner's physician for the borough of Manhattan, who testified about the autopsy on Rice. Cause of death, in his opinion, was intense congestion in the lungs caused by some "irritant" gas.

The Defence Attorney fought hard to stop the jury believing the possibility of chloroform having been administered. He put a series of searching questions to Dr. Williams. If chloroform had been administered in the manner described by Jones, would not parts of Rice's face have been blistered? Would there not have been some inflammation and congestion of the eyes? Dr. Williams shook his head. "Not necessarily," he said. "It would depend on the degree of the liquid saturation, and whether any of the liquid was brought into contact with the face or the eyes."

So the medical experts continued with their evidence for day after day, and, despite gruelling cross-examinations, they refused to be shaken. Six handwriting experts followed each other into the witness box to swear that Rice's signatures on the questioned documents were forgeries. They had been traced from genuine signatures. Enlargements of the forged signatures and genuine ones were displayed in court, and the experts used them to provide a wealth of evidence which supported their opinions: the questioned signatures showed "a cramped and unnatural writing" . . . "breaks in continuity, retouchings, and pen-lifts".

Judge Goff, Recorder of the County of New York, was meticulously impartial in his summing-up—reviewing the evidence and outlining the law without giving the jury any indication of his personal opinions about Patrick's innocence or guilt. However, the jury took little time to find Patrick guilty of first-degree murder. That was on March 26, 1902. His attorneys filed the customary motions for a new trial and in arrest of judgment. These were overruled, and on April 7 Patrick was told he would die in the electric chair.

However, for the next six years Patrick stayed in prison while his friends used pressure and legal ploys to secure his release. This expensive exercise finally met with success—on November 28, 1912. Governor John Dix, just before the expiration of his term of office, granted Patrick an unconditional pardon. Dix explained that "the hostile atmosphere which surrounded the defendant when he was tried precluded a fair trial", and added, "there has always been an air of mystery about the case".

Dix stated that Patrick's release had been recommended by the State Superintendent of Prisons and, as an additional reason for his surprising action, said: "In 1910 the Medico-Legal Society of New York published a brochure of their researches and concluded that the condition of Rice's lungs as found on postmortem could not have been caused by chloroform."

There were violent protests about the governor's decision, and many people suspected corruption. None of that mattered to Patrick, who considered his 12 years' imprisonment punishment enough. As for Jones—the man who had actually committed the murder—he had been given his full freedom shortly after Patrick's conviction. Like Patrick, he was never heard of again by the general public.

Today, three miles from the centre of Houston, Texas, stands the famous Rice University which received an endowment of some ten million dollars under the 1896 will signed by William Marsh Rice. Fifteen hundred pupils, who are charged no tuition fees, qualify from there every year with degrees such as Bachelor of Arts, Bachelor of Science, Master of Arts, and Doctor of Philosophy.

If Patrick's lethal scheme had succeeded, there would be no Rice University. Instead, William Marsh Rice would have had some type of monument – "costing not less than $5000" – on his grave.

THE MONUMENT EXISTS too, . . . built on the campus of the Rice University – but not courtesy of Albert Patrick.

RICHARDSONS, THE

For years the Richardson brothers and their gang of vicious hoodlums terrorized all south London with their remorseless violence. For the sake of "security" they beat and mutilated all potential informers—calmly munching fish and chips as their victims bled and writhed in agony. Any juror would have been brave indeed to vote for conviction. . . .

THE FRATERNITY OF TORTURE

THE most notable factor about the appearance of 32-year-old Charles William Richardson in the prisoner's dock of London's Central Criminal Court was that it ever happened at all. Many people – especially senior officers of Scotland Yard – had long thought it the proper place for Richardson to be. But most had suffered the frustrating belief that he would never be seen there – and Charles William Richardson himself had held it, as a matter of faith, that he would never cross the Old Bailey's threshold.

Not only was he among the most vicious of London's criminal thugs, but he was one of a select underworld band who had taken almost total security measures to ensure that no witness would dare to point a finger at them and say: "These men are evil – and I can prove them to be so."

In Richardson's case the "security measures" involved torture to "persuade" the would-be informers to maintain their silence. So it was that Richardson was as much surprised as the authorities, that April day in 1967, when he found himself arraigned for trial.

With seven of his henchmen – the "Richardson Gang" – he stood charged with the violence and intimidation with which he had built, over several years, a criminal empire in the densely packed tenement and high-rise housing estate areas of London that stretch south from the Thames.

On the charge sheet he was described as a "company director". But, as the evidence was to show, his "company" consisted of a motley collection of executives who made their profits from shady deals, and whose "labour relations" were based upon the theory that dissident employees or business associates were best kept in line by being stripped naked and given electric shock treatment.

Latter-day Capone

Richardson moved in a criminal world that was a scaled-down replica of the Prohibition era of Chicago and its mobs, and he liked to think of himself as a kind of latter-day Al Capone. As he stepped into the dock in his £50 suit there was an air of arrogance on his chubby features. This was reinforced by the deliberately careless manner in which he bore his stocky, boxerlike frame. When the charges of violence were put to him he snapped out: "Not guilty."

The Crown had decided to concentrate on the torture and other forms of violence, and not upon the actual criminal activities of the Richardson gang. Mr. Sebag Shaw, leading the prosecution, made that clear to the jury in the first few moments of his opening speech. Charles Richardson, he told the 11 men and one woman in the jurybox, was the dominant leader of a "somewhat disreputable business fraternity" who operated through a number of phoney companies.

"But," he said, with a wave of his arm, "this case is not about dishonesty or fraud; it is about violence and threats of violence. Not, let me say, casual acts of violence, committed in sudden anger – but vicious and brutal violence systematically inflicted, deliberately and cold-bloodedly and with utter and callous ruthlessness."

Beatings and torture of people who upset Richardson – or who were even suspected of jeopardizing his "business" career – ensured that no one ever complained to the authorities about south London gangsterism. Such methods had succeeded for years until, finally, some of the sufferers had told their disgruntled stories to the police.

The first of the alleged victims to be seen by the jury was Jack Duval, born in Russia in 1919, and a one-time French legionnaire. He acknowledged that he had come to the Old Bailey that day from prison, where he was serving a three-year sentence for an airline tickets fraud.

Duval was asked to recall a day in 1960, and did so in tones that suggested it was the unluckiest day of his life. That was the day on which he was first introduced to Richardson – in the Astor Club, off London's Berkeley Square. Very soon he was serving his apprenticeship as European representative for one of the gang's "companies" – whose main purpose was to import Italian-made nylon stockings on credit and then omit to pay the bills. His efforts were not of a high standard, and he was recalled to London.

He duly reported to the Richardson headquarters in south London's Camberwell, where he was greeted by Edward Richardson, the gang leader's younger brother, who "punched me in the face. Then, when I fell down, I was beaten with golf clubs. When I asked what I had done to deserve that, Edward Richardson said, 'You just do as Charlie tells you.'"

Later, still serving as a loyal employee, he was sent to Germany to order goods on credit for the Common Market Merchants Ltd. – another of the Richardsons' concerns.

"I was in Germany for about eight weeks," said Duval wistfully. Then, once again, his return to "head office" turned out to be a far from festive occasion. The greeting he received from Charles Richardson was in the traditional gang fashion. "As I entered the Camberwell office," said Duval, "Mr. Richardson hit me with his fist, and I still have the mark on the side of my nose from his ring."

Relating his ordeal

Members of the jury peered at Duval to see the scar. But, in the excitement of relating his ordeal, he was moving his head too rapidly from side to side. "When I came to," he recalled, "I found I had been relieved of my watch, ring and wallet containing 200 dollars. Mr. Richardson was sitting behind his big desk with chairs all around, like a court."

But "Mr. Richardson" was far from behaving with the decorum of a judge. He was, in fact, selecting knives from a canteen of cutlery, and throwing them in the direction of a Mr. Alfred Blore – the manager of Common Market Merchants. The knives, some of which were striking Blore in the arm, were intended to draw Blore's attention to his business failings.

According to Duval, Richardson "kept saying to Blore: 'I'm the boss and if I tell you what to do you will do it.' Mr. Blore asked, 'What have I done, Charlie?' Naturally, I was quiet; sitting in my corner. Mr. Blore was screaming: 'Don't do it to me!'" The crux of the matter, Duval explained to the jury, was that "Mr. Blore came in as a director of Common Market Merchants and he did not

---

THE WEST END Astor Club in London's Berkeley Square. It was here that new gang members were recruited before beginning their apprenticeship in one of the "companies". Jack Duval was to regret the day he was introduced to Charles Richardson.

want to run the company under the orders of Mr. Charles Richardson."

Other cronies of Richardson, minor "executives" of the company, had been lurking on the fringes of the bizarre Camberwell office-cum-courtroom, and two were ordered to go to Common Market Merchants' office in Cannon Street (in the square-mile business section of London called "the City") "and collect the stock and books and make it look as if there had been a robbery". The reason for that, Duval drily testified, was that by then Mr. Blore "was covered in blood", and if any questions were asked it would be said that he had been attacked during the supposed robbery.

Mr. Geoffrey Crispin, defending Richardson, suggested that it was Duval, and *not* Charles Richardson, who was the real gang leader. Duval agreed that he had lived a life of fraud, involving large sums of money. But he denied that in the fraudulent companies run by the gang he was, as Mr. Crispin put it, "the guvnor".

A guest of Her Majesty

Sharply, Duval told the lawyer: "I have never been the boss. I have worked for Charles Richardson because I had to." But, continued Mr. Crispin, Duval was hoping to receive a large sum of money by selling his life story to the newspapers. Duval had a swift answer to that. "I am," he said, haughtily, "at present a guest of Her Majesty and cannot indulge in any business activities while I am in prison."

Duval was followed into the witness box by a nervous, 38-year-old Polish-born businessman, Bernard Wajcenberg, whose dealings with Richardson and his "firm" had also been of an unhappy nature. He, it appeared, had sought business "references" about Richardson from the police—a move which had met with Richardson's disapproval. At a meeting in the notorious Camberwell office—at which Wajcenberg was "so paralyzed with fear I could not speak"—Richardson told him: "You have ratted by making inquiries about me from the police. If you don't pay £5000 you will not get out of this office alive."

To add weight to his threat, Richardson showed Wajcenberg a cupboard stocked with knives, axes, and a shotgun. Hoarsely, the witness told the jury: "Richardson grabbed me by the lapels and said, 'When I go berserk you know what happens.'" Wajcenberg did know and took swift steps to borrow £3000, which Richardson accepted in settlement.

ARROGANCE characterized the tough appearance of Charles Richardson, which was reinforced by the careless way he carried himself. He was sentenced to 25 years and his brother, who was already in prison, to 10. Charles was released in 1984.

Derek John Lucien Harris, another business associate of Richardson's, was not so fortunate as Wajcenberg. He had been selected as victim for the most sophisticated form of torture employed by the "firm" — torture by electric shock. Harris testified that this had happened in June, 1964, when he was negotiating the sale of a company to Richardson, and called at the Camberwell office to collect money owing to him.

Since Richardson was in the habit of receiving, rather than paying, money, this was an unwise approach by Harris — who was taken by some of the gang's gorillas to a nearby warehouse. There Richardson greeted him with the pained comment: "I like you, Lucien, and I don't want to hurt you." Then, aided by another member of the gang, he proceeded to beat Harris up. On tiring of that, the gang boss muttered orders to a couple of his men, who left and returned a few minutes later. One carried a parcel of scampi; the other a hand-operated electric generator of the type used for testing car spark-plugs.

Bound and gagged

"Everyone," Harris recalled, "began eating. After he had finished, Charles Richardson screwed his thumbs in my eyes. It was very painful, and I could not see for some moments. On Richardson's instructions my shoes were removed, and my toes were wired up to the generator. Roy Hall [another member of the gang] turned the handle, and the shock caused me to jump out of my chair, and I fell to the floor.

"After that I was stripped except for my shirt, and the shock treatment was repeated. As I rolled on the floor Richardson said the generator wasn't working very well and orange squash was poured over my feet. Then I was bound and gagged and given further electric shocks to various parts of my body. Finally, Richardson said I was to be taken to the marshes where I gathered I would be killed and dumped under a pile of refuse."

As he was dressing after the "treatment", Harris said, Richardson pinned his left foot to the floor with a knife. On the instructions of the judge, Mr. Justice Lawton, Harris then removed the shoe and sock from his left foot and rested the foot on a chair in the witness box. For the next 10 minutes the attention in the courtroom was wholly concentrated on the Harris foot. First the judge came down from his bench to examine it, then the members of the jury filed past it, in pairs. Finally, it was surrounded by the barristers on both sides of the trial, Crown and defence.

Two scars were visible on the foot, and Harris pointed to each during the inspections and repeated, again and again: "The knife went in there and came out here."

Altogether, he said, his session in the warehouse torture chamber lasted for six hours — at the end of which the mercurial Richardson "apologized and then gave me £150".

Next another victim of the shock treatment, a man named Benjamin Coulston, told the court that he, too, had undergone a six-hour torture ordeal. He was stripped naked, some of his teeth were torn out with a pair of pliers, lighted cigars were stubbed out on his arms and legs, and he was "toasted" on face and body by a closely held electric heater. As an endpiece to the session he was bundled into a tarpaulin sheet, along with two 14-lb. weights, and from inside the shroud he heard Richardson say: "Get rid of him."

Coulston stared at the jury with saddened eyes. "I thought I was going to be dumped in the river," he said. "And all the time this was happening Richardson and the others were drinking, laughing, smoking and enjoying the fun." But, luckily for him, Richardson wearied of the episode once the victim's terror had been savoured and ordered him to be released. "He gave me a new shirt," said Coulston, "and his brother, Edward, drove me home."

Other victims came to the witness box to recount similar experiences in the firm's office and warehouse. One man — who had been beaten and burned and had his toes broken — heard the screams of another sufferer as he lay in a hole,

LAUGHING, drinking, smoking and enjoying the fun . . . while the victim suffered the agony of shock treatment and "toasting" with an electric heater. Then Charles (right) would give the victim a new shirt, and brother Edward would drive him home.

beneath a trap door, into which he had been thrown when his torturers had finished with him.

The highlight of the trial came on the morning on which Richardson himself finally entered the box to tell his own story. Tough and self-assured, his defence was based on the simple line that all the evidence against him was perjured. Duval's story was an example, and he blandly told the jury: "It is something out of a storybook and never happened at any time. It is a ridiculous allegation that I should beat him up just to do what I told him to."

Had he ever attacked anyone? he was asked. He looked around the courtroom with the smile of a man who would endeavour, patiently, to answer all nonsensical questions. Of course he had never attacked anyone. "Never had a cross word," he declared. "They are a lot of clever fraudsmen, putting these allegations and getting out of their own frauds by blaming me for these incidents."

On a table in the well of the court stood the electric generator said to have been the principal torture machine. But Richardson eyed it as though it were some totally mysterious piece of equipment. "That's the only one of those I've ever seen," he insisted. "I have never owned one, and I don't know anyone who has." He looked at the machine again. "It's a conspiracy," he said. "It's a tissue of lies. These people have ganged up against me."

Alive and well

One moment of humour came when prosecuting counsel, seeking information about a potential witness whom the police had been unable to trace, asked Richardson: "Is this man alive and well?" With mock exasperation, Richardson retorted: "You keep asking me all the time if people are alive and well, and I object to it. It has a very serious inference!"

Richardson was followed into the stand by his henchman Roy Hall, who was alleged to have operated the electric generator. But, like his boss, he firmly declared that he had never before seen such a machine. What was more, he added, he had never seen the two victims, Harris and Coulston, "never in my life before I saw them in the magistrate's court. I am an innocent, hard-working man. Prosecution witnesses have tried to frame me."

The jury witnessed a parade of other gang members alleged to have acted as assistants to the chief torturer. One was the man said to have attempted to draw a victim's teeth with pliers, and who succeeded only in tearing the man's gums. Again, he had done nothing, seen nothing, knew nobody. On the day that the loudest screams were being enjoyed by the scampi-eating gang—and the electric generator was emitting its agonizing stream of current—he was busy putting flowers on the grave of his wife's father.

For the Crown, Mr. Sebag Shaw summed up this, and similar defence evidence, as "poppycock produced in the hope of creating a smokescreen through which you, the members of the jury, would not be able to see. But this trial is concerned with matters of the gravest import to society. If the charges made out are well founded, it reveals a canker in our midst which, if unchecked, would undermine the civilized society in which we live." Of Richardson, he said: "He was the man of power who could get things done and who could succeed by his methods where other methods had failed."

But it was on the 38th day of the trial—the longest trial so far in British criminal history—that an important and significant announcement came from the judge. He had been informed, he said, that threats had been made to members of the jury that "there had better be a disagreement in the Richardson case". One threat had been hastily whispered to a juryman's 75-year-old mother as she waited at a bus stop. Similar "warnings" had been given to other jurymen by telephone.

Mr. Justice Lawton, careful to preserve the fair-trial rights of the prisoners, told the jury: "Whatever has happened must have been done without the co-operation of the defendants, most of whom have been in custody since last July.

"But, unfortunately, whenever there is a trial of this kind it attracts publicity, and there are busybodies, evil-wishers, misguided acquaintances and friends who will interfere. When they do interfere there is a danger that a jury might take the view that what did happen came about as the result of the intervention of the defendants. Now that I have pointed out the position to you I am confident that no such view will be taken by you."

All the same, the judge went on, a special police telephone post had been set up with a secret number for jurymen to ring immediately, at any hour, if they were approached again. "A police patrol car will be on the scene within minutes," Mr. Lawton added.

New trial threat

The judge repeated his concern over the issue in his detailed summing up of the trial. There was "not a scrap of evidence," he warned, that Richardson and his fellow defendants had been parties to the jury threats, and the jurors must put the matter out of their minds in reaching their verdicts. He reminded the jury of the importance of a unanimous decision. "If you cannot agree, there will have to be a new trial," he told them. "Just think what that will mean."

Mr. Justice Lawton spent three days on his summing up—one of the longest addresses ever made from the bench—and on June 7 the jurors retired for nine hours and 26 minutes. As they finally filed back into court, many of them showing signs of fatigue, the eight men in the dock stared anxiously at them. The list of charges was long, and it took time for the foreman to deliver the several verdicts. Richardson and five other gang members were found guilty of some—although not all—of the charges against them.

Richardson, pronounced guilty on nine counts, told the judge, "I am completely innocent of these charges." But he and the rest still had to wait before hearing their sentences. Mr. Justice Lawton said he would hand down verdicts the following day. Meanwhile he discharged the jury "from your long, wearisome and worrying time" but added: "You are not concerned with sentencing, but having regard to your long connection with the case you might like to be in court to-morrow."

The jury accepted his invitation and were back at the Old Bailey the next morning to hear the judge sentence Charles Richardson to 25 years' imprisonment. Mr. Justice Lawton told him: "I have come to the conclusion that no known penal system will cure you but time. The only thing that will cure you is the passing of the years.

Sadistic disgrace

"I am satisfied that over a period of years you were the leader of a large, disciplined, well led, well organized gang, and that for purposes of your own material interests, and on occasions for purposes of your criminal desires, you terrorized those who crossed your path, terrorized them in a way that was vicious, sadistic and a disgrace to society.

"When I remember some of the evidence of your brutality I am ashamed to think that one lives in a society that contains men like you. It must be clear to all those who set themselves up as gang leaders that they will be struck down by the law as you are struck down."

Richardson stared, tight-lipped, at the judge as the sentence was delivered. Then, as three police officers formed a guard around him to take him to the cells below the courtroom, he turned to the jury and snarled: "Thank you—very much!" Sentences ranging from eight to ten years were given to the other guilty defendants. Edward Richardson, the gang boss's brother, collected one of the 10-year sentences, which was to follow the five years he was currently serving for other offences.

It was the end of the notorious Richardson gang, and it had been achieved through the concentrated efforts of a team of 100 policemen. As his last duty in the trial the judge called before him the dozen senior detectives of the team—including young, blonde Woman Police-Constable Gillian Hoptroff.

Mr. Justice Lawton told the police team: "I want to thank all of you on behalf of the court—and I think I am speaking on behalf of every law-abiding citizen in this country—for the work you have done in breaking up one of the most dangerous gangs I have ever heard of."

Hewlett-Woodmere Public Library

The Dido Smith Fund